"Dr. Barton has not only written the history of Negro literature of the period but has sought to find out what its psychology told us about the Negro mind in its social aspects . . . . . she has gone below the surface and produced a work which was hailed as a model in its unrelenting and searching analysis of the expression of race consciousness in modern American fiction . . . Her main question was the social adjustment or maladjustment of the Negro in the U.S.A. since 1900, as mirrored in the literature (1900–1930)."

Professor S. B. Liljegren
University of Upsala, Sweden, 1948
Studia Neophilogica, Vol. XXI

"The paradox of the Black artist has always been an awareness of the 'absurdity of existence' and a creative and courageous response to racial hardships and human suffering. As long as he and she can continue to wrest meaning out of meaninglessness the slave may yet become the emancipator, the wasteland may yet bloom."

—From the Prologue

BLACK VOICES

in

AMERICAN FICTION,

1900-1930.

Rebecca Chalmers Barton

DOWLING COLLEGE PRESS
Oakdale, New York

12/1976
Am. Lit

For further information contact

Dowling College Press
Oakdale, New York 11769

Library of Congress Catalog Card Number: 76—10511

Printed in the United States of America

ISBN No. 0-917428-00-5

PROLOGUE

This 1976 publication, *Black Voices in American Fiction 1900–1930,* has roots in the past calling for the author's explanation and acknowledgements. I carried out the research between 1930 and 1932 and completed the writing in 1933, in satisfaction of the thesis requirements for my Ph. D. degree. I undertook an analysis of the variations of race consciousness among Black Americans and an appraisal of their literary accomplishment during a highly productive thirty-year period. *Black Voices* is, in fact, a study of the correlation between the group experience and its fiction, from 1900 to 1930.

Such a pioneering project was undertaken with the encouragement of my late husband, John R. Barton, Professor of Sociology at the University of Wisconsin, who maintained "way back then" that women were persons and should follow their professional interests with as much zeal as men. To him I owe a life-long gratitude for this early lesson in "doing my own thing." Also supportive were my friends, Emmy Louise Manniche and Peter Manniche, former President of the International College in Denmark.

Fortunately, this attitude was shared by the well-known scholar in comparative literature, Professor S. B. Liljegren of the University of Upsala, Sweden, who considered the resultant study of a then unexplored field of such importance that he arranged in 1934 for a few privately printed copies to be circulated among scholars in his field here and abroad. Most of them, familiar with the works of Dreiser, Upton Sinclair, Ernest Hemingway, Sinclair Lewis, Sherwood Anderson and William Faulkner, did not realize that these writers had Black American contemporaries such as W. E. B. DuBois, Charles W. Chesnutt, James Weldon Johnson, Paul Laurence Dunbar and that versatile group associated with the "Negro Renaissance" of the 1920s, exemplified by the fiction of Rudolph Fisher, Langston Hughes, Jessie Fauset, Nella Larsen, Claude McKay, Eric Walrond and Jean Toomer, and by the critical essays of Dr. Alain Locke of Howard University.

Since the response to my choice and treatment of the material was favorable, I was urged by family, colleagues and friends at the time to seek publication of this thesis. However, the immediate responsibility of two small children in the aftermath of the depression, soon followed by the advent of World War II, brought more pressing problems than book publications.

It is only after a long career of university and college teaching and writing about Black authors, within the framework of my field of comparative literature, that I now agree to the timeliness of this publication here and now, in its original thesis form, without additions or annotations. In this way present-day scholars, students, and, beyond them, concerned readers can begin to discover for themselves, across the years, the variety, scope and creativity of these early twentieth-century Black writers of fiction too often neglected and ignored in our presentation of American literature, and too often still unknown because of their "out-of-print" status.

Once more I am indebted, this time to my daughter, Eloise Barton Nelson, to my son, Norman Barton, and to those many Black and non-Black friends and colleagues who have reminded me so continuously that I was "ahead of my time" in my scholarly pursuits, that my doctoral dissertation does not project as some sort of "period piece" today, that my insights and judgements can still "stand up on merit alone" as relevant in this day of Black pride, Black expression and Black Studies. Although they agree that some of the typography and orthography may well seem dated to modern eyes, they stress the fact that the contents still ring true—perhaps too true, since apparently no one else since then has written a critical work of the Black fiction of that period in any depth.

Furthermore, this same group of "true believers" emphasizes that my name did become recognized in this whole field with the 1948 publication by Harper and Row (then Harper Brothers) of my book entitled *Witnesses for Freedom: Negro Americans in Autobiography (1900–1945)*. Although this second study has been out of print for some time, it can at least be found in most major libraries in this country and overseas, is well known as a reference book and is listed in most current anthologies of Afro-American literature, whereas in contrast my thesis from 1935 is unavailable except to a very small circle. Since my point of view and approach, as well as my original research, have often been incorporated in contemporary literary studies, I see that interested writers and readers anywhere and any place should also have access to that first study.

During my forty-five-year perspective on Black authors I have been fortunate on several counts. Many of the early Black authors I covered gave me personal encouragement through interviews and correspondence. Every institution in which I taught allowed me to include these works in my courses. Most important of all, my students from 1936 to 1976, of whatever race, creed, color, sex or age, have always given thoughtful attention to this subject matter, whether at the International College in Denmark, at the University of Wisconsin, at the University of California at Santa Barbara. or presently at Dowling College in Oakdale, New York. In my present status as a Professor Emeritus of English at Dowling College I continue to teach Afro-American as well as English literature.

However, it takes more than interest and moral support to realize a project such as the present publication in the present economy. For this reason I am greatly appreciative of the practical assistance offered by the Dowling College Press and its Director, Gloria Schetty-Plante, and by Women's Time Publications, Inc. and its Managing Editor, Andrea Wandelt.

In addition, my special and warm thanks go to Elizabeth Brandeis Raushenbush, a good friend of forty years, who has considered it so important to secure publication of this book that she has generously helped to bring it about, despite inflation. To her I dedicate it, not merely because of her indispensable support, but also because of our many shared beliefs and activities through storm and stress. During a fifteen-year period in Wisconsin in which she served as Chairperson of the Governor's Migratory Labor Committee and I served as the Executive Director of the Governor's Commission on Human Rights, we learned together that one hundred deeds are worth more than one thousand dreams of equal opportunity.

Perhaps this present book is one such deed which can help set the literary record straight and open the door more widely to new approaches beyond the inbred racist bias in our culture as a whole. Black authorship did not start with Richard Wright's *Native Son* in 1940 and end with Ralph Ellison's *Invisible Man* in 1952 and James Baldwin's novels in the 1960s. For more than three centuries Afro-American literary voices have been heard in this land by those who would listen. As Langston Hughes observed so perceptively in the 1920s, "I, too, sing America," an urgent reminder in our Bicentennial year.

The paradox of the Black artist has always been an awareness of the "absurdity of existence" and a creative and courageous response to racial hardships and human suffering. As long as he and she can continue to wrest meaning out of meaninglessness the slave may yet become the emancipator, the wasteland may yet bloom.

Rebecca Chalmers Barton
Dowling College, 1976

CONTENTS

PREFACE

The American Negro of today is in a peculiar and dramatic position. Underneath him is crumbling the old order, while the nature of the new order in process of construction has not yet been clearly defined. His status in the old order, however stifling and disagreeable to him, at least possessed the virtue of certainty. The master who held him as a slave and the science which judged him as inferior re-enforced each other in establishing firmly his necessary rôle of subordination. And the attitude of mind, the psychology of the relation between white man and black man had become far too deeply rooted in the mores and customs, in the emotions and reactions on both sides suddenly to be swept away by the external occurrence of that war which secured the national emancipation of the slaves legally. The fact of the definiteness of conviction embodied in the traditional system can be judged by the number of years it has taken for the minority to force any modification. It was not until fifty years after the close of the Civil War in 1865 that the new attitudes it was supposed to engender began to assert themselves to any noticeable degree, and undoubtedly a still longer period of time will pass before the older attitudes will be regarded as nothing but curious vestiges.

In thus restraining the momentum and yet not preventing the approach of different and iconoclastic attitudes, the traditional view now contributes to that general complex of uncertainty with which every Negro of today must reckon. The period of transition which he is still undergoing generates uncertainty. That the attitudes of different sections of the country towards him should vary is relatively simple to apprehend, shaped by local economic interests or social customs, as in the case of the manufacturing North, and the agricultural aristocratic South. The more liberal attitude of the North, shown by its comparative willingness to accept the Negro laborer immigrating from the South on a fresh and more unbiased basis, can largely be explained by its negative lack of the slave tradition and institution, and its positive desire for economic gains. But when, in addition, the Negro finds a great fluctuation of attitude on the part of different groups and individuals *within* any one section, this tends to a state of confusion and an intensification of the natural conflicts he himself has already in endeavoring to crystallize his changing status. This state of ferment, this restless seeking for a new equilibrium based upon saner first principles is in keeping with the formulation of those terms heard so frequently of late, „The Negro Renaissance", and the „New Negro", while the expression of this spirit is found with increasing vigor in the Negro literature of the present century.

To an unusual degree this literature reflects the Negro mind occupied with the problems of adjustment to a more or less resisting environment and facing these problems in all the different ways called for by changing time, place, and situation. There has evidently been no question of separating literature and life in the case of the Negro whose daily experiences have been so strongly conditioned by racial factors and by all the emotions thus brought into play that he seemingly finds it quite natural for them to appear in the same light in his work as an artist. His literature has been and is touched by the fact of race prejudice and has been responding according to the dictates of a richly developing race consciousness. His reaction towards injustice and discrimination, towards segregation and exploitation, towards lynching and disfranchisement, his feeling about his own limitations, achievements, potentialities and possible participation in American life, his conception of his natural capacities, originality and aspirations, all this and much more leave on his art impressions, whether distinct of outline or only vague in suggestion. On establishing contact with the production of Negro writers during this century one is struck by the lack of uniformity of these impressions. For example, the Negro's essays and biographies may reveal his rational theories on the subject of race directly while his poetry gives access to the depths and nuances of emotional response.

But the most fertile field of literature open to an observation of this variation is that of fiction in general and the novel in particular. This is partly due to the prolificacy, especially since the World War, of this type of literature which thus allows a wide range for variation. It might also be explainable in the light of the great flexibility characterizing the novel as a medium of art. Direct articulation of the author's particular grievances through the mouths of his characters, implications of injustice through the choice of his setting or the creation of atmosphere — these ways of expression and many more are available to the novelist. At one time the consciousness of race has resulted in the obvious cruder „problem" form, at another it is so sublimated as to be realized only as a brooding spirit.

And this variation has a direct connection with that already mentioned as taking place in the group life. There is not only change in both instances, but the same kind of change. Just within the three decades since 1900 we discover that all the major attitudes held by Negroes in regard to their status have a correspondence in the novels written by Negro authors. The correspondence appears to result from the influence of one upon the other, rather than from mere accident, but it would be difficult perhaps impossible to determine on which side the major responsibility for this connection rested. Obviously certain life experiences have reflected themselves immediately in the stories written by these same Negroes, but on the other hand literature has inevitably often had a direct effect on the group psychology, giving it some new bent or twist and thus modifying the group experience in some way.

Unquestionably it is a case of interaction between the two forces. Taking this for granted, and without making the futile endeavor to capture the beginning or end of a vicious circle, we are free to concern ourselves with the problem of the correlation itself. In other words, the object of this investigation is not to attempt to ascertain the relative proportions to which literature and life influence each other, but to isolate for observation similar attitudes wherever they exist.

Growing and simultaneous acquaintance with the nature of the group experience of the Negroes in America and with the body of literature generated by them led to a gradual recognition of the surprising number of these parallel phenomena. This recognition was at first a faint and general one, but further acquaintance with the material gave it definite form and created the desire to trace this correlation in detail. The best method of procedure seemed to be first, to analyze systematically the major reactions of the Negroes to race prejudice by studying the development of their group life, and second to use these as a basis for comparison in measuring the degree and kind of race consciousness extant in the most important works of fiction.

It is quite clear to see that any such object of study cannot be separated from the so- called „race problem", weaving such a scarlet thread into the complex pattern of American society. The race consciousness of the colored American can be regarded as the response to the race prejudice of the white American, and between the two forces the „problem" comes into being. And at present this „problem" is being regarded in the United States so much more from an objective and rational than from an emotional and subjective point of view that this investigation can be quite in harmony with it. A new scientific spirit is at work. There is a demand for facts and figures, statistics and research, to replace the popular notions and traditional generalizations. The methods and conclusions of the old race-theorists are being criticized by many on the grounds of inadequacy. The dangers of generalization not only about one race in comparison to others but about a race as such are being discussed. This means that the scientific minded American nowadays hesitates not merely to make sweeping statements about the inferiority of the Negro race in relation to the white race but in addition about the similarities of the Negroes to each other. And finally, along with this recognition of tremendous differences of characteristics from color to intelligence among the Negroes as a group is coming a conviction on the part of many of the fallacy of the „race" concept in any case. To such conclusions does the attempt to regard the „race problem" without the customary emotional bias seem to be leading.

This disinterested approach is not alone a departure from the antagonistic but from the sentimental treatment of the Negro in American life. It countenances the „Uncle Tom's Cabin" spirit of sweetness and love no more than the Ku Klux Klan spirit of jealousy and mistrust. Emotionalism underlies both, and emotionalism, presumably, is to be avoided in an impartial consideration. In so far as white America is stressing the need for objectivity in its greatest race problem it is only expressing its general tendency to value things scientific, and in particular, the scientific method. The extent to which the material development of the country has proceeded is the result of more than an instinctive response to vast material resources. It is due to a passionate belief in the tangible and concrete, a conviction that figures are essential, that facts are finger posts to truth, and that truth is to be found only through experimentation in each given situation. This conception of truth as unfixed, as subject to change in the face of new evidence has become part and parcel of the American experience. Since the recognition of truth as changeable leads to an inevitable questioning of long-established truths it is to be expected that the new spirit of inquiry will turn its searchlight not only upon problems of sex and marriage, religion, education, industry, war and peace, but also upon those of race where equally and similarly it will demand the burden of matter-of-fact proof, freed from the taboos imposed by tradition and from emotionalism of one kind or another.

A corollary to the felt need for scientific evidence is the desire for *internal* evidence. The former treatment of the race problem in the United States has not included any consideration of what the Negroes might think of the matter. That would have been considered as ridiculous as consulting a dog on his preference in the matter of bones. Thus, indicative of change is the current assumption on the part of white students of race questions that the Negroes themselves should be consulted and considered as genuine sources of information and understanding. Rather than reading books about Negro ways and doings written by white authors, as previously, why not read those written by Negro authors, is the question which occurs. Obviously one of the most effective roads to understanding will be through their spontaneous expression in art where so often the more important unconscious as well as conscious reactions are captured. Here is opportunity for internal evidence of an intimate and vivid character. It is this opportunity which the present study grasps by considering only that fiction produced by Negroes themselves. For the last decade white writers such as Julia Peterkin, Du Bose Heyward, Carl van Vechten, and Roark Bradford have been widely accepted as interpreters in art of the Negro consciousness, just as Harriet Beecher Stowe, Joel Chandler Harris, and others were accepted in their day. But the assumption of this investigation is that in many ways the Negro is his own best interpreter, and can furnish unique and first hand material. Now that he is becoming so articulate, it behooves us to pay attention and listen instead of drowning him out by the sound of our own voices.

But a very significant point is that when the searching spirit, prompted by its desire for objectivity, for facts, for internal evidence, turns for help towards the Negroes themselves, it is met by an identical spirit of inquiry already at work within the ranks. This means that white critics have access not only to the more emotional reactions of Negroes in art and literature but in addition to the self critical analysis of Negro leaders and thinkers concerning the development of race consciousness within their group. Negro scientists and scholars have not been sitting back idly in preparation for that day when they would be investigated from the outside. Negro sociologists and historians have been busy during the last ten or twenty years formulating their own theories and advancing their own interpretations of their group history. They have been submitting themselves to self-analysis and consequently developing their own definite ideas about themselves. Obviously the process has been painful at times, since the disinterested approach is admittedly easier to maintain towards another, as in the case of the white scientist in relation to the Negro group, than towards oneself. At the same time the Negro has the advantage of knowledge obtained at first instead of second hand and more value may attach to it because of this chance for greater authenticity, as long as the perspective has been carefully preserved. But at the essential points in the race problem, the scientists of today, whether of light or dark skin color, seem to be meeting. Therefore in attempting to evalute the situation from the Negro's point of view it is often possible to depend upon the conclusions of scholars from both groups, interchangeably. This is true of the scholars where it would not be true for the writers, for it is the very essence of science to require clear eyesight in place of those rose colored spectacles which are frequently an asset to the aesthetic achievement of an artist.

Emotional control cannot fail to inject a healthy current of air into the stale issues of race, and the Negro's own formulation of attitudes, whether independently or in conjunction with the white scientist, into new race theories and principles has a decided importance for the present study. Before we can comprehend the thought-currents of the present-day Negro literature, it is essential to have at least a general idea of the concepts of sociological and psychological import which Negro scholars are attaining. It is helpful to become acquainted with the nature of their investigation into the present position of their group in American life as something explainable only by the light of past development and conditions, and only by means of a scientific analysis of cause and effect.

Therefore in the first part we shall consider what changes have *actually* occurred in the psychology of the group life, according to the estimation of Negro thinkers themselves, and in the second part we shall observe the expression of the same race consciousness, of these corresponding mental attitudes, in the outstanding works of fiction by Negro writers.

It is impossible in the limits of one study to apply the illustrative method and to make a thorough and detailed examination of the whole mass of fiction so copiously produced by Negroes in the last three or four decades. Much of it is of such a repetitive nature that it is possible to choose representative works. Although this is a sociological and psychological study, the method of selection has the additional advantage of providing material which has more claims to literary value than the rest, most of which is rather worthless in that respect. And this has importance for our purpose after all in that it offers the best opportunity for observing whatever literature might exist untouched by racial issues. The greater the literary attainment the less possibility there will be of finding sociological matter which is so difficult to embody in artistic form. Therefore applying this test while keeping in mind the need for material reflecting general tendencies, we shall concentrate on works which are both representative and outstanding.

PART ONE

RACE CONSCIOUSNESS IN THE GROUP EXPERIENCE

Definition of the Term.

The phenomenon of race consciousness demands the existence of two disharmonious groups for its development. Both groups may experience strong self-feeling in relation to each other, and to that extent both can be said to possess something akin to race consciousness, although strictly speaking it may be national or class consciousness. But the members of a group which is in the superior position in relation to the other are not forced through circumstances to acquire such a heightened consciousness and sense of unity with their particular group as those of the weaker or suppressed group where there is a need for these means of survival. Theirs is that type of self-assurance which may be described as racial, national, or class *pride.* The hereditary lord and the victor through force of arms assume their innate right to superiority through the very fact of their superior status externally, so that their self-feeling becomes as instinctive as that underlying „the divine right of kings" hypothesis, and therefore more unconscious than in the case of the resentful serf or the vanquished. In contrast, these have to re-enforce their self-feeling consciously and often with great effort in the face of constant suggestions of inferiority. The undesirableness of their position is continually thrusting itself into their awareness, and consequently it is more natural to describe their reactions to the dominant group under the term of race consciousness.

In this present study, therefore, race consciousness is

treated as a condition applicable especially to a so-called inferior or „out-group". This is because it is this group and not the superior or „in-group", which is on the defensive, and because race consciousness, like any other type of consciousness, intensifies as the result of conflict necessitating protective armor. Whenever experience contains stimuli of a harsh and unpleasant nature the reactions become more acute and vital. A baby's awareness of hunger is much stronger than his awareness of comfort and warmth. Under the pressure of one, he becomes extremely cognizant of self, under the lulling of the other, he may fall to sleep and thereby lose consciousness.

Race consciousness is thus further defineable as a psychological phenomenon heightened by any disturbing economic, social, and political factors in the environment. If acquiescent to the suggestions of „inferiority" on the part of the dominant group, the race consciousness is at a low ebb. Resistance and rebellion are the signs of its acceleration. The greater this becomes, the more the position of the superior group is threatened. This means that any passive assumption of superiority must give way to active steps towards assuring its perpetuation. The feeling of superiority has often been an excuse for a feeling of prejudice against what has been regarded as inferior, but this feeling of prejudice must express itself less in attitude and more in action in proportion to the challenge it meets. Thus we have an endless process in which race prejudice fosters race consciousness which in turn fosters the race prejudice, and so on, with oppression and rebellion in constant action and reaction.

But if there were no original assumptions of superiority within the strong group, and no consequent setting of limitations to the position and activity of the weak group, there would develop no virile race consciousness which depends for its creation upon a sense of need in the presence of a danger. Energizing this danger is the spirit of hostility exhumed by race prejudice. Therefore some consideration of the nature, causes, and forms of prejudice is required before real insight into the complexities of race consciousness is possible.

Analysis of Race Prejudice: Stimulus.

In analyzing their own position in American life, **Negroes** have realized this. Due to a desire to understand the problems of their race more clearly, Negro scholars have turned to an examination of race prejudice as a necessary first step. They begin with a recognition of the difficulties attendant on such an examination, because prejudice is so linked up with human emotions of an explosive character and yet so apparently rational on the surface. But since their method of procedure is to subject all „apparent reasons" to scrutiny, they immediately find a flaw in the time-honored justification of prejudice as something instinctive. They suggest that **perhaps it is** dependent upon circumstances and not upon hereditary factors, that perhaps a white child is not born with a dislike for individuals of another skin-color after all. „Prejudice is a state of mind," writes Kelly Miller, a Negro sociologist, „Some affect to believe that it is an innate passion paralleled with instinct, and is therefore unalterable. Others maintain that it is a stimulated animosity modifiable by time, place and condition, and is on the same footing with other shallow obliterative feelings."[1]) These „others" among the Negroes are rapidly increasing in number at present, supported by the observations of experimental psychologists in dealing with children, and by the theories of white scholars. In the recent collection of **Negro** essays and stories, „Ebony and Topaz", an article was included by Professor Ellsworth Faris, head of the Department of Sociology at the University of Chicago. It was included obviously because his views are in accordance with the growing sentiment of Negroes on this point: „Race prejudice has often been asserted by popular writers to be instinctive or hereditary. While this is apparently a complete misstatement it is a very excusable one. The error arises from the normal tendency of unsophisticated people to confuse the customary with the natural. When children grow up in a community they take on the customs and

---

1) **Survey Graphic. Vol. VI. No. 6. March, 1925:** *The Harvest of Race Prejudice.* p. 682. K. Miller.

attitudes prevailing, some of which are very old while others are quite recent in origin. But the children can make no distinction between the new and the old and when the attitudes have become second nature they are often thought of as innate or natural. It is said to be "in the blood'."[2]) One proof against the instinctive view often used is that the average European white man exhibits none of the American's prejudice on meeting the Negro. His own particular position is not threatened or undermined, and therefore he experiences no prejudice, in spite of being white.[3])

If environmental instead of instinctive, then the causes must be sought. What we ordinarily consider as instinctive is often the spontaneous response to the unknown and strange. A vague uneasiness based on ignorance of the nature and possible action of the unknown creature threatens our sense of security and leads us to envelop ourselves in a protective feeling of superiority towards it. But if it were only a matter of individual response here and there, race prejudice would never become a social force. It is when the majority of individuals in a group re-enforce their individual fears to the point of consolidation that prejudice finds roots in the mores and traditions. The feeling of security it seeks to preserve necessitates a resistance to change. It is the spirit of conservatism at work, the desire for the preservation of the „status quo". It differs from class and caste prejudice only in its object. The attitude of hostility and the motive of self-preservation are the same. In fact it is a commonly accepted view to-day that race prejudice is the outgrowth of previous class conflict. „Race theories did not develop until the relations between groups raised class problems."[4]) Rationalizations were made to maintain the existing social system through a dislike of having to rearrange status. In the case of the Negroes, the slaves were

---

2) Ebony and Topaz. p. 90.

3) The Annals of the American Academy of Political and Social Science. Vol. 140. No. 229. Nov. 1928. p. 336.

4) Ibid. p. 1.

the lowest social and economic class. Because they happened to be black, the association between „lower" and black was easily made and then intensified when National Emancipation upset the established stratifications. The European immigrant also finds himself repeatedly in the lower class, but he is able to escape from it far more easily than the Negro, largely because there is not the obvious distinction of color to identify him unmistakably with this class.[5]) When there is no color barrier, then there is a possibility that those very democratic traditions of America which originated as a reaction to European class domination and which cherish „logcabin" presidents may increase chances for the success of the poor man. But the taboos which have been built up around a dark skin are too strong to be dispelled in this way even when faced with the inconsistency of a partially applied doctrine of equality and freedom.

„The Negro is all right in his place" thus becomes an oft-repeated slogan in the South. If the Negroes in the South had been content to remain in the subordinate position tradition had alloted to them, then the probability is that such active racial antagonism would not have developed. It is where the Negro has sought to enter new fields of occupation already sacred to white Americans that he has met the greatest opposition.[6]) Competition in the economic sphere is obviously one of the most fundamental conditions for the increase of prejudice. There are numerous other possible spheres, cultural, religious, social etc.. But whether the struggle be for money, work, bread, or for position, status, social prominence, conflict is an integral part of the experience, and prejudice will not disappear until the conflict decreases.[7])

From this sociological point of view, prejudice can be considered a natural and normal phenomenon in the sense that crime, poverty, automobile accidents, suicide, and epidemics are

---

5) Annals. p. 3.

6) Ibid. p. 15.

7) Ebony and Topaz: *The Natural History of Race Prejudice.* p. 90.

natural and normal![8]) However, as Negroes point out, the prejudice cannot be mitigated or controlled as easily as the other phenomena, not merely because the unwelcome effects are less noticeable to the superficial glance, but mainly because of the obscuring clouds of „rationalizations" which have sprung up to perpetuate the attitude. The real motives, such as envy, hate, or fear, are often even unconscious since it is human nature to justify one's conduct in the best possible light. Many white Southerners claim instead of antipathy to have an actual fondness for Negroes and their distinctive folk-ways — but always with that significant qualification: as long as they keep in their places. Many others experiencing prejudice would even refuse to accept this descriptive term for an attitude which they sincerely regard as arising from sound theory and conviction. Likes and dislikes are defended by arguments which are results of and not real reasons for the preferences and prejudices.

According to Negro students of the subject, the chief rationalization supporting the attitude of whites towards blacks in America is the assumption that the Negro is biologically inferior, an assumption likewise held towards the „foreigner" or immigrant on American shores as useful in the process of Americanization, but less drastically applied. The science of the nineteenth century, in keeping with the prevailing evolutionary doctrines, supported this assumption. Reference was made to his African background. The classical anthropologists maintained that social evolution follows a unilinear course, that people of simple culture today give us insight into the past evolution of modern man, and that primitive culture reflects an incomplete and arrested development.[9]) The African was regarded not only as primitive but as „savage". The smaller average of brain size and the keener sensory powers in contrast to the white race were considered as proof of his identification with the lower animals. His lack of emotional control, of capacity for intellectual concentration and abstract thinking marked

8) Ebony and Topaz. p. 89.
9) Ebony and Topaz. Frazier E. F.: *Racial Self-Expression*. p. 119.

him as limited.[10]) His peculiar physical characteristics such
as thick lips and kinky black hair and black color, branded him
as inferior. The difference of his culture was another indication
of a difference in capacity. „The Africans do not build their
houses, tend their flocks, herd their cattle, train the youth, or
appease the gods in the same way as the European or Americans, then they must be inferior beings fit only for the exploitation of their so-called superiors or swept from the face of the
earth if they resist the interlopers."[11]) In both physical and
mental traits there were found differences to support a theory
of inequality.

The idea of the superiority of the Nordic race was based
on the belief that its material and social progress was far
greater, that it would be impossible, for example, to name
woolly headed Caesars, Napoleons, Newtons, or Columbuses. The
whole course of history shows the dominance of the Nordic
type, which is inquisitive, adventurous, courageous, free-think-
ing and individualistic, and therefore pioneer, explorer, and
conqueror. The influence of popular white writers like Madison
Grant and Lothrop Stoddard in encouraging this white superiority complex is often recognized by Negro scholars. Mr. Grant
regretted the sentimentality of the „Brotherhood of Man" doctrine, and regarded the doctrine of the Declaration of Independence that all men are created free and equal as just a
noble utterance by men who were thinking across the seas and
not in terms of the Indian at their back door and the Negroes
they were holding as slaves. Mr. Lothrop Stoddard in his book,
„The Rising Tide of Color", pointed out the danger to white
civilization of the dark races. Both men had an alarmist psychology, stressing by the use of numerous arguments the peril to
the Nordic race if the inferior races were not strongly repressed. Micegenation could only be a menace to the stability of the
more highly specialized and cultivated white race.

Finally, reference to Christianity and the will of God was

---

10) Ibid. p. 119.
11) Woodson, Carter G.: *The Negro in Our History*. p. 7.

made. The Bible gave texts to support the institution of slavery: „There were, moreover, Southern churchmen who were busy writing treatises on the inferiority of the Negro and the wisdom of Providence in subjecting them to servitude in keeping with the Noachian 'Cursed be Canaan'. Preaching to Negroes, they explained the ancient proclamation: Japheth shall dwell in the land of Shem, and Ham shall be his servant. Servants therefore obey your masters."[12])

The inferiority of the Negro was regarded as proved not only by the evidence of history, biology, cultural anthropology, Christianity etc., but by the evidence of experience in modern times. The freed slaves were not able to live up to the responsibility of their independence. They were too ignorant and lazy and servile to become self-respecting, self-supporting citizens. Psychological tests proved an average mental capacity lower than that of the whites, criminal records showed that the crime rate for Negroes was higher than that for the whites, health statistics revealed that the Negro death rate was high, indicating weak, inferior stock. Primitive stock could never adapt to complex, modern life. The standard of living was exposed as far below that of the whites witnessing to an innate inability to attain to their cultural level. Wherever better standards, wherever achievements of an intellectual and artistic nature could be found, it was among the increasing mulatto group and was due directly to the infusion of white blood. The mulatto was regarded as superior to the Negro group because of his white blood, and inferior to the white group because of his dark blood.

As a consequence of the point of view supported by all these "rationalizations", it was very natural for race prejudice to express itself as it did. When it was no longer possible to keep the Negroes in their right places through established institutions, such as slavery, then other devices had to be found. Segregation could keep them in their places geographically, disenfranchisement could keep them in their places politically, exclusion from trade-unions and skilled jobs could keep them in

12) Woodson, Carter G.: *The Negro in Our History*. p. 227.

their places economically. The activity of the Ku Klux Klan and the custom of lynching would check their immorality through fear. Exclusion from theatres, libraries, schools, and restaurants frequented by whites would prevent the unpleasantness of mixing socially. This would also limit the chances for cultural presumptions on the part of the Negroes. The provision of poor housing, mediocre educational facilities, and low wages was in keeping with the inferior character of the recipient. The danger of casting pearls before swine was constantly held in mind by those white people, North or South, liable to race prejudice.

Having tried to recognize in this way the nature and forms of race prejudice, its real and rationalized causes and effects, Negro thinkers turn to the study of its reaction on the Negro. This is the problem which holds perhaps the greatest interest for them. It is virgin territory simply because formerly the subject has not been of interest to the whites. The other side of the picture has not been worth seeing. But now the impartial view of science calls for complete evidence.

Stages in Race Consciousness: Response.

The history of the varying reactions of the American Negroes to race prejudice is the history of the growth of their race consciousness. Their changing moods and their attitudes in the face of social repression are intimately linked up with their changing status. Their reactions to the American environment from the time of their introduction as slaves at the beginning of the seventeenth century to the present year form several main tendencies. There has been what might be called a period of acceptance and submission, of defence, of offence, and finally a tendency towards non-resistance.

Submission.

Submission was a natural reaction for the slaves. Outnumbered, subjected to a new language, new customs, new social organization they experienced mental confusion. The hard forced labor, the insufficient food, and the heavy punish-

ments produced a state of intimidation.[13]) The breaking up of
Negro families by sale and the difficulty of winning freedom
by escape or purchase, or of securing any legal protection
caused a general feeling of hopelessness and despair about the
situation. It tended gradually to lead to an unquestioning
acquiescence with the system, as is usually the case when no
possibility of change has yet been envisioned. Fear paralyzed
action and encouraged inertia, until the habit was firmly fixed
among the masses.

It became a question of accepting the inevitable and of
seeking human happiness only within these narrow limits.
Some compensation was necessary. They found it in the consolation of religion. Religion became an escape from reality. The
Christianity of white America opened up to them at the
critical moment. It taught them that suffering was a thing to
be endured as a part of God's will for them, it promised them
abounding happiness in the future life. It suggested to their
minds a comparison of their lot with that of the Israelites
under the Egyptians, and comforted them with the offered love
of a Heavenly Father. They gained strength to submit with
patience by remembering the life of Jesus. Emotional outlet
was furnished by the evangelical type of religion they accepted,
and a certain amount of color and beauty was introduced into
their lives through the choral singing in harmony, the fervent
preaching, and the warm fellowship with other Christians. And
here was one point where as a rule they were not repressed in
any initiative they took. Many white masters, whether opportu-
nists or sincere Christians themselves, could not fail to see, or
at least sense, the advantage of a Christianity which taught
the duty of humility to their slaves. The interpretation of Christianity which the Negroes received only confirmed the status
quo. Jesus, the Man of Sorrows, was presented, and not Jesus,
the iconoclast. The pious Uncle Toms and the faithful Mammys
flourished under such a regime. There were innumerable
instances of affectionate relationships between white family

---

13) Woodson, Carter G.: *The Negro in Our History.* pp. 224—225.

and slave conditioned by the benevolence of the one and by the willing and obedient attitude of the other. Submission was found to be expedient since it evoked kinder treatment. It was a case of making the best of a bad lot.

This was usually facilitated by their own feeling of inferiority. The lowness of their estate was impressed upon them not only by their position as slaves but by the constant suggestion on the part of the dominant group. Without any education or knowledge of the facts, they were susceptible to the repeated statements concerning their native incapacity. Public opinion was strong enough to sweep along a majority of the Negroes. Even those who were casting off the shackles at this time often suffered secretly from the effects of a defeatist psychology.

Defence.

But gradually the pendulum swings. When it was no longer the minority but the majority which stood as free men, it became increasingly easy to offset the unfavorable suggestions and to challenge the old assumptions. Therefore for fifty years after the close of the Civil War in 1865 the prevailing attitude is one of denial. The period of Reconstruction put the Negro on the defensive. Here was his chance. The white world as a whole was skeptical, nevertheless here was his chance. This was no time for escapes and illusions. It was a time for facing concrete issues and for actual facts. The struggle for adjustment and self-preservation demanded a new psychology. The building up of some self assurance was essential.

Yet such a process is not completed in a few years. During the first part of the period of Reconstruction the gloomy interpretations of the nineteenth century science were at the height of their prestige, strengthened by the evident failure of migrating Negroes to succeed in urban industrial life. The Negroes as a group experienced an increasing resentment of injustice, but as a rule were inarticulate in their own defence. But at the end of the nineteenth and the beginning of the twentieth century there is a burst of protest and refutation, strengthened by the reactionary measures of government and state at this time, and continuing with decreasing zeal up to the present day. The occasion is ripe for meeting argument with counter-argument, prejudice with counter-prejudice. Explanations for seeming inferiority are on every hand. References to real achievement and worth are constant. And of course they pushed ahead to extremes in many cases. Such a Negro scholar as Arthur Schomburg recognizes this when he writes: "The blatant Caucasian racialist with his theories and assumptions of race superiority and dominance has in turn bred his Ethiopian counterpart — the rash and rabid amateur who has glibly tried to prove half of the world's geniuses to have been Negroes and to trace the pedigree of nineteenth century Americans from the Queen of Sheba."[14])

A more balanced type of defence characterizes the work of many twentieth century Negro scholars. They are attempting to show the reverse side of the old racial arguments. Although their motives and conclusions partake of the defensive, they make every effort to remain objective and cool. Their success is often noticeable in their tendency to collaborate with white scientists. In the *Annals of the American Academy of Political and Social Science* and in magazines under white ownership, articles by Negroes appear side by side with articles by white men, and the same is true in the case of distinctively Negro publications. Authorities such as Professors Park, Reuter, Goldenweiser and Boas in America and Professor Leo Frobenius of Germany are continually used.

The first defence, then, is a biological one. That the Negro is biologically inferior is open to question. Physical characteristics such as stature or skin color are subject to change according to environmental influence, often depending upon nutrition, habitual activity, or climate.[15]) The size of the brain is reduced through poor nourishment and the function of the brain depends on nerve cells and fibre which are only a part

---

14) Survey Graphic. Schomburg, Arthur: *The Negro Digs up his Past.* p. 672.

15) Reuter, E. B.: *The American Race Problem.* pp. 24—25.

of brain mass. And it might be added that there is an effective defence even without resources to this explanation, since actual investigation shows that many murderers have large brains, and that the average size of the white woman's brain is smaller than that of the Negro man's.[16]) There is therefore no proof that there is a direct connection between size of brain and mental capacity!

In regard to those other "repugnant" physical traits, „Man's skin color is partly determined by exposure, mostly by an inherited mechanism which regulates pigment — — Pigment is probably a waste product of cell metabolism. It contains iron — — Our ancestral skin was probably dark — — Pigment increased in the Negroid types and decreased in the Mongoloid — — 'High and low' skin color is as sound biology as grading planets by color would be sound astronomy — —"[17]) The typical features of the white race are not always as far removed from those of animals as are the Negroes'. The European has retained "the hairiness of the animal ancestor while the Negro is comparatively free from it."[18]) As to its quality, "Kinky woolly hair is found in no apes or monkeys. Straight black hair is. The kink is the 'highest' type, the straight black the 'lowest' — — The Negro scores with his thick out-turned lips. No men in the world have such human lips as the blackest Africans. Thin lips are primitive, 'low', apish — — There is no known fact of human anatomy or physiology which implies that capacity for culture or civilization or intelligence inheres in this race or that type."[19])

The inclination of Europe and America to consider the African as a heathen and savage is often due to insufficient knowledge and misrepresentations. Travellers have been mostly casual observers, hesitant to make long visits or proceed into the interior because of the strangeness of the climate and cul-

---

16) Boas, Franz: *The Mind of Primitive Man.* pp. 26—28.
17) Dorsey, George A.: *Why We Behave Like Human Beings.* pp. 40—43.
18) Boas, F.: *The Mind of Primitive Man.* p. 22.
19) Dorsey, G.: *Why We Behave Like Human Beings.* pp. 41—43.

ture. Public functionaries were not to be relied upon, either. They had more chance for detailed observation but at the same time were more biased by their position. The evidence of missionaries could not often be taken as impartial. "It would be unwise to expect that partisans of a certain religious system seeking to uproot another can be depended upon to report definitely on the virtues of the people whom they would proselyte."[20]) It is necessary, then, for modern scholars to investigate Africa, its peoples and its culture, accurately, and at first hand.

As a result, there is a tendency to discard the word "primitive" in favor of the word "preliterate" in speaking of the African peoples. This is because it is now felt that the essential difference between primitive and modern man is the absence of a written tradition in the first case. People of simple culture on observation seem to be as logical as people of complex culture in the realm of secular activities. "The sensory powers of primitive peoples as well as their capacity for emotional control and abstract thinking do not appear to differ essentially from those of civilized man."[21])

The fundamental point of departure from the older scientific school is the new emphasis upon environment. There is a repeated stress laid on the importance external conditions can have in modifying not only physical and mental traits but also the so-called culture of a race. The mistake is often made of "confusing advance in culture with brain improvement."[22]) The general course of historical events with different environment and opportunity can explain variations in cultural achievements more adequately than the theory of differing racial mental traits.[23]) Complex situations call forth complex responses. The extent of the ability will depend upon the extent of the demand. "It is a serious, though common, scientific blunder to seek the explanation of social phenomena in the facts of race. It is never

20) Woodson, Carter, G.: *The Negro in Our History.* pp. 5, 6.
21) *Ebony and Topaz.* Frazier, E. F.: *Racial Self-Expression.* pp. 119—20.
22) Woodson, Carter, G.: *The Negro in Our History.* p. 9.
23) Boas, F.: *The Mind of Primitive Man.* p. 29.

scientifically permissible to explain culture facts by a resort to biological data without first exhausting the possibilities of explanation on the cultural level."[24])

A simple civilization may be caused by isolation. When there is little stimulus from the outside the same time-honored customs are preserved. There is a growing general agreement today that "cultural advance is due to the contact of peoples rather than the flowering of the genius of a particular racial stock."[25]) The ancestors of highly advanced races were not superior to primitive men as now observed in places cut off from modern civilization. Therefore the difference is only a time difference, and negligible when viewed from the perspective of centuries.

Furthermore, culture is inter-racial. No people has its "own" exclusive culture. It is a combination of cultural inheritance, and new acquisitions assimilated and developed in acceptable forms.[26]) The conqueror "learned the arts of life from the conquered, and carried on the work of civilization."[27]) All civilizations have borrowed. The Greeks were the continuators of an inherited older Oriental culture. Agricultural methods came from Asia. The wheel, domestication of the horse, modern astronomy came from the Babylonians, Hindus, and Egyptians. The invention of glass is from Egypt. Spectacles came from India. Paper, highly significant, came from China. Races have never remained in isolation, are never pure, and rarely originate more than about ten per cent of their culture. Momentous ideas may often come from what we regard as primitive races. The notion of the zero figure was originated by the Mayas of Central America. It was unknown to Europeans until they borrowed it from India. A marked sense of historical perspective is common to Chinese and Europeans. Ancient Romans,

24) *Annals.* Reuter, E. B.: *The American Mulatto.* p. 39.

25) *Ebony and Topaz.* Frazier, F. A.: *Racial Self-Expression.* p. 120.

26) *Annals.* Frobenius, Leo: *Early African Culture as an Indication of Present Negro Potentialities.* p. 153.

27) Boas, F.: *The Mind of Primitive Man.* p. 6.

modern Germans, and Japanese have in common the talent for rationalistic organization of administrative affairs.

The superiority of any particular race or culture is being explained as due to circumstance. Nearly every race at some time has had a belief in its superiority, the Jews with their religion, the Egyptians, the Greeks, and the Chinese with their discoveries of printing and gun powder. To-day it is the Anglo-Saxons, and a thousand years from now no one can say who it will be. The white men are superior in wealth through control of natural resources, and in knowledge through the opportunity to build on the experiences of those preceding. They have the power and the energy to expand and control due to a combination of favorable conditions.[28]

Not only is superiority explained as due to environment rather than biological factors. The idea of superiority as such is questioned. People differ in their opinions as to what constitutes superiority. The Chinese ideal of learning and education, the Oriental habit of contemplative thought and the African capacity for rich emotion may provide as important elements to civilization as the practical, healthy aggressive qualities of the Anglo-Saxon. It is hard to say which racial qualities are most desirable. Generosity and the capacity to coöperate are as essential to survival as intelligence.[28]

And, as a last thrust, the theory of race itself is called to account. One criticism is that the term has been used far too loosely as applying not only to the main divisions of mankind but also to "nations, linguistic stocks, or cultural groups."[29] In these cases the apparent homogeneity of the group is to be explained in sociological rather than biological terms, by customs, language, and political traditions rather than by physical traits in common.[30] And even when restricted in usage to distinguish these principal human types, many of the leading Negro and white scholars are agreeing that it is a hypothetical concept. "The increasingly certain dictum of sci-

---

28) *An Introduction to Sociology.* (Davis and Barnes). pp. 840, 843.
29) Herskovitz, M. J.: *The American Negro.* p. 67.
30) Reuter, E. B.: *The American Race Problem.* p. 29.

ence is that there are no 'races' in any exact scientific sense; that no measurements of human beings, of bodily development, of head form, of color and hair, of psychological reactions, have succeeded in dividing mankind into different recognizable groups: that so-called 'pure' races seldom, if ever, exist and that all present mankind the world over are 'mixed' so far as the so-called 'racial' characteristics are concerned."[31]) For the sake of convenience the term "race" is still generally used, but there is a belief that it cannot be of scientific and practical value unless it refers to a kind of average of a group of individuals who exhibit a relative sociological or biological homogeneity subject to change with changing conditions. There can be no hard and fast lines. The interpretation must be so broad as to allow for the constant creation of new "races" on this basis, according to the appearance of a new social or physical type.

From this point of view it would be fallacious to regard the Negroes as a closed racial group inclusive of the American Negroes. Not only has the Negro in Africa undergone a process of crossing with European and Oriental stock centuries ago which prevents the existence of any "pure" Negroid race to begin with, but in addition the American Negro reveals characteristics which throw doubt on the correctness of his classification in the same category. Generalities about Negroes and the attempts to identify them all together are misguided. "The so-called American Negro is probably less than twenty-five per cent of pure African descent. There is reason to believe that over seventy per cent of these so-called Negroes are descendants of American whites and that forty per cent of them have as much white blood, as Negro."[32]) A peculiar diversity of ancestry is found among the Negroes now living in the United States, native born or immigrants from the West Indies, Haiti, Latin

---

31) *Annals.* Du Bois, W. E. B.: *Race Relations in the United States.*
   p. 6.
32) Ibid. p. 10.

America, or Africa, "people of Spanish, French, Dutch, Arabian, Danish, Portugese, British, and native African ancestry."[33]) The Caucasian through the white man and the Mongoloid through the American Indian have joined with the African Negro to form a unique combination.[34])

The resultant product can be regarded as a distinctive race in a relative sense. Certainly there are psychological and social forces making towards the cohesion of the group as evidenced by its "Renaissance" movement, while the physical type shows a rather surprising uniformity in view of the mixed origin. It is a type which seems to lie "half way between the characteristic features of the parent stocks" so that "the American Negro resembles all of his ancestral types and yet is none of them."[35]) But his distinctiveness must always be realized as impermanent. as due to a peculiar set of conditions in the past and present which may be radically transformed at any time. For instance, mutual racial dislike on the part of colored and white people in America has been instrumental during the last two or three generations in discouraging inter-marriage between the two groups. The environmental factor of forced and then voluntary isolation has had its biological effects. But „this American Negro type will never be established if the bars which prevent racial mixture are broken down, or if for any unforeseen reason there should be a large migration to this country of pure Africans who would mingle their blood with that of the American Negroes."[36]) Inhabitants of a changing world, they formulate no closed radical group any more than did the Africans subject to the Eastern migration of Arabs, or the Anglo-Saxons subject to the conquest of the Normans or the native born „Nordic" white American subject to the influx of Central and Southern European immigration. No group of peoples ever has a guarantee of that isolation essential for the maintenance of any „racial purity."

33) *The New Negro*. Domingo, W. A.: *Gift of the Black Tropics.* p. 341.
34) Herskovitz, M. J.: *The American Negro. p.* 4, 33.
35) Ibid. pp. 52, 49.
36) Ibid. p. 50.

Such new conclusions about race, whether fully accepted as yet or not, constitute an entrenchment of their defence position serviceable in emergency. It has been preceded by a temporary acceptance of the American Negro's identification with the larger Negro race and an attempt to offset any assumptions as to its biological and cultural inferiority, an attempt supported by reference to the hitherto unrecognized importance of environmental influence. But now many Negroes in America fortify themselves still further in the face of continued attack. Racial arguments on one side tend to gain strength before racial arguments on the other, but to fall flat before the denial of „race". Supported by the research work of scholars like Boas and Herskovitz, they suggest that perhaps it is not really necessary, after all, to clear themselves in the light of their African ancestry, that they form a peculiar type of their own in the making of which the „superior white race" itself has its undeniable part, in spite of its avoidance of responsibility, that they must therefore be judged strictly on their own merits as a group. This judgment should include a recognition of individual differences within the group at present and of the possible modification of the group in the future through fluctuating conditions. The past should not claim at the expense of the present situation, especially when the past is so problematical. Function is more important than structure.

In this way leaving muted points of anthropology and biology as well as a consideration of the Negro in relation to his origins and his African background, and focussing upon the social situation of the Negro in America now, the critics continue to apply the environmental test. A favorite method of proving the natural inferiority of the Negro has been the use of intelligence tests. But this is admittedly to-day a complex field of investigation and no one conclusion can go without challenge from a diametrically opposed conclusion. The findings of psychologists have revealed the greatest variety and this cannot help but suggest the need of caution in generalizing about the difference between the mental capacity of black and white. "The Negro may be the intellectual inferior of the white racial stock, but to date no one has marshalled in proof of the position any body of evidence that has scientific validity."[37])

Psychological tests provide a convenient device for grading individuals but they do not as yet measure real intelligence. The results are too dependent upon the effects of the particular individual's training and environment. Difference in schooling, in occupation, in economic status, social contacts and opportunities in general, will inevitably contribute towards certain differences in the quality of the answers given by individuals. Otherwise how can the fact be explained that the Northern Negroes have better ratios than the Southern Negroes. It is true that the average score for white school children has been higher than that of Negro children, but „the casual and offhand manner in which the testers have in general assumed a common environment in terms, say of income of parents, is an adequate and conclusive demonstration of their failure to appreciate the almost infinite complexity of social stimulation, and the large end results that may come from small and apparently trivial differences in initial stimulation."[38])

In regard to health, Negro scholars point to the fact that the expectation of life is as high today as that of the American white man thirty years ago, and is improving steadily. The higher death rate can be explained first, by exposure to a temperate instead of a tropical climate, then by ignorance, poverty, and lack of medical attention, by bad housing, overwork, and insufficient food and clothing, conditions which are still more prevalent among Negroes than whites, rather than by inherent susceptibility and biological weakness.[39]) A recent general improvement in social and economic conditions thus accounts for the declining death rate from their most prevalent disease, tuberculosis.[40]) The difference between the races is thus not

---

37) Reuter, E. B.: *The American Race Problem*. p. 92.
38) Ibid. pp. 91, 83.
39) *Annals*. Dublin, L. I.: *The Health of the Negro*. p. 82.
40) *Annals*. Landis, H. M. R.: *Tuberculosis and the Negro*. p. 86.

unalterable and racial in cause, but due to historical and environmental experiences which are modifiable.[41])

There is an acknowledgement on the part of Negro leaders such as Du Bois and Booker T. Washington, that their race has a higher crime rate than the white race in America. This seems to offer support for the generally accepted popular notion of criminal tendencies in the Negro, explained by his „inherited depravity", his barbarian background, his racial brutality, or what not. But there is a growing insistence on the need of probing behind the crime into the cause. Granting that the Negroes, on receiving their freedom and being introduced to city and industrial life, had a large percentage of criminality, explanations are numerous. In many cases, "these emancipated slaves were victims who had been bred deliberately in sloth, ignorance, poverty and crime,"[42]) with practically no political or industrial training. They were not equipped for freedom to begin with, and since Emancipation they have been provided with only inadequate and inferior educational facilities in spite of equal taxation. Some connection between a high degree of illiteracy and illegality is natural. Ignorant parents and poor schools cannot train and supervise children in the right way so as to avoid juvenile delinquency, that starting point of more serious offences. In addition the number of criminals is swelled because of the fact that there are not enough institutions in the United States for the care and isolation of feeble minded and defective Negro children who are thus a potential source of danger to the community. And aside from delinquents and defectives, average Negroes have an incentive to crime just in their restricted circumstances and undesirable location.[43]) Race prejudice of the white inhabitants has segregated them in those sections of the cities where the material and moral standards are lowest, and has limited their activities. Outlet through crime is to be expected, especially when educa-

41) Reuter, E. B.: *The American Race Problem.* p. 186.

42) *Annals.* Du Bois, W.E.B.: *Race Relations in the United States* p.8.

43) Reuter, E. B.: *The American Race Problem.* pp. 361—362.

tion in the ways and technique of crime is all too available from the surroundings, and anti-social suggestions sink into the fertile soil of that mental and moral confusion attendant on the abrupt change from a supervised agricultural to an independent industrial mode of life.

Furthermore, the will to believe on the part of many white communities magnifies the actual extent of criminality. The American public is often so conditioned by such organs of public opinion as the cinema and daily press that it is more than ready to suspect the Negro of crime. The white citizen is frequently quick to accuse, the officers of the law quick to arrest without sufficient grounds. There seems to be evidence to the fact that the Negro law-breakers whether real or imaginary meet discrimination on the part of the law-courts, so that they are not only often convicted more frequently than white men arrested for the same offence, but also are given heavier sentences which in turn breeds crime.[44]) With less education and money, with more temptation to crime, with the attitude of the average judges and juries, lawyers and policemen already prejudiced against them, it is to be expected that the apparent criminality exceeds that found among the white race. But the authenticity of the quantitative method in ascertaining the real tendency towards crime among Negroes is assailable, under the circumstances.

That the mulattoes as a group seem to possess a certain superiority to the full-blooded Negro group is again admitted. In industry and business, the professions, and the arts, the outstanding men are of mixed blood. Out of a list of about 250 Negro leaders thirteen-fourteenths were attested to have part white ancestry.[45]) The facts are indisputable, and the black man of genius is regarded as an exception. But even here the biological interpretation is considered inadequate. The very fact that there *are* cases of full-blooded Negroes of marked achievements, even if not frequent, throws doubt on the theory

---

44) *Annals.* Sellin, T.: *The Negro Criminal.* p. 59.
45) Reuter, E. B.: *The Mulatto in the United States.* pp. 379—380.

of innate inferiority in the race as such. Such exceptions as Phillis Wheatley, the first recognized Negro poetess, and Paul Laurence Dunbar, to many the greatest of the Negro poets, Professor Kelly Miller, an outstanding sociologist, and Dr. Robert Moton, the famous educator, seem to indicate no inherent and inevitable limitations due to their relatively pure African descent.

Negro and white students are suggesting that the question is not so much a qualitative as a quantitative one. The black man who rises to success of some kind can hold his own with the best from the mulattoes. But he does not rise so often. This suggests an external explanation in a possible difference of attitude and opportunity presented to the two groups from the outside. And here indeed, is found the heart of the problem. From the very start there have been less discrimination against and more favorable conditions for the mulatto. In the days of slavery the white master would naturally be partial to his relative's or his own mulatto child, giving him education and special privileges and often freeing him when mature.[46] At worst, the mulattoes were treated as servants rather than slaves, and used for lighter tasks around the houses of the white peoples which at the same time developed more initiative and sense of responsibility. There was a chance to absorb more of the culture of the white group through direct observation and contact.[47]

Aside from being better equipped in this way for the test of freedom, the mulattoes have had a potent psychological factor working in their favor. There was a wide-spread assumption on the part of white Americans that they were superior to their black brothers. It was a natural assumption on the part of those who, in many cases, had actually contributed their own „superior" white blood, and it could not but affect the opinion of the Negroes themselves. It encouraged a feeling of

46) Herskovitz, M. J.: *The American Negro*. p. 60.
47) *Ebony and Topaz*. Reuter, E. B.: *The Changing Status of the Mulatto*. p. 108.

inferiority among the full-blooded Negroes and a feeling of self-confidence and worth among the mulattoes, helping to establish them as the dominant group with the continued opportunity for fuller development.[48]) Quite apart from the question of accuracy, such an assumption fostered a tradition of mulatto superiority which in turn influenced marriage selection. Since the mulatto has a more desirable social status, the mulatto woman is often sought for marriage more quickly than the black one.[49]) Since racial prejudice seems to increase with increase of black pigmentation, there is observable a tendency on the part of black-skinned Negroes to offset their handicap through mulatto marriages, which if not directly accruing to their advantage at least will insure more favorable conditions for their lighter-skinned children. This means that often the black Negroes of superior ability are admitted and contribute their endowment to the mulatto class, in this way providing a certain ground for the contention of the mulatto biological superiority. The mulatto group has had every advantage working in its favor to include the best of both groups. Yet it is necessary to consider it primarily as a social group and not as a biological type. And there is every reason to believe that with lessened prejudice and equalized opportunities the full-blooded Negro will no longer need to accept such predominant mulatto leadership. Already the restraining effects of the traditional public opinion are being loosened. In proportion as the popular notion of race inequality is broken down and the faith of the Negroes in themselves is built up, the circumstances making for the exclusive advantage of the mulatto will disappear.[50])

And basically the two groups find themselves unavoidably bound together in a common cause. From the white point of view the mulatto is still a Negro, as long as he has a discoverable

48) Reuter, E. B.: *The Mulatto in the United States*. pp. 376—378.

49) Herskovitz, M. J.: *The American Negro*. p. 62.

50) *Ebony and Topaz*. Reuter, E. B.: *The Changing Status of the Mulatto*. p. 110.

drop of Negro blood in his veins and therefore is still an inferior creature. In his contacts with the modern white world, it
is rather barren consolation to be considered a little less inferior to darker Negroes as long as he is in spite of this assigned
to the same general category. It is a case of the leopard and his
spots. Therefore, from the point of view of defence, Negroes of
all shades of color find need of joining forces.

It is as a group, then, that they present their qualifications
for a place in American life. The contention that any person
possessing Negro blood is unable to adjust satisfactorily to
the white man's civilization in America affects them all alike,
and draws forth numerous denials. Their striking capacity for
adaptation is constantly cited. Through a long history of ad-
versity, the American Negro has been schooled in the ways of
survival, one of the first requirements of which is as quick
and complete an adjustment as possible to the new and usually
hostile environment. In this respect he stands in marked contrast to the American Indian who could not submit himself to
the customs of the white man and thus continued to resist,
paying the price with almost complete extinction.[51]) But the
Negro had a more protective psychology. The result is described
graphically by one of the ablest Negro scholars: „Torn from
his native culture and background, he was suddenly precipitated
into a complex and very alien culture and civilization, and passed through the fierce crucible of rapid, but complete adaptation to its rudiments, the English language, Christianity, the
labor production system, and Anglo-Saxon mores. His complete mental and spiritual flexibility, his rapid assimilation of
this new culture, in most cases within the first generation, is
the outstanding feat of his group career and is almost without
parallel in history."[52]) Instead of introducing factors of non-
conformity, from the first there was a general acceptance of
the American institutions and standards. Without this loyalty

---

51) Moton, R. R.: *What the Negro thinks.* pp. 64—65.
52) *Annals.* Locke, Alain,: *The Negro's Contribution to American Art
and Literature.* p. 234.

and predisposition towards coöperation, the Negroes might have constituted a real danger to the equilibrium of the United States, as their numbers and awareness of the situation grew. White Americans have received from the Negroes an unrecognized blessing through that very power to adapt which they deny exists. „The lower standard of living" may still hold true for the Negro in comparison with the white group as a whole, but it is approximating the higher standard more closely with every decade, and in the face of so much progress under unfavorable conditions, the thinking Negro to-day finds himself wondering how much more it might be under favorable conditions.[53])

For the thinking Negro is taken up with this idea of progress. His defence towards the white world would be considered inadequate even by him if it consisted only of a proof of his assimilative and adaptive capacity. At best this would be only a negative virtue. And the facts seem to support a belief in more than passivity. The opinion held by Lord Bryce is upheld: that the Negroes made more advance during the first thirty years of their freedom than has ever been made by an Anglo-Saxon group in a similar period of time. And the last two decades have seen an even greater acceleration, with the World War as a real starting point for conspicuous economic and industrial progress. Beween 1915 and 1930 a million and a half Negroes moved North and citywards. The cutting down of foreign immigration and the greater demands of war industry gave the Negro an opening in industry. By an anomaly, the war thus proved beneficial in his case. There was a great call for Negro labor which was not unanswered, but it was not mere opportunism on the part of the Negro, or an escape from a combination of poor crops and terrorism in the South. „The wash and rush of this human tide on the beach line of the northern city centers is to be explained primarily in terms of a new vision of opportunity, of social and economic freedom, of

---

53) *The World Tomorrow*, June, 1929. Locke, Alain: *Negro Contributions to America.* p. 255.

a spirit to seize, even in the face of an extortionate and heavy toll, a chance for the improvement of conditions."[54])

There have been material and tangible results. After the Civil War the Negroes were estimated to have owned 12,000 homes, 2,000 businesses, 20,000 farms, 2 newspapers, and their wealth was evaluated at $ 20,000,000.[55]) At the end of 1929 they owned 700,000 homes, 70,000 businesses, 232,000 farms, about 500 newspapers, with a wealth evaluated at $ 15,000,000,000.[56]) When they first reached the North they were confined to unskilled labor, since they were regarded as unfit for industry. Gradually they have worked their way into semi-skilled and often skilled work, and the trade unions which were almost universally hostile at first, are beginning to recognize their growing ability and power.[57]) In fact, their success has forced „a tendency towards some admission of the Negro into the higher skilled and even the executive ranks of American industry.[58])

Similarly educational gains can be pointed out. There has been an improvement of educational facilities, equipment, and standards. 4,174 Rosenwald schools alone have sprung up in 17 of the Southern states, the Negroes themselves having contributed four million dollars towards them. Howard, Fisk, and Atlanta Universities are of established sound reputation.[59]) There are 10,000 graduates each year from American colleges and universities, and there are at least 45,000 Negro teachers, 3,500 physicians, and over 1,000 lawyers, in addition to those in other professions including scientists of international repute such as Professor George Carver and Professor Ernest Just.[60])

---

54) *The New Negro.* Locke, Alain: *The New Negro.* p. 6.

55) Davis and Barnes: *An Introduction to Sociology.* p. 843.

56) *The New Republic.* Aug., 7, 1929. Bagnell, Robert W.: *Two Decades of Negro Life.* p. 304.

57) Ibid. p. 305.

58) *Opportunity.* May, 1930. p. 138.

59) Ibid. p. 138.

60) *The New Republic.* Bagnell, Robert: *Two Decades of Negro Life.* p. 304.

In general the claim is that the Negro has been giving ample indications of a capacity not only for passive adjustment but for positive achievement, and, still more, that this achievement has gone beyond the limits of the group to add to the larger American life. From the time when the slaves constituted America's first great labor force, the Negroes have been contributing to its civilization, oftentimes unconsciously and usually in the face of resistance and skepticism, yet nevertheless effectively. The material welfare of the United States owes a debt to the presence of Negroes, Negroes who have participated in all the wars, nursed the white babies, dug in the fields, cooked the food, and worked in the factories. From this point of view, there is no real justification for the prevailing conception that the Negro is a liability rather than an asset, that he is a permanent dependent in national life.

Even more than the material are the artistic contributions to America stressed and evaluated. These came often as a reaction to white civilization originally, but usually something distinctive and new was added. „The irony of the situation is that in folk-lore, folk-song, folk-dance, and popular music the things recognized as characteristically and uniquely American are products of the despised slave minority."[61]) For example, the spirituals were the outcome of the slaves' contact with Christianity. Their sorrows found emotional outlet in these songs permeated with religious fervor and colorful imagination, until their genuineness and sheer artistry have commanded recognition. "They have outlived the particular generation and the peculiar conditions which produced them; they have survived in turn the contempt of the slave owners, the conventionalizations of formal religion, the repressions of Puritanism, the corruptions of sentimental balladry, and the neglect and disdain of second-generation respectability. They have escaped the lapsing conditions and the fragile vehicle of folk art, and come firmly into the context of formal music. Only

---

61) *The World Tomorrow.* June, 1929. Locke, Alain: *Negro Contributions to America Life.* pp. 255—256.

classics survive such things."[62]) And to-day modern music is being influenced by Negro gifts. For example, a fundamental element in the music of the present is jazz, and jazz proper, though fostered in an encouraging American environment, is thoroughly American Negro. The original songs were the "Blues" and jazz became "his spiritual picture on that lighter comedy side, just as the spirituals are the picture on the tragedy side."[63]) The question of the intrinsic value of jazz is another matter. Many modern Negroes would deny that jazz could be regarded as a commendable offering to any civilization or could be viewed as a genuine form of art, while pointing to the fact that the American public nevertheless treats it as indispensable to music and the dance and to that extent should be ready to appreciate and recognize its Negroid origins. It is not to be denied that jazz as a popular art is playing an important rôle in the present civilization of America, whether or not in its culture.

It is anticipated that the Negro will influence American culture in the present and future as he has in the past. There will be more men of the calibre of Countee Cullen, Roland Hayes, Paul Robeson, and Henry Tanner. The Negro poet, actor, musician, and artist are stepping more and more into the foreground. Instances of Negro elements in American life could be indefinitely multiplied, forming the sole theme of books by Negro writers such as Dr. Du Bois' "The Gift of Black Folk", and subsidiary themes of books such as Dr. Moton's "What the Negro Thinks", and Dr. Locke's "The New Negro".

Offence.

But of late years the Negro seems to have grown weary of defending himself by resorting to explanation and counter-argument, by listing his virtues and potentialities. Perhaps it is futile to expose his handicaps to those who caused them and his triumphs to those who oppose them. There comes a time

62) *The New Negro:* Locke, Alain: *The Negro Spirituals.* p. 199.
63) *Survey Graphic.* March, 1925. J. A. Rogers: *Jazz at Home.* p. 665.

when one wonders why one should have to justify his existence, after all. The motive has been to instigate a more friendly public opinion and to secure a better place under the sun. But in the last analysis, the fault is not one of omission or commission on one side. The other side has also its share in the responsibility for evil days. The injustices of the dominant group have been forced upon the weaker group. But the patent success of the process should perhaps call forth in place of a consciousness of superiority, a consciousness of guilt. White Americans are concerned about the "race problem", forgetting in their strategic position that it takes at least two groups to make such a social problem. After all, Negroes begin to ask, who started the trouble? If the white group had left the Negroes of Africa in peace, all would have been quite otherwise. The Negroes were not even voluntary immigrants like the Europeans. They were forcibly introduced into the country and therefore not to be held answerable for its consequent resentment.

The feelings of fear and perplexity, of hopelessness, and despair, or of humbleness and apathy which led to the early state of submission on the part of the majority of Negroes were superceded by feelings of pride. With the growth of this pride there has been a natural tendency among many to desert the defensive for an offensive position, to carry the battle into the camp of the enemy. The spears are sharp and the arrows are barbed, for the sense of injustice is great. In fact the contention is that the very existence of this injustice practised by the white group is enough to throw doubt upon its right to assume superiority. It is a question as to whether the two are compatible. "This failure and apparent disinclination of the privileged group to employ their own professed moral and ethical standards when dealing with Negroes has been sufficient to cast a cloud over the title to superiority claimed by those who see in white nothing but good and in black nothing but evil."[64])

---

64) Moton, R. R.: *What the Negro Thinks.* p. 26.

If the white people in America did not profess to ideals, or even if they admitted to inconsistency, the case would be altered. There is something to condone in an out and out materialist who makes no secret of his self-seeking intentions. He will use whatever means necessary to attain his ends but at the same time will not depend upon an unearned sense of virtue for stimulus. Many of the old slave-drivers exercised unspeakable brutality over their charges, but they did not pretend to be other than the powerful animals they were. It was not so simple for more cultivated and educated types. "For it never was pleasant — this thing of disposing of the slave in the land of the free and the home of the brave, where all men are created equal and endowed with equal rights to life, liberty, and the pursuit of happiness."[65]) The only possible way for them to reconcile slavery with Christianity, and an exclusion policy with democracy was by building up a huge structure of rationalizations founded upon hypocrisy.[66])

This is the main indictment which the Negro brings against the average American citizen: his failure to square his conduct with his principles, and his refusal to recognize this failure. From the very first, the Negro asserts, America has shown an astonishing power to avoid the subject. The only way in which the Declaration of Independence could be peaceably formulated was by passing over the issue of slavery. Even then there was the inevitable minority demanding justice, but the compromise selected by the majority in dealing with such a controversial matter was to omit all reference to it.[67]) Their silence sanctioned the institution and, now that economic and social conditions in the nation long ago forced the abandonment of the slavery system, their silence continues to sanction modern substitutes. It is a question as to whether the debt-slavery in which the ignorant Negro farmer in the South is easily involved to-day is much more preferable to the body-slavery of old. Share-crop-

65) Moton, R. R.: *What the Negro Thinks.* p. 29.
66) *Survey Graphic.* March, 1925. Miller, Kelly: *The Harvest of Race Prejudice.* p. 682.
67) Moton, R. R.: *What the Negro Thinks.* p. 47.

ping and peonage are common. Exploiters are quick to seize their advantage, for "so long as the best elements of a community do not feel in duty bound to protect and train and care for the weaker members of their group, they leave them to be preyed upon by these swindlers and rascals."[68]) Again, the prominent white citizens in a Southern community may not soil their hands directly in the work of the Ku Klux Klan, but their encouragement or even their failure to protest allows the supreme injustice of lynching to be practiced over and over again and allows attitudes to survive which were able to defeat the recent Anti-lynching legislation. And yet, the charge continues, they can sit in their church pews on Sundays and listen complacently to the gospel proclaiming the brotherhood of man. It seems to the Negro as if one white hand were upholding the glory of the land of opportunity, and the other were crushing his right to vote in most Southern states, or pushing him into inferior schools and houses, into separate vehicles and communities, where even the public taxation for improvements which he has helped to pay avails him little.[69]) Such a double standard of ethics fostered by race prejudice is bound to weaken the moral fibre of the dominant group, lead to national disgrace and open the way for undesirable international effects. A chronic state of hypocrisy and injustice is disastrous to the society which cultivates it.[70])

Strong prejudice will not only blind people to a sense of right but will destroy their power of discrimination. They will be unable to differentiate between individuals of an unpopular race and will classify them all under one stereotype, whether they are educated or ignorant, capable or ignorant, rich or poor. Therefore the Negro on the offensive finds another vulnerable spot here. It is not alone a weak moral sense, which they claim to discover in their opponents but a weak intelligence. Is it not

---

68) Du Bois, W. E. B.: *The Souls of Black Folk.* p. 171.
69) Moton, R. R.: *What the Negro Thinks.* Ch. V & VI. pp. 69—99, 100—126.
70) *Survey Graphic.* Miller, Kelly: *The Harvest of Race Prejudice.* p. 682.

a form of mental laziness or dullness, they ask, to make
sweeping generalizations about the Negro group, including all
members on the same low level without any distinctions. The
superficial white observer is challenged for his glib remarks
about the bad conditions of the masses. Granting this, "there
is certainly on the one hand adequate historical cause for this,
and unmistakable evidence that no small number have, in spite
of tremendous disadvantages, risen to the level of American
civilization. And when, by proscription and prejudice, these
same Negroes are classed with and treated like the lowest of
their people, simply because they are Negroes, such a policy
not only discourages thrift and intelligence among black men,
but puts a direct premium on the very things you complain of,
— inefficiency and crime. Draw lines of crime, of incompetency,
of vice, as tightly and uncompromisingly as you will, for these
things must be proscribed; but a color-line not only does not
accomplish this purpose, but thwarts it."[71]) Even if a certain
amount of prejudice were always inevitable or desirable as an
incentive in a society, it should at least be on individual and not
on race grounds, directed against stupidity and coarseness
rather than against the kind of complexion one has by accident.

Solutions.

But whether the Negroes take the defence or offence position, whether they extol the virtues of their own group or
denounce the vices of the other group, whether they bear
resentment and indignation or appeal to either the conscience
or reason of the "in-group", they are faced with a common
problem. This period of denial, this urge towards resistance
and assertiveness evolves along with it a certain sense of responsibility. A way out must be found. The need for solutions
is pressing. No matter what the causes and effects of race
prejudice, the condition is real and must be faced on this
ground. Given the disease and diagnosis, what about the
treatment and cure. In the days before the Civil War religion

---

71) Du Bois, W. E. B.: *The Souls of Black Folk.* p. 187.

was the only solution for the majority, and Emancipation the only solution for the more thoughtful and capable minority. But to the restless souls who come later this religion is regarded as a deceptive panacea without healing powers, and Emancipation as a hollow freedom without content. There was no new heaven and new earth awaiting for them ready-made, in the chaotic times of Reconstruction. Their changed status found ready a host of new problems demanding new adjustments, and supported by an even more virile prejudice than before. Very early in their experience as freed men Negroes came to realize the firmly rooted nature of prejudice which prohibited sudden or quick removal but which nevertheless should not prohibit some sort of mitigation in keeping with the need.

Obviously no thinking and self-respecting Negroes then any more than now were content with the three popular nineteenth century solutions for dealing with that problem of four million released slaves: deportation, extermination, or amalgamation.[72]) There has been at different times a certain vogue for colonization, actually attempted in Haiti and Liberia culminating in the recent Back-to-Africa movement headed by the notorious Marcus Garvey.[73]) But few American Negroes have had any desire to leave the land in which they have been born and raised to settle in a foreign and distant place. It might have been a different case with the first generation, but the second and third generations know nothing but America and therefore consider it as their home. And even if they are treated as unwanted children in this home, they have refused equally to accept the second alternative of extermination. In spite of poor treatment they have persisted in surviving. This was against the general expectation about the Negro after the Emancipation. "He was expected to dwindle progressively in numbers until his final disappearance, but he is still here and his numbers continue to increase."[74]) The question of amal-

---

72) Moton, R. R.: *What the Negro Thinks.* p. 240.

73) Woodson, Carter G.: *The Negro in Our History.* pp. 304, 434, 554.

74) Moton, R. R.: *What the Negro Thinks.* p. 240.

gamation is more complicated and has been given much more consideration. But the concensus of opinions, whether favorable or unfavorable to the idea, is that it can be only a theoretical and ultimate solution. As long as two different races live in proximity intermarriage is bound to take place, but it will always be opposed as an open practice by the "respectable" group on both sides, and it can only prove such a gradual solution of the race problem that it has no immediate and practical value.

In view of what they held were inadequate suggestions for their treatment, it is natural that Negroes should develop their own theories as to the wisest course of procedure. As the nineteenth century draws to a close, two types of leadership, two schools of thought, two general attitudes begin to take shape. One is what might be characterized as opportunistic and utilitarian, the other as idealistic and ultimate in its aims, the one willing to compromise, the other scorning compromise, the one optimistic of mood and tactful in method, the other rebellious of mood and militant in method. Dr. Booker T. Washington was the guiding spirit of the first, Dr. W. E. B. Du Bois of the second.

The philosophy of Booker T. Washington was hopeful and invigorating. He tried to show to thousands of his race that it might be considered a certain advantage to belong to an unpopular race in so far as it could serve as a needed spur towards greater achievement. He claimed as a great human law that "Merit, no matter under what skin found, is, in the long run, recognized and rewarded."[75] His own career from obscure poverty and parentage to a nationally and even internationally recognized position appeared to give startling confirmation of this law. And the secret of his power seemed to lie in his emphasis upon the next step, firmly and accurately taken. He regarded a better future for his people to depend upon slow and careful building from bed-rock.

To him, this meant a primary concern with their economic

75) Washington, Booker T.: *Up from Slavery.* p. 41.

welfare, which in turn required a concentration on their industrial training. In order to hold their own with white men, they must develop greater skill and efficiency. Good jobs and good pay will not be available to the untrained worker. It is not until the black worker can make bricks or build a house or repair an automobile as well as or better than the white worker that he can expect to be received on the same level. And it is not until he has won economic independence and security through this means that he can expect to be approved by the community. He must have education to succeed in this scheme, but it must be industrial and not cultural. Rather than being educated away from his environment he should be given instruction that he could use immediately in the first necessary step upward.[76]) "Cast down your buckets where you are," was his repeated cry to his race. Vocational education has become such a slogan in the modern world that the pioneer work of this Negro educator back in the nineties seems to have found justification outside the boundaries of his particular race.

The "uplift" program of Booker T. Washington gained additional prestige because of the approval it occasioned among the white people. Here at last was evidently a solution on which both sides could agree. White philanthropists readily contributed towards the foundation of industrial schools in the South, and white audiences listened to the speeches of this Negro leader with enthusiasm. But there were those skeptics among the Negroes who were quick to point out the secret of his and his program's popularity: He did not antagonize white people by presuming equality. He spoke of the Negro's duties rather than his rights. For the Negroes to become better workmen could only improve the material welfare of the nation and could not endanger the spiritual welfare as long as they kept their subordinate places peacefully. And this is exactly what Washington proposed and even more, for, "in our humble way, we shall stand by you with a devotion that no foreigner can approach, ready to lay down our lives, if need

76) Woodson, Carter G.: *The Negro in Our History*. pp. 440—441.

be, in defence of yours, interlacing our industrial, commercial, civil, and religious life with yours in a way that shall make the interests of both races one. In all things that are purely social we can be as separate as the fingers, yet one as the hand in all things essential to mutual progress."[77])

There were many keen-minded Negroes at the beginning of the twentieth century who could not fail to regard such a point of view as compromise. It eased the consciences of the white people by giving them opportunity for a helpful attitude which at the same time was moderate enough not to strain their tolerance to the breaking point. It provided channels of activity for the onward sweep of the black people while carefully proscribing the width and depth and length of these channels. To be sure it was positive and a step beyond submission, yet there was something too cautious, too unimaginative, too humble and conciliatory in its very nature to satisfy more radical minds. Such a tradition had grown up around Washington that it took courage even to express criticism of his ideas. But leadership for the opposition was found in the outspoken opinions of Dr. Du Bois whose influence was and is to-day potent in developing the other general attitude towards solution.

The feeling of this second group is that there is no way out except by winning full rights as American citizens. The Negro cannot fulfil his duties satisfactorily until he is allowed his just opportunities for unlimited self-development and participation in national life. While recognizing the values offered by the first group, not an inch of other values must be relinquished according to Dr. Du Bois' direct statement. "So far as Mr. Washington preaches Thrift, Patience, and Industrial Training for the masses, we must hold up his hands and strive with him, rejoicing in his honors and glorying in the strength of this Joshua called of God and of man to lead the headless host. But so far as Mr. Washington apologizes for injustice, North or South, does not rightly value the privilege

77) Washington, Booker T.: *Up from Slavery.* pp. 221—222.

and duty of voting, belittles the emasculating effects of caste
distinctions, and opposes the higher training and ambition
of our brighter minds, — so far as he, the South, or the
nation, does this, — we must unceasingly and firmly oppose
them."[78]) And this opposition is not even tempered by the
Washington type of optimism. Often a mood of bitterness
permeates it, caused by the realization of the overwhelming
odds it must struggle against or by the utter absurdity and
cruelty of the attitude which necessitates it.

To-day the constructive elements of Washington's ideas
appear on the educational side in the work of Dr. Robert Moton,
now principal of the Southern industrial school started by
Washington, and on the organizational side in the ameliorative
and practical methods of the National Urban League. Dr. Moton
stresses the continual dependence of the Negro on the white
man. "For all that the Negro has accomplished so much to-day,
there is a definite limit to his achievements without the practical support and coöperation of the white man," and, because
of the latter's advantageous position, „the idea of Negro domination is a political scarecrow, unworthy of intelligent constructive statesman-ship."[79]) "The moderation of the Negro's desires" must be remembered. Because his whole past experience
in the United States has shown his tendency to adapt and compromise, the problem of his status in American society should
be treated by "conference and adjustment" rather than by
heated legislation. The reason why Dr. Moton finds grounds
for hope is that this very process is now going on in the South,
that the conscience of the South, especially its cultured and
superior group, is so aroused of late years as to lead to the
formation of the Interracial Commission, and that here at last
white man and black man are actually conferring and coöp-
erating peacefully together on racial issues. He and his adher-
ents find new strength in the belief that the silent majority
of intelligent white people, especially since the crisis period of

---

78) Du Bois, W. E. B.: *The Souls of Black Folk.* p. 59.
79) Moton, R. R.: *What the Negro Thinks.* p. 266.

the World War, are beginning to join voices with them in their plea for justice. The keynote of Dr. Moton's solution is direct coöperation between the races, with the diplomatic policy of "leaving to the future the handling of such problems as may still prove too difficult to approach."[80]) Throughout twenty years the National Urban League, under Negro leadership, with its magazine "Opportunity", has applied this theory. It is concerned with local, urban, industrial conditions as they affect the Negro, and it joins with white organizations in attempting to adjust immediate issues in the wisest possible way.

But it is this very tendency to limit the immediate issue to the modest and easily attainable, and to assume the slowness in the reaching of eventual and more ambitious goals as inevitable which provokes the criticism of the radical group. No Negro of balanced judgement takes issue with the fundamental belief and the final idea of Dr. Moton when he writes: "At the bottom of his heart the Negro believes that he has capabilities of culture and character equal to those of any other race; he believes that his gifts and endowments are of equal worth to those of any other people; and even in the mingling of racial strains, however undesirable it might seem to be from a social point of view, he would never admit that his blood carries any taint of physiological, mental, or spiritual inferiority. However long it may take, therefore, through however many generations of social progress it may extend, the Negro expects ultimately to live in America with such freedom of movement, such equality of opportunity, and such measure of common respect for his person and personality as will leave him even though distinguished in physical characteristics, without any lower status than that of the average American citizen."[81]) But many take issue with the conservative postponement of this ultimate bliss.

The left-wing movement to-day finds more unhampered room for action in the North than in the South. Undoubtedly

---

80) Moton, R. R.: *What the Negro Thinks.* pp. 261—265.
81) Ibid. p. 239.

the more tactful approach started by Booker T. Washington is largely conditioned by the greater barriers raised by greater prejudice in the Southern states. In New York City there is not the same price to be paid for radicalism. It has a center for its aggressive method in the National Association for the Advancement of Colored People, and its periodical, "The Crisis", organized twenty years ago to take active measures for securing political and legal equality. The work of this association leads to inevitable coöperation with the whites, especially when it must come in repeated contact with governmental departments in its efforts to win complete franchisement, to illegalize lynching etc.. But the stress is upon the recognition and exercise of the initiative and talent *within* the group. The weary distance to absolute justice cannot be shortened by too much reliance on outside aid.

One of the best ways to stimulate this potentiality of the group to its maximum capacity and accelerate evolution in the United States environment is by arousing its pride. Consequently the outstanding Negro men of this second school of thought often utilize conscious devices to that end, considering them in the light of a solution, since pride is an antidote to prejudice. This explains the Negro's increasing emphasis on history, for example, during the last two decades. A sense of the past is much more essential to the Negro than to the white American because he needs some sense of stability as a compensation for persecution. He needs to feel a continuity with past achievements of his race in America, to learn about actual but usually unknown facts which crush his old shame and nourish his pride and ambition. Access to such facts, freed from the old taint of propaganda, is facilitated by their own historians, and a publication like the "Journal of Negro History" and books like "The Negro in our History" by Dr. Woodson provide a healthy background of scholarship and research for a popularizing process.[82]) "That the Negro

---

82) *The New Negro*. Schomburg, Arthur: *The Negro Digs up His Past*. p. 236.

has been throughout the centuries of controversy an active collaborator, and often a pioneer, in the struggle for his own freedom and advancement"[83]) is a startling and invigorating realization to many young Negroes in the schools to-day, especially when it is supported by a quantity of concrete instances.

But in re-discovering and in re-interpreting the past so that it becomes a living force in their experience, Negroes find themselves drawn to another and more distant source. Beyond the confines of America in space and time looms up the continent of Africa with all its secrets as to their cultural past slowly unfolding under the probing touch of the twentieth century. If white America insists upon identifying them with Africa, regardless of how remote from it the product of several generations in America may feel, at least there cannot be the same stigma associated with it as previously. The Negro now has ample scope for experiencing pride as he comes to appreciate the qualities of his race expressed hundreds of years ago. Formerly he preferred to keep silence about his origin. "But a new notion of the cultural attainment and potentialities of the African stocks has recently come about, partly through the corrective influence of the more scientific study of African institutions and early cultural history, partly through growing appreciation of the skill and beauty and in many cases the historical priority of the African native crafts, and finally through the signal recognition which first in France and Germany, but now very generally, the astonishing art of the African sculptures has received."[84]) The timeworn paintings on cliffs, the masks, the unearthed pottery and ivory carvings, and the harmonious compositions in stone and metal all show a combination of feeling, imagination, and skill in art which could be associated with savage crudity only by a distorted view.[85])

---

83) Ibid. p. 232.
84) Ibid. p. 237.
85) Woodson, Carter G.: *The Negro in Our History.* pp. 567, 573.

The coöperation complex of the first method of solution, whether directly or indirectly, encourages an ideal of conformity, while the impulse towards independence and pride in the second method of solution encourages an ideal of uniqueness. The argument of the first group is that coöperation between a suppressed and a dominant group always involves a balance of power in favor of the stronger, and the smoothness of the so-called coöperation can best be facilitated by trying to approximate its standards. No matter how far he may go to bring about justice, the white man is at present the ruler of America, and the arbiter of its civilization, and therefore the best way for others to obtain desirable conditions for existence there may be by living on as amenable terms as possible with him. This would mean a rather complete acceptance of his gods. Wherever the Negroes set up their own gods, at least in conspicuous places, there will be friction again. Thus, many Negroes of the present day are not only claiming a power of adaptation to white civilization but are considering the advantages of it. It is conformity for a purpose, as a means to an end.

The extreme expression of this tendency is seen in the phenomenon called "passing". Many individuals who theoretically are supposed to belong to the Negro race bear none of the distinguishing characteristics, and due to the preponderance of their white ancestry can easily pass as belonging to the white race. The process of transferring from one race to another is simplified in the crowded, fluctuating and impersonal nature of the modern city. Thousands are prompted to take the step. When they see white men in possession of privileges denied them as a race, when they have always heard the argument that physical differences from these white men are the proof of racial inferiority, and when they are free from these differences themselves, it is natural that they should wish to escape and merge in the identity of the white group. They become like them not because of an urgent desire to associate with white people as such, but because of the longing for release from the burden of race. "Thus, under the protection of their white skin they can enjoy the comforts of travel and residence, can avail themselves of public service obtained at a price, and indulge their tastes in public entertainments and diversions without obtruding themselves upon the privacy of other individuals, or interfering with their enjoyment of the same thing, while at the same time they avoid for themselves what are wholly unnecessary and altogether unreasonable slights and discriminations. In this way they move about with perfect freedom ,giving no offence to others and not being offended."[86]) The way towards professional or financial advancement is now open to them, and self-development in any direction is no longer circumscribed. The solution for them has become only a limited, individual solution, and is of course not applicable on a large scale, but the very fact that so many choose to cross the borderline between black and white indicates the pressure towards conformity which the American atmosphere causes. It is an ironic situation that through his very efforts to isolate the Negro by associating *difference* with *inferiority*, the white man often encourages the Negro's attempts to minimize the first in order to escape the second. As we have already seen in the tendency of dark-skinned Negroes to compensate by mulatto marriages, a premium is frequently recognized as attached to a light skin, the lighter the better. It seems that the white man might stand more chances of keeping the alleged purity of his group intact, if he admitted that virtues could also be attached to a black skin.[87])

But the strength of the movement working against conformity is revealed by the very fact that by no means all the individuals qualified to "pass" as white people avail themselves of the opportunity. There are countless Negroes of light, tan or white complexion who prefer to stay outside the pale. Their sense of past racial achievement and present ability, their feeling of worth in their own right have aroused a pride and loyalty for their race which only intensifies with opposition,

86) Moton, R. R.: *What the Negro Thinks.* p. 229.
87) Ibid. p. 233.

and stifles any temptation to take the easier path on a personal
score. They have joined with their darker friends and relatives
in a new group solidarity seeking a unique culture of its own.
Instead of accepting even unconsciously the Anglo-Saxon assumption of its inferior characteristics, this group is putting
a new value on these same characteristics until they are almost
glorified.[88]) From the beginning of the twentieth century when
Dr. Du Bois first flung his challenge at Booker T. Washington
this way of thinking has been having a growing impact upon
the race problem. Radicals of all kinds, young writers and
artists, journalists, various professional men swell the ranks
of the non-conformists. With the New York community of Harlem as a center, there is even a geographical foundation for
their cultivation of uniqueness. Segregation, as long as it is
voluntary and not forced by law and public opinion, can be
sanctioned to a certain extent as an agent both in promoting
group solidarity, encouraging to latent powers, and in providing
a soil for the growth of distinctive racial gifts and temperament, of original artistic contributions, of a special philosophy
of life.

The spirit of this group is marked by a strong idealism,
by a belief in the existence of other than material values as
well as a belief in their possession of them. They feel that
those who seize an opening to desert their race are usually
prompted by a materialistic outlook, by a primary wish to gain
the good things of this world. But, if such ones do not become
too lulled by worldly success and comfort, the opinion is that
they will often grow homesick for the vitality and color, for
the rhythm and beauty, for the warm emotions and spiritual
vision of their people. For this group stresses a capacity in the
Negroes for living abundantly and richly, with imagination
and fervor, which is exceptional in the land where the machine
is master and the dollar is god. The suffering which racial
prejudice has brought upon them is regarded as deepening to
their experience and as a source of that particular kind of

---

88) *Ebony and Topaz*. Frazier, F.: *Racial Self-Expression*. p. 120.

wisdom born from pain. Instead of letting themselves be crushed by it, they intend to use it as a means of insight into the nature of life, as an inspiration towards struggle and attainment, whether expressed in deeds or through art. The old attitude of defeat in the face of prejudice has been firmly replaced by an attitude of victory. To this group pride and self-reliance are not only justified, but the only means of solution.

Between conformity and non-conformity is the middle way. Here belong many critics and students who see the truths and yet the dangers in both extremes. While attracted to the courage and romance of the radical philosophy, they feel the impossibility and folly of applying it completely in American life. It is largely dependent on the idea of group-solidarity and there are several obstacles in the way of achieving that. The Negroes have no distinctive language to help foster their uniqueness. Their religion in creed is the same fundamentally as that of the white group. There is no complete geographic isolation or centralization in one part of the country.[89]) On leaving their particular community they find themselves in a white world which is suggesting that the only claim they have for being a distinctive group is their color, and that this is nothing to arouse pride. Their manners, habits and customs are typically American, and they cannot escape from a certain economic and cultural dependence on the white people. They have not as much inner content to nurture their separate group life in America as national groups composed of immigrants from the Old World. Too great insistence upon withdrawing into their race would be an unhealthy escape and would damage the chances of winning group efficiency by a balanced adjustment to the larger environment, for "any nationalistic program that made the Negro seek compensations in a barren racial tradition and thereby escape competition with the white man, which was an inevitable accompaniment of full participation

89) Reuter, E. B.: *The Mulatto in the United States.* p. 382.

in American culture, would lead to intellectual, spiritual, and material impoverishment."[90])

On the other hand, race values are too important not to preserve, and if the Negroes tried to identify themselves as fully as possible with white America, they feel that there would be a cultural loss. The skepticism as to any uniqueness of race temperament which has biological roots may be justified, but there is plenty in the distinctive social experience of the group to account for it and to give it tangible substance. The solution becomes one of being both a Negro and an American. It is the belief of many that this middle course can be taken, that the Negro can still be his individual self and yet coöperate in American life. If the building up of some group tradition is encouraged only as long as it is harmonious with fuller participation in national culture, then it can be a center from which creative activity can radiate. From this point of view, "the radicalism of the Negro is no limitation or reservation with respect to American life; it is only a constructive effort to build the obstructions in the stream of his progress into an efficient dam of social energy and power."[91]) And in this way, competition and coöperation could play their essential rôles in Negro life together, alternately stimulating and modifying, until a state of equilibrium was reached which would be its own solution.

Non-Resistance.

But recent years show that the possibilities of various reactions to race prejudice are not yet exhausted. Beyond the battle line are those who refuse to fight. Above the debate of controversial issues are those who follow the way of non-resistance. They are not concerned with defence and offence, problems and solutions, for they stand clear-eyed and free in spirit, and that is enough. Their ideal is the "New Negro" who in daily life may rebel and at times seek points of smooth contact

90) *Ebony and Topaz*. Frazier, F.: *Racial Self-Expression*. p. 120—121.
91) *The New Negro*. Locke, Alain: *The New Negro*. p. 12.

with white America, according to the particular situation, and yet who has something within him which neither success nor failure along those lines can touch. "The old Negro, we must remember, was a creature of moral debate and historical controversy. — — So, for generations in the mind of America, the Negro has been more of a formula than a human being — a something to be argued about, condemned and defended, to be 'kept' down, or 'in his place' or 'helped up', to be worried with or worried over, harassed or patronized, a social bogey or a social burden. The thinking Negro even has been induced to share this same general attitude, to focus his attention on controversial issues, to see himself in the distorted perspective of a social problem."[92])

But now comes fresh light and an emergence on a higher level. "Until recently, lacking self-understanding, we have been almost as much of a problem to ourselves as we still are to others. But the decade that found us with a problem has left us only with a task. The multitude perhaps feels as yet only a strange relief and a new vague urge, but the thinking few know that in the reaction the vital inner grip of prejudice has been broken."[93]) When the individual ignores prejudice or is indifferent to it, then it loses effectiveness. When added to a cultivated independence is a philosophical stoicism and disinterestedness springing from the mind rather than the will, the personality remains intact. It is the younger generation which seems to have certain untapped inner resources essential for the achievement of this ideal, but even here only a few have been able to gain such difficult self-mastery. The "New Negro" then signifies as yet a tendency more than a group, a tendency which is found working in the older generation as well, among scholars and writers, and among many leaders in the radical and even the conservative groups. Rather than existing as a definite and finished type, the "New Negro" reveals a leavening spirit expressing itself partially in one individual and more

92) *The New Negro.* Locke, Alain: *The New Negro.* pp. 3—4.
93) Ibid. p. 4.

fully in another, until those who become most possessed by it enter into the probation period out of which a new type begins to appear. Such a type could not hope to form more than a minority for a while, since the spiritual demands of a non-resistance which is still positive while passive in the use of force are too great for the masses of the people to meet.

But for those who can in this manner transcend race prejudice, the world seems to take on a new aspect. The energy which would otherwise be absorbed by race conflict is now free to seek constructive ways. There are signs of rebirth of that creative instinct which may have motivated their race long ago in its ancestral home and which is now influencing an artistic movement felt to be in the nature of a renaissance. "If then it is really a renaissance - and I firmly believe it is, we are still in the hill - town stage, and the mellowness of maturity has not yet come upon us."[94]) But the very realization of something unfinished and growing is evidently a greater spur toward the self-expression of these individuals who no longer speak for the Negro but simply and calmly as a Negro. They do not stress being white, brown, or black in color as the important thing. They are first and foremost individuals who use race experience as they use other forms of experience as a factor in the development of personality, and as a basis for expression. Their keenness of insight makes them quite aware of the harshnesses attendant on race relations, but at those times when they are inescapably confronted with some aspect of the race problem, they prefer to use the weapon of irony instead of indignation or abuse. Their power of objectivity protects them from the heat of the conflict, and projects them into regions where the air is cooler and more invigorating. Racial prejudice becomes a phenomenon to be observed dispassionately and even laughed at, but not a destroyer of inner security and peace.[95])

---

94) *Ebony and Topaz*. Locke, Alain: *Our Little Renaissance*. p. 118.
95) *Annals*. Bond, H. M.: *Self Respect as a Factor in Racial Advancement*. p. 24.

Such a serenity of mind might well be claimed as no new achievement. In the days of submission, many of the blackest slaves, with Uncle Tom as the classic example, seemed to have possessed it back in the eighteenth and nineteenth centuries. They could bear the hardest blows of the overseer and the harshest treatment of the slave dealers with evident fortitude and even detachment. But the difference lies in the source of the two attitudes. The inner control of the slave is regarded as the concomitant of his escape into religion, while that of the "New Negro" is felt to come as the result of self-knowledge. The one was dependent on a power greater than and external to himself, the other feels self-sufficient in his own right. The spiritual capacity of the slave came from his faith in supernatural aid instead of from his conviction of the limitless resources within himself. He regarded himself as an inferior being, utterly helpless without his God, whereas the "New Negro" senses a power to create the world in his own image.

The Process of Change.

In fact, the fundamental difference between the psychology of submission and of non-resistance is so great that it is a striking reminder of the transformation the years have brought. We have seen in this chapter that the Negro observer, viewing the trend of his race's experience in America, is aware of this great change, occurring within a comparatively small span of time. From the day of the slave to the day of the "New Negro" he discovers many different and fluctuating attitudes, reactions, and moods on the part of his people struggling for self-preservation in the face of antagonism. From the white group has come the race-prejudice, from the black group race-consciousness. The stimulus, prejudice, in spite of certain changes in form and expression dependent on the particular setting and time seems to have remained more of a constant in its fundamental feeling of antipathy and distrust than the responses which have met it, responses fluctuating from smouldering resentment through counter antipathy to indifference, friendliness, or pride. This is to be xepected since the status of the in-group is regarded as fixed as long as it uses the same kind of prejudice for protection, whereas the out-group has no fixed status and must achieve it through growth and struggle and a variety of means. Growth posits perpetual change. It would be ineffectual to rely upon the same kind of race consciousness. Different kinds must be tried and rejected and tried again. If the Negro sees no hope of securing a decent place in American society by one approach he will of course experiment with another, until the time when, as this "trial and error" method is modified and controlled more and more by trained and seasoned intellects, the goals are obtained.

The variable nature of race consciousness among the Negroes might also be partially explained on the grounds of inner conflict. The nature of the Negro seems to show a predisposition towards receptivity and patience, towards coöperation rather than competition. It has been suggested that some connection may be drawn between this characteristic and his Ethiopian background. The Ethiopians in Africa with their quiet and peaceful agricultural life centuries ago presented a marked contrast to the neighboring Hamitic men with their pastoral life involving a struggle for existence and the development of the brave, masterful, practical type. The Ethiopian was absorptive and assimilative, inclined towards the emotional and the mystic, the Hamitic aggressive, materialistic, and rational. "The Ethiopian culture has always given to the African the capacities of a deep emotional life, of soul, of expansiveness; the Hamitic has given him those of vitality and a healthy outlook upon life. No one can understand the potentialities of present-day Negroes in Africa and America, and no one can clearly imagine the course of their further development who does not keep ever in mind the fact that they are the visible expression and form of the Ethiopian culture."[96]) Throughout the history of the American Negro these Ethiopian characteristics have survived, but as they have seemingly proved

---

96) *Annals*, Frobenius, Leo: *Early African Culture as an Indication of Present Negro Potentialities.* p. 162.

unsuited alone to cope with the exigencies of a different and inimicable environment, they have come to form a predisposition rather than remaining as clearly defined and strong characteristics. In another environment the Negro found himself able to lead a peaceful existence and still maintain his personal integrity and his individual values. But in the American environment the Negro came to realize that leading a peaceful existence could only establish more firmly his original status in America of slave and inferior.

Thus a conflict may have been aroused between his natural way of life, fixed in age-long mores, and the demands made on him by his new situation. To avoid distasteful suppression, competition became more and more inevitable. A certain amount of compromise and agreement was necessary from the first, and natural inclinations have not only encouraged this approach but have often caused Negroes to revert to it, after the other approach has been tried. But as years have brought them more intimate knowledge of the American environment and more experience and surety, their acquired traits of self-assertion have begun to find expression at the expense of the natural traits. This process has been hastened by their immediate contact with the different cultural traits of other groups which has tended to modify and enlarge their own set of values, and by the adaptation of successive American-born generations to the prevailing American mores. To-day for example, in the same community will be found West Indian, African, and thoroughly American Negroes. The competitive and materialistic trend of their surroundings has long ago left an impress upon the American Negroes, whereas "the outstanding contributions of West-Indians to American life is the insistent assertion of their manhood in an environment that demands too much servility and unprotesting acquiescence from men of African blood."[97]) In such ways can the provocative influence from white America and from Negroes of different background turn the African Negro into a rebel and a non-conformist.

---

97) *The New Negro.* Domingo, W. A.: *Gift of the Black Tropics.* p. 349.

But the natural and the acquired characteristics have been difficult to reconcile in the short course of three centuries and of only a little over half a century of freedom, and it has often been a case of fluctuating between the two poles. Under such conditions any type of race consciousness evolved at one time or by one group was subject to the danger of a reaction. It is not until the twentieth century that any one clear and dominant type of race-consciousness has given signs of crystallizing into some state of permanency.

The obvious explanation for this would be that there must be greater prejudice to-day which is requiring a stronger and more unified defence. Although this is partly true among some white groups, especially the poor and uneducated groups who have most to fear from Negro progress, there is lessened prejudice each year among intelligent white American citizens who have come to recognize, whether grudgingly or not, and often substantially to encourage the capacity and achievements of the black group. These are providing a leaven, North and South, towards the eventual mitigation of prejudice in the masses, but the process is of course slow and meanwhile the Negroes cannot stand aside and wait. A real reason, then, for the heightened race consciousness of this decade is the Negro's accelerating desire for unhampered living, and impatience to satisfy it. The diminishing of white race-prejudice has been negligible in proportion to the increase of Negro ambition and standard of values until the point has been reached where the disparity between the wish and the chance for fulfilment has been too great not to cause growing dissatisfaction among Negroes. This in turn breeds a virile race-consciousness.

The awakening to better possibilities and the restlessness which accompanies it have spread through the masses of Negroes not only because of the influence from external events, such as the World War with its resultant opportunities for Negroes in economic and industrial life, but because of internal leadership. Negro thinkers are aware of the need to cultivate among their people high ideals and a discontent with half-gods. They feel that attainment in their own case as well as that of the group is possible only by the exercise of a race consciousness which is positive and vibrating with power, and which is no longer a mere instinctive response to the immediate situation. With the vision of wisdom, they are helping to produce an attitude on a rational basis, guided and tested by the best thought of the group.

Before this century little attention was paid to the question of race consciousness while much more was said about prejudice. This only reflected the general tendency to disregard the Negro's side of the question, the story of his reaction to prejudice, as unimportant. Race consciousness always existed in some form or other, but it was only experienced directly and not recognized as such. But now,with deliberate analysis and thought investigating and directing it, the awareness becomes doubled. Not only is one conscious of certain feelings on encountering race prejudice, but one is conscious of being conscious.

The first three tendencies towards submission, defence, and offence are by no means dead or triumphantly superseded by the present tendency towards non-resistance. Movements are never as clear-cut or mutually exclusive as that. There are many Negroes now who hold one or the other earlier attitude towards their American surroundings. The masses of the exploited peasantry in the South, for example, retain a defeatist psychology identifiable with that of the slave regime. But as the impetus of education and leadership is felt, more and more the left hand of the individual Negro comes to know what his right hand is doing. He comes to recognize whether he is conforming because of fear or rebelling because of anger at injustice, whether he is on the offensive or defensive, submitting to white repression for expedient purposes or ignoring it through pride. And his openness to influence from a more effective type of race consciousness is in proportion to the clearing of his vision. In this way, Negro leaders have opportunity for capturing tendencies in a formula, for moulding group opinion, and for giving the strengthening race consciousness such a shape that it emerges in our day for the first time as a measurable reality.

PART TWO

RACE CONSCIOUSNESS IN FICTION 1900—1930

Wherever race consciousness is conditioning the point of view and the purpose of the individual writer, his literary production will bear witness to the extent and nature of this influence. If we find no traces then we can conclude that the race consciousness is at a low ebb, that it has been subtly and effectively sublimated in its expression, or that it has been transplanted by other and stronger psychological factors. In the particular case of the American Negro, we will turn to his important works of fiction during the last thirty years and attempt to ascertain whatever correlations exist between their psychology and this force of race consciousness already conspicuous in the group experience. The method of procedure will be to analyze them under three aspects:

1. The type of milieu the writer presents to us: the natural, the physical and geographical setting with its human contents, that is, the kind of people who live and breathe within these borders.

2. The sort of person who rises up at his touch and stands outlined against the horizon, on whom the light is concentrated and the burden of the action depends; the characteristics of the individual who emerges from the mass.

3. The nature of the mood which his created world as a whole evokes, through milieu or kind of character or interaction of the two; the sort of emotion aroused and the effect produced by style, technique, manner of treatment, by the particular line and color combination.

Difference in point of view will necessitate difference in treatment of these three aspects of the novel or work of fiction. If an author has a defeatist psychology or an acquiescent acceptance of the status quo the temper of his novel would be quite otherwise from that of the writer with a purpose who chooses his milieu, the type of his characters, and the development of his plot with the intention of stimulating some very definite emotional reaction in his readers, such as disapproval or open dislike, warm sympathy or a broader sense of justice. Willa Cather, with her concern for the creation of atmosphere on the artistic side and her interest in human psychology generally on the intellectual side, is at liberty to evoke at will the spirit of the middle western prairies, the hills of Mexico or the vastnesses of Canada and to portray the inner conflicts of different human beings from vital and instinctive peasant girl to skeptical professor or zealous Catholic priest. But the urge to reform which dominates the motives of a writer like Upton Sinclair will tend towards an almost compulsory preoccupation with the large American city and its ever typical groups struggling in economic, political, and racial competition, whether capitalist is pitted against worker in the relentless industrialism of Chicago, or conservative against radical, native born against immigrant, in the Sacco-Vanzetti city of Boston.

We have seen that the marked characteristic of the history of race consciousness among the American Negroes from the time of their introduction in any large numbers during the seventeenth century to the present era is change, accelerating in recent years, and that that process is by no means complete. It was also clear that transition in their psychological attitudes has seemed to depend not merely on the fluctuation of certain external conditions, and on attitudes on the part of the dominant white group, but on special influences at work within the Negro group itself at various times, so that when we make such broad and general distinctions as the periods of submission, defence, offence, and non-resistance, we must recognize them as the results of interplay between inner and outer forces. In the first part we have endeavored to isolate for observation the most important of these inner and outer forces which have formed general tendencies and gone into the making of this complex phenomenon of race consciousness.

Although at any one time all tendencies may be claimed as present in the group, it is true that even the comparatively short space of the thirty years of this century has contained the ebb and flow of certain dominant rhythms. Today we may find the subservient Negro type next door to the aggressive type battling for his rights, and yesterday the calm voice of the man of science was already audible beside the emotional outbursts of the religious enthusiast. But although it is one peculiarity of movements always to be overlapping, it is another peculiarity to crystallize their own unique forms out of the surrounding medium. And therefore it has been possible to isolate these psychologies of race consciousness at least to that point where we are free to observe any correlation between them and literary types.

In studying these literary types, it is impossible to sever the creation from the creator. Although we are not free to claim that any author speaks directly through his characters, or that the expressed ideals and evident purpose of his book coincide with his own private opinions, nevertheless what we see in his work is at least a reflection of some point of view he has chosen to adopt for the moment, and to that extent elucidates his conscious motives in writing. The kind of characters, of milieu, and of mood presented in any work of fiction may not tell us much about the real *man* behind them but they will indicate where he as *author* stands in relation to the changing thought currents of his century. Finally, authors together with their books are bound to divide and fall into separate groups according to the likenesses between them.

Chapter 1. MILIEU

The aim of this chapter as stated is to study the various kinds of milieu presented to us by different Negro writers in order to aid our understanding of the particular type of race consciousness each embodies. The author's choice of setting and of people within that setting provides a key to the whole meaning and purpose of the book and to the secret of its psychology.

Plantation-Slave.

Up to the beginning of the twentieth century, the attempts at fiction made by Negro authors showed a certain fondness for the plantation life of the South. The background was familiar and provided the most natural medium for the movements of their simple folk characters. Although the national emancipation in the sixties meant that the masses of Negoes were no longer tied to the large plantations of their Southern white masters, according to the actual course of events during the first decade of freedom a considerable number of Negroes, confused by the idea of their new status and untrained to meet its responsibilities, remained on their former masters' grounds in the capacity of servants. This perpetuated an acquaintance with this particular milieu and facilitated the ability of later writers, both Negro and white, to use it for artistic purposes. And it was natural that the plantation pictured was usually the ante-bellum plantation, because it was then that its characteristics were observable to the richest degree.

Thus in Paul Laurence Dunbar's collection of short stories at the end of the nineteenth century, "Folks From Dixie", we have a typical scene of love and courtship, of religious conversion and rivalry among the slaves of Mas' Rob's plantation.

At first glance the picture may present a rather bleak aspect: "It was winter. The gray old mansion of Mr. Robert Selfridge, of Fayette County, Kentucky, was wrapped in its usual mantle of winter sombreness, and the ample plantation stretching in every direction thereabout was one level plain of unflecked whiteness. At a distance from the house the cabins of the Negroes stretched away in a long, broken black line that stood out in bold relief against the extreme whiteness of their surroundings."[1]) But a closer knowledge of the inhabitants of these rough little houses, and their customs and interests, makes us realize the strength and the warmth of the community life. The little Baptist meeting house where they met for Sunday services and prayer meetings may have been equipped only with the rudest of hard benches, but the singing and praying and "getting of religion" which occurred under its roof transformed it to a place of cheer and even fascination. At ordinary times the preacher could color the atmosphere satisfyingly with his descriptions of „the harp-ringing heaven of bliss or the fire-filled home of the damned", and at revival meetings this emotional spirit was so intensified that "interest, or perhaps more correctly speaking, excitement ran high, and regularly as night came round all the hands on the neighboring plantations flocked to the scene of their devotions."[2])

Religion has a competitor in this intimate community, for the temptations towards fine dress and flirtations and all the worldly impulses connected with love making are bound to conflict with purely spiritual concerns! But whether they are praying for salvation or vying with each other to win the desirable mate, their ways are simple and wholesome, and their reputations of good report. They are portrayed as a simple and unpretentious folk, good humoured, kindly, and generous of impulse, satisfied with humble standards and seeking improvement in Christian virtues. As a group their greatest sins are an inclination towards gossip or towards jealousy, and even

---

1) Dunbar, P. L.: *Folks From Dixie.* p. 3.

2) Ibid. pp. 6—7.

these are robbed of any possible sting by their delicious naiveté:
"She noticed, too with a pang, that Phiny had tied a bow of red
ribbon on her hair. She shut her lips and only prayed the harder,
But an hour later, somehow, a ribbon as red as Phiny's had
miraculously attached itself to her thick black plaits."[3])

Here we have a self-contained group study, a little world
which, though in fact enslaved and dependent, nevertheless is
leading a distinctive life of its own. We gain a sense of a contented and yet active little community, absorbed in its own
peculiar type of humorous and emotional experiences and
usually in contact with the white world in a superficial and
exterior way.

The same is the case with the stories in Charles W. Chesnutt's "The Conjure Woman" which appeared in 1899. The setting of old communal plantation life is vividly presented
through the reminiscences of the venerable ex-slave, Uncle Julius. It is not before the end of the nineteenth century that a
white gentleman from the North goes down South to North
Carolina with its slow ways, old run-down plantations, ram-
shackle houses and dirt roads, and starts up a long neglected
grape culture. But after he discovers the old Negro about the
premises and takes him into his services as a coachman, the
interest shifts entirely from the white owner and the present
aspect of the plantation, as the tales which Uncle Julius relates
call up the pre-war days when he was living among many other
slaves on the same plantation. It is true that the white masters
often appear through these series of sketches, but rather as
"deus ex machina" than as an integral part of the doings and
feelings of the Negro group.

But it is made plain that any seeming lack of contact or
interest on the part of the Negro world for the white world
is due to the forced isolation and realization of inferior status
rather than to any positive dislike. In fact, both Dunbar and
Chesnutt in several stories provide us plenty of illustrations of
the devotion and loyalty of slaves to masters, when given oppor-

3) Ibid. p. 17.

tunity. This is a milieu where peace and duty and faithful love hold sway. In the sense of benevolence and of despotism which these scenes from slavery days give, it is evidently the first rather than the second condition of which the Negroes are conscious. There is indeed an idealization of the old master-servant regime in "A Family Feud" and "The Intervention of Peter" where it is the slave who enters into his white family's affairs in such a way as to save delicate situations. The affectionate devotion of such a type is symbolized in the glowing memories of old Aunt Doshy, a former trusted slave in a wealthy and aristocratic Kentucky family: "Aunt Doshy was inordinately proud of her family, as she designated the Venables, and was never weary of detailing accounts of their grandeur and generosity. What if some of the harshness of reality was softened by the distance through which she looked back upon them; what if the glamour of memory did put a halo round the heads of some people who were never meant to be canonised? It was all plain fact to Aunt Doshy —."[4]) Here Aunt Doshy stands to us not as an individual but as the embodiment of a certain group attitude.

And these same group characteristics persist, although with less clarity, even in those stories of „Folks From Dixie" where Paul Laurence Dunbar abandons a direct treatment of the plantation. We see the same type of Negroes, living as free people in independent communities, but still maintaining similar interests. The church is still the centre of excitement in "The Trial Sermons on Bull-Skin" and courting against obstacles is still an absorbing pursuit in the small Negro town of Miltonville. The communal life has much of that simplicity, intimacy, warmth and humanness which the old plantations contained. And again, in cases where Negroes have moved northward or westward into white towns, the loyal habit patterns instilled by the Christianit, of former years can prompt an ex-slave, although after considerable conflict, to act generously and lovingly towards the former master now destitute and in

---

4) Dunbar, P. L.: *Folks From Dixie.* pp. 137—138.

despair, as in the account of "Nelse Hatton's Vengeance". Or the implanted instincts of tenderness and responsiveness to love among each other can, in the case of "Jimsella", again after some struggle, prevent a domestic disaster in the midst of a large city environment so menacing to the preservation of the immigrating Negroes' old plain and contented domestic habits. By nature, then, the simple uneducated Negroes of these stories are possessed of the old-fashioned moral and religious virtues. But the most fitting atmosphere for their freest exercise is suggested to be that of the ante-bellum plantation.

Although the intimate group life reflected in Chesnutt's plantation stories exhibits the same essential qualities of devotion and kind heartedness, the Christian motive and influence are subordinate. "The Conjure Woman" reveals another important characteristic of the untutored slave psychology which Dunbar practically neglected, and that is, the predisposition towards superstition. There are still the humble hopes and fears, loves and rivalries occupying the attention of the group, but it is the clever conjure woman or the powerful conjure man, who is the dominant force in this milieu, and not the persuasive and ardent preacher. These Negroes believe in the efficacy of charms more than they do in the efficacy of prayer. "-De lef' hin'-foot er a grabeya'd rabbit, killt by a cross-eyed nigger on a da'k night in de full er de moon"[5]) will as surely bring luck as the "baby doll, wid a body made out'n a piece er co'n-stalk, en wid splinters fer a'ms en laigs, en a head made out'n elderberry peth, en two little red peppers fer feet"[6]) created by the magic of the conjure woman brought disaster to "Hot-Foot Hannibal". In an emergency there is even such powerful aid to be had from the conjure woman as a life charm made perhaps of some strands of one's own hair, a piece of red flannel, and a few roots and herbs all tied together in a little coon-skin bag. "'You take dis cha'm,' sez she, 'en put it in a bottle er a tin box, en bury it deep unner de root er a

5) Chesnutt, Charles W.: *The Conjure Woman.* p. 135.
6) Ibid. pp. 207—208.

live-oak tree, en ez long ez it stays dere safe en soun', dey ain' no p'isen kin p'isen you, dey ain' no rattlesnake kin bite you, dey ain' no sco'pion kin sting you. Dis yere cunjuh man mought do one thing er 'nudder ter you, but he can't kill you. So you neenter be at all skeered, but go 'long 'bout yo' bizness en doan bother yo' min'."[7])

This is the world where haunts walk abroad unmolested. Those of two lovers of tragic fate may linger about for years: "his ha'nt en Mahaly's hangs 'round dat piece er low groun', en eve'body w'at goes 'bout dere has some bad luck er 'nuther; fer ha'nts doan lack ter be 'sturb' on dey own stompin'-groun'."[8]) And grey horses can always see such specters if they appear on Friday![9]) In such an atmosphere miracles are not to be wondered at. When Negroes are changed into trees or animals, such as a mule, a black cat, a gray wolf, or when a little pickaninny is changed into a humming bird it is all quite natural to Uncle Julius as he narrates. For what otherwise could be expected in a community where the powers of magic were not only understood but utilized in the ordinary course of events? "She could wuk de mos' powerfulles' kin' er goopher,— could make people hab fits, er rheumatiz, er make 'em des dwinel away en die; en dey say she went out ridin' de niggers at night, fer she wuz a witch 'sides bein' a cunjuh 'oman."[10]) And such a witch was doubly to be respected because her control extended not only over human beings but over birds and animals. The hornets will sting for her, the sparrows keep watch for her, and the rattlesnakes poison for her.[11])

It might seem plausible that the group life of these plantation slaves was regulated into ways of peace and pleasantness if not through fear of white masters then through fear either of God or the powers of magic. A superstitious Negro might be expected to walk the straight and narrow path, so as

7) Chesnutt, C. W.: *The Conjure Woman.* p. 174.
8) Ibid. p. 192.
9) Ibid. p. 203.
10) Ibid. p. 15.
11) Ibid. pp. 50, 151, 175.

to divert any possible occasion for the use of punitive supernatural forces against him, just as well as the Christian who
covets his chances for heaven. But somehow we acquire the
impression that this peculiar group temperament is more basic
and has an independent existence of its own underneath all
external stimuli. Dunbar and Chesnutt make us feel that if
Christianity had never been introduced among them and if
superstitions had never gained such a hold on their imagination they nevertheless would continue to inhabit their primitive
and isolated milieu in a manner of life instinctively simple,
natural, and harmonious.

But, from the point of view of these writers, civilization
can corrupt as the horizons spread. Paul Laurence Dunbar has
already hinted in several stories of the dangers to this folk
type presented by a more complicated world. But the fact does
not take on clear contours until Dunbar leaves the field of the
short story for that of the novel. The American Negro novel
begins with these two authors together with the beginning of
the century, and it is significant to observe that with this new
form of writing comes a new milieu. This is easily to be understood. Plantation life submitted itself most gracefully to the
tale. The milieu was too circumscribed to allow for dramatic
action or complicated plot. Life was episodal, and the interest
lay in situation and incident. But as Negroes move townward,
northward, and cityward the novel becomes the adequate form
of expression for the growing complexity of human character
and action in a world which is not only wider but wickeder.

In Paul Laurence Dunbar's novel, "The Sport of the Gods",
published in 1902, we have a direct example of a changed and
corrupting milieu. The fact is emphasized by contrast. In the
first chapters we are shown a typical Negro family in the
South, now in the capacity of servants rather than of slaves,
but with much of the same type of faithful slave-master relationship. The home is well-furnished and comfortable, the
father and mother satisfied with their positions and their
bright and attractive children. But the scene shifts to New
York and everything is quite otherwise. There can be no doubt

that the milieu is far more fascinating. The tall buildings, the lights, and the crowds are new experiences, and when the provincial has mastered his fear or loneliness, "the subtle, insidious wine of New York will begin to intoxicate him. Then if he be wise, he will go away, any place, — yes, he will even go over to Jersey. But if he be a fool, he will stay and stay on till the town becomes all in all to him, until the very streets are his chums and certain buildings and corners his best friends. Then he is hopeless, and to live elsewhere would be death. The Bowery will be his romance, Broadway his lyric, and the park his pastoral, the river and the glory of it all his epic, and he will look down pityingly on all the rest of mankind."[12]) The mother, symbolizing the conservatism of the older generation, might fear the bigness, "for she knew that there could not be so many people together withou a deal of wickedness,"[13]) but the younger generation was eagerly receptive to new influences. When young men down South dressed up in the evening, the limits of the environment usually meant that it was either for church or family visiting, but here the young son saw that they evidently had other and more exciting pastimes. "In the moment that he recognized this, a revelation came to him, the knowledge that his horizon had been narrow, and he felt angry that it was so."[14]) Especially on young people, then, whose ways are not set, can this new milieu work disaster.

It is the age-old tragedy of the provincial in the big city: "Whom the Gods wish to destroy they first make mad. The first sign of the demoralization of the provincial who comes to New York is his pride at his insensibility to certain impressions which used to influence him at home. First he begins to scoff, and there is no truth in his views, nor depth in his laugh. But by and by, from mere pretending, it becomes real. He grows callous. After that he goes to the devil very cheerfully."[15]) An increasing knowledge of city ways brings an inevitable acquain-

12) Dunbar, P. L.: *The Sport of the Gods*. pp. 82—83.
13) Ibid. p. 86.
14) Ibid. p. 87.
15) Ibid. p. 88.

tance with the underworld, and this underworld is an ever present factor in Dunbar's novel. One of its typical products is "The Banner Club" described as "an institution for the lower education of Negro youth" and patronized by all sorts of men, educated and uneducated, honest and dishonest, parasites looking for victims, and politicians for votes, artists for inspiration and reporters for news: "Of course the place was a social cesspool, generating a poisonous miasma and reeking with the stench of decayed and rotten moralities. There is no defence to be made for it. But what do you expect when false idealism and fevered ambition come face to face with catering cupidity?"[16])

No longer have we a sheltered Negro group atmosphere. The interest is still centered on Negroes of humble station in life, but they are inextricably bound up with the surrounding white world. In cosmopolitan New York this would obviously be true, while in the small Southern town of mixed population the races are constantly knocking against each other. This fact involves more daily friction and introduces the virile germs of prejudice into the milieu. It is not alone the big city which brings troubles to unsophisticated Negroes, but it is the small Negro-White town in the South with its atmosphere of gossip, pettiness, envy, and mutual racial distrust which can perhaps less suddenly and conspicuously but nevertheless seriously damage the development of the Negroes. Dunbar has already indicated this in the first part of his novel where we observe suspicion at the heart of the small town.

Small Southern Town and Ignorant Masses.

And perhaps it is for this reason that other early novel writers have concentrated on the Southern small town. In comparison Dunbar was a little premature with his utilization of New York. It was not necessary yet to go to the big Northern cities, for there was a challenging and unused milieu still in the South, with plenty of problems and complexities pertaining

---

16) Dunbar, P. L.: *The Sport of the Gods*. pp. 116—118.

to it. The logical step from the plantation Negro milieu was the Negro-white town so characteristic of the Southern states. And this is the step taken by Chesnutt as a novelist.

Characteristic of these towns is an unprosperous condition at the close of the nineteenth century which undoubtedly has bearing upon certain other undesirable features. In Chesnutt's "The Marrow of Tradition", (1901), the Virginian town of Wellington has suffered economic reverses: "Twenty years before, Wellington had been the world's greatest shipping port for naval stores. But as the turpentine industry had moved southward, leaving a trail of devastated forests in its rear, the city had fallen to a poor fifth or sixth place in this trade."[17]) Far more backward is Clarendon in "The Colonel's Dream", (1905). The run-down condition is apparent at first glance when one finds cows grazing on the empty lot between the bank and post-office, "pigs sleeping in the shadow of the old wooden market-house, the lean and sallow pinelanders and listless Negroes dozing on the curbstone."[18]) Isolated from centres of commerce, with practically no mills or mines in the surrounding territory, the town is largely agricultural and very dependent on the expensive import of Northern product in return for its shipments of raw cotton. Unemployment is the result. One old Negro states the dilemma aptly: "De w'ite folks says de young niggers is triflin' cause dey don' larn how to do nothin'. But what is dere fer 'em to do? I kin 'member when dis town was full er black an' yaller carpenters an' jiners, blacksmiths, wagon makers, shoemakers, tinners, saddlers an' cab'net makers. Now all de fu'nicher, de shoes, de wagons, de buggies, de tinware, de hoss shoes, de nails to fasten 'em on wid — yas, an' fo' de Lawd! even de clothes dat folks wears on dere backs, is made at de norf, an' dere ain' nothin' lef' fer de ole niggers ter do, let 'lone de young ones.'"[19]) Clarendon possessed cotton and corn merchants, dry goods and grocery

17) Chesnutt, Charles W.: *The Marrow of Tradition*. pp. 141—142.
18) Chesnutt, Charles W.: *The Colonel's Dream*. p. 16.
19) Ibid. pp. 97—98.

stores, a courtyard and a jail, many saloons and many churches; the merchants along with their customers are continually going into bankruptcy, the farmers are burdened by heavy mortgages or debts. The idea of using surrounding natural resources and building up a cotton industry and thus revivifying the material condition of the town is too strenuous. There is no spirit of ambition, efficiency, or thrift, and the methods of work in daily life generally are shiftless and old-fashioned: "No one could do anything in a quarter of an hour. Nearly all tasks were done by Negroes who had forgotten how to work or by white people who had never learned."[20])

In an atmosphere of idleness and unprosperity race prejudice is shown to thrive. Thwarted white men are pictured as having to find an outlet for their discontentedness and an explanation for their poor circumstances which will not cast reflection on their own limitations. "There was always some extraneous reason given — the War, the carpet baggers, the Fifteenth Amendment, the Negroes,"[21]) but most frequently the Negroes. For the Negroes are ever present and their faults are obvious to the whites. Their inefficiency is regarded as a drag on the South: "Six niggers can't get one horse up without twice as many white men to tell them how. That's why the South is behind the No'th. The niggers, in one way or another, take up most of our time and energy. You folks up there have half your work done before we get our'n started."[22]) And inefficiency is only one sign of a deteriorated and degraded people, who according to the Presbyterian minister of Clarendon, representing in religious phraseology general public opinion, are not fit for assimilation, cannot be deported, and therefore must be encouraged towards extinction: "'It is God's will. We need not stain our hands with innocent blood. If we but sit passive, and leave their fate to time, they will die away in discouragement and despair. Already disease is sapping their

20) Ibid. p. 105.
21) Ibid. p. 108.
22) Ibid. p. 72.

vitals. Like other weak races, they will vanish from the pathway of the strong, and there is no place for them to flee. When they go hence, it is to go for ever. It is the law of life, which God has given to the earth. To coddle them, to delude them with false hopes of an unnatural equality which not all the power of the government has been able to maintain, is only to increase their unhappiness. To a doomed race, ignorance is euthanasia, and knowledge is but pain and sorrow. It is His will that the fittest should survive, and that those shall inherit the earth who are best prepared to utilize its forces and gather its fruits."[23])

But meanwhile, before this eventual solution arrives, there is the immediate problem of keeping the Negro in order. The major interest of both Clarendon and Wellington is not commerce but politics, and seemingly the strength of this interest depends on the fear of Negro rights. In both towns the fight for Negro disfranchisement is the crucial political issue. The Negro was held as unfit to participate in government because of lack of education and experience, because of criminal tendencies, and because of incurable mental and physical inferiority, therefore the vote in his hands was dangerous to the community.[24]) For political equality leads to social equality and social equality to intermarriage and a train of evils.[25]) Social equality is so unthinkable that any means is justified in avoiding it. Thus we see an editor of Wellington pacifying his conscience as were many other leading citizens: "This was not difficult to do in politics, for he believed in the divine right of white men and gentlemen as his ancestors had believed in and died for the divine right of kings."[26])

On the surface it would seem that the various types of people presented by this milieu would cause class as well as race divisions. Among the white group alone there is the conservative and aristocratic type of Southern gentleman, the

23) Ibid. pp. 164—165.
24) Chesnutt, C. W.: *The Marrow of Tradition*. p. 31.
25) Chesnutt, C. W.: *The Colonel's Dream*. p. 194.
26) Chesnutt, C. W.: *The Marrow of Tradition*. p. 34.

educated and self-reliant man without family tradition, and the "poor white" class aspiring and successfully climbing to wealth, public office and social recognition. If living alone in one community, undoubtedly there could be no basis for unity among them. On one side would be condescension and scorn, on the other envy and competition. But in these Southern towns they have the Negroes as a common enemy storming the citadel and therefore must unite in defence. They have different motives and views of life, but they can be in harmony on such a question as the urgency for Negro disfranchisement and the inferiority of Negroes in general. And in this way distinctions between various types also existing among the Negroes are minimized and fitted into one scheme. We find the old-fashioned Mammy and the devoted servant as remnants of the old regime, and the subservient opportunistic Negro belonging to the clown stereotype, or the patient helpless Negro worker, and finally in "The Marrow of Tradition" we have the introduction of the new emancipated and educated type of professional Negro with ambition and capacity. But again it narrows down to a race rather than a class problem, since the white point of view standardizes them, cataloguing them all under the general classification of "nigger". "It was a veritable bed of Procrustes, this standard which the whites had set for the Negroes. Those who grew above it must have their heads cut off, figuratively speaking — must be forced back to the level assigned to their race, those who fell beneath the standard set had their necks stretched, literally enough, as the ghastly record in the daily papers gave conclusive evidence."[27])

Thus it is plain that as Negro writers turn from the environment of the old plantation to that of the town, sophistication and conflict and complexity are taken as replacing the former characteristics of naiveté, peace and simplicity. And, on the whole, the core of the situation is found to lie in race relationships. Other possible sources of conflicts in urban life seem to be dwarfed before this issue. The milieu has no longer

27) Chesnutt, C. W.: *The Marrow of Tradition.* p. 61.

an atmosphere of relaxation but is instead throbbing with tension. Life is not to be enjoyed but to be endured as a problem.

And the possibilities of this milieu for the novel have had too strong a hold on the imagination of the Negro author to be exhausted with the first years of this century and the work of Dunbar and Chesnutt. In succeeding years other backgrounds become more popular, but as late as 1924 a novel appeared which at present may be regarded as the end product of the process begun by these earlier writers. In "The Fire in the Flint", the scene is laid in the nineteen twenties in place of the eighteen nineties and the small town is therefore somewhat changed on the surface, even in such an important aspect as its economic state: "Situated in the heart of the farming section of the State, with its fertile soil, its equable climate, its forests of pine trees, Central City was one of the flourishing towns of South Georgia. Its population was between eight and ten thousand, of which some four thousand were Negroes. The wealth and the prosperity depended not so much on the town itself as it did on the farmers of the fertile lands surrounding it."[28]) And here is the cotton mill which Clarendon lacked, while there is plenty of active trade, industry, and material progress among the population. It is not the former type of sleepy backward town, for the lure of American business has touched it and money making, bootlegging and sex have proved even more fascinating pursuits than politics.

But material well-being is not spiritual well-being, and the mental outlook of this modern town is just as limited and trivial as that of Clarendon or Wellington. There is a "Main Street" pettiness and vulgarity characterizing it: "A typical Southern town — reasonably rich as wealth is measured in that part of Georgia — rich in money and lands and cotton — amazingly ignorant in the finer things of life. Noisy, unreflective, their wants but few and those easily satisfied. The men, self-made, with all that distinctly American term implies. The women concerned only with their petty household affairs and more

---

28) White, Walter F.: *The Fire in the Flint.* p. 32.

petty gossip and social intercourse. But, beyond these, life was and is a closed book. Or, more, a book that never was written or printed." Culture and the finer graces of life were something quite foreign to such an atmosphere: "The companionship and inspiration of books was unknown. Music, even with the omnipresent Victrola, meant only the latest bit of cheap jazz or a Yiddish or Negro dialect song. Art, in its many forms, was considered solely for decadent, effete 'furriners'. Hostility would have met the woman of the town's upper class who attempted to exhibit any knowledge of art. Her friends would have felt that she was trying 'to put something over on them.' As for any man of the town, at best he would have been considered a 'little queer in the head,' at the worst suspected of moral turpitude or perversion."[29])

The economic problem is gone from the town but the race problem evidently lies too deep to be removed with it. Once more appear various kinds of white people, ranging from the doctors, lawyers, and bankers to the "poor whites", and once more they are united in their common hatred of "niggers". And the poorer and more ignorant the white man, the greater the fear and jealousy, until we find that among the underpaid, poorly housed, sickly white mill hands in "Factoryville" "there was but one strong conviction, but one firm rock of faith to which they clung — the inherent and carefully nurtured hatred of "niggers" and a belief in their own infinite superiority over their dark-skinned neighbors."[30]) Separated from the squalid Factoryville by railroad tracks is "Darktown" with similar muddy unpaved streets and dilapidated shacks where the poor class of Negroes was forced to live, and on the edges of this district are the few better homes inhabited by the few educated and ambitious Negroes. As in the case of "The Marrow of Tradition", we find a rising type of Negro, the intelligent man of capacity, but similarly he is fitted into a stereotype by the well-to-do white residents on the hill, by the small tradesmen,

29) White, Walter F.: *The Fire in the Flint.* p. 39.
30) Ibid. p. 38.

and by the factory workers. Even the Negro farmers in the outlying districts do not escape this blanket of prejudice, so that we get a picture of their ruin at the hands of the white land owners and exploiters.

We are not surprised to discover that in such a state of tension between the races the Ku Klux Klan should play an active part in this milieu. It is to be expected that white citizens looking for ways and means of subjugating Negroes should hit upon the device of reviving that old secret organization. It seems oblivious to the fact that it cannot arouse the same emotions in the Negroes of the nineteen twenties as in those of the eighteen nineties: "Perhaps the clearest indication of how little the South realizes the changes that have taken place in the Negro is his recrudescence of the Klan. Where stark terror followed in the wake of the Klan rides of the seventies, the net result of similar rides today is a more determined union of Negroes against all that the Klan stands for, tinctured with a mild amusement at the Klan's grotesque antics."[31] Nevertheless, for all practical purposes, it has sufficient power to accomplish its aims even without help from the old weapon of superstition. And undoubtedly a large part of the explanation for the leaders' revived stress upon mystery and secret ceremony is because of the influence they have in bringing uneducated white members to the fever pitch of race prejudice: "Stodgy, phlegmatic, stupid citizens by day, these by night went through the discomforts of so unprepared a meeting-place, and through the absurdities of the rites imposed upon them by clever rogues who extracted from them fees and donations for the privilege of being made to appear more silly than is usually apparent. Add to that gullibility a natural love of the mysterious and adventurous and an instinct towards brute action restrained only by fear of punishment, by a conjuring of bogies and other malevolent dangers, and one understands, at least in part, the presence of these three hundred 'white, gentile, Protestant' citizens of Central City at this meeting."[32]

31) White, Walter F.: *The Fire in the Flint.* pp. 173—174.
32) Ibid. p. 123.

Perhaps the most pernicious aspect of race relations shown within the close confines of the small town is the way in which the poor and ignorant white citizens are pitted against the Negroes. Because they are motivated so exclusively by instinct instead of reason they provide fertile soil for the suggestions of more prosperous and intelligent citizens who wish to use them for the more unpleasant tasks involved in Negro suppression. Consequently, "they opposed every move for better educational facilities for their children, for improvement of their health or common status or welfare in general, if such improvements meant better advantages for Negroes. Creatures of the fear they sought to inspire in others, their lives are lived in constant dread of the things of evil and terror they preached. It is a system based on stark, abject fear — fear that he whom they termed inferior might, with opportunity, prove himself not inferior."[33]) And the functioning of this system is seen most clearly in the activity of the Ku Klux Klan where propaganda is consciously utilized by the leaders and where the followers are whetted to commit deeds of bloodshed and violence, if necessary in pursuit of their awakened sense of duty as white Americans.

Within the ranks of the Negroes themselves there are also discouraging conditions revealed. The masses, still illiterate and seeking outlet in emotional religion, still with a mind-set of inferiority in relation to their white neighbors, have no faith in the possibilities of their own development under whatever leaders their group produces. A white doctor or lawyer must of course be better than a Negro doctor or lawyer. Professional men of their own skin-color for that very fact were to be mistrusted: "This slave mentality, Kenneth now realized, imbued upon generation after generation of colored folk, is the greatest handicap from which the Negro suffers, destroying as it does the confidence in his own abilitiy which would enable him to meet without fear or apology the test of modern competition."[34]) And, when conditions are such that a Negro

33) Ibid. p. 126.
34) Ibid. p. 48.

must think first of all of saving his own skin, a lack of coöperation in group effort, and a desire instead for inconspicuous submission according to the long established terms, are to be anticipated. As a result of "the evasions, the repressions, the choking back of natural impulses the Negro practised to avoid trouble" in the South, he has learned the lessons of caution and expediency.

The inevitable consequence of this state of affairs in this small town is to darken the very atmosphere. When hypocrisy and ignorance, fear and hate on both sides are the rules of life, the result can be nothing less than depressing. Walter White portrays repeatedly the gloom and the hopelessness of a scene which is saturated throughout with the poison of race prejudice.

"The Fire in the Flint" is only a late example of that type of problem novel where the atmosphere in general is close and stifling. The very fact that the background of these novels is limited geographically only intensifies the impression. Within the boundaries of the Southern small towns, strong emotions are seething and throwing off fumes which, lacking outlet, only continue to thicken the surrounding medium. One is inclined to contemplate the necessity of such things as fresh air and open spaces.

Urban-Cosmopolitan and Cultured Middle Class.

Any such need is answered by the sense of expansion in the milieu presented in 1912 by James Weldon Johnson's "Autobiography of an Ex-Coloured Man". In many ways this book can be regarded as a milestone in the course the Negro novel has taken. It introduces an entirely new chapter in the Negro novelist's treatment of milieu. For many years after the appearance of this fictional autobiography the note was struck for a broader and even cosmopolitan touch. No longer was the action localized in the South, either on the plantation or in the small town. Urban life in all its varieties is now depicted, with the large city as the centre of attention. The Northern or Western city is chosen in preference to the Southern, and the evident emancipation from the use of the South as background does not stop in its course with other parts of America but proceeds to a use of European cities as well. The effect is kaleidiscopic, especially when the scene shifts from one city to another and from one continent to another within the bounds of one novel.

Thus James Weldon Johnson transports us from the agricultural South to urban Connecticut where his hero grows up, and, after a brief episode in the Southern city of Jacksonville, back North to the sophisticated underworld life of New York, then to Europe with Paris, London, and Berlin as bright spots, finally returning to New York and its whirling activity. We are now removed from the local and provincial atmosphere where time moved slowly and a variety of happenings was unknown. There in no stagnation or monotonous round of events in the modern city, whether it be in the United States or in Europe: "New York City is the most fatally fascinating thing in America. She sits like a great witch at the gate of the country, showing her alluring white face and hiding her crooked hands and feet under the folds of her white garment — constantly enticing thousands from far within, and tempting those from across the seas to go no farther. And all these become the victims of her caprice. Some she at once crushes beneath her cruel feet; others she condemns to a fate like that of galley-slaves; a few she favours and fondles, riding them high on the bubbles of fortune; then with a sudden breath she blows the bubbles out and laughs mockingly as she watches them fall."[35]) The fascination exerted is often positive as well as negative and destructive. The beauty of Paris is felt as intoxicating: "Paris became for me a charmed spot, and whenever I have returned there, I have fallen under the spell which compels admiration for all of its manners and customs, and justification of even its follies and sins."[36]) In this novel as in subsequent ones we see the Negro susceptible to that fever

---

35) Johnson, James W.: *The Autobiography of an Ex-Coloured Man.* p. 89.

36) Ibid. p. 129.

of modern life which thirsts for contact with the city rather
than with the soil. There is danger inherent in its very nature,
but it is sweet danger for him as he finds that "the crowds,
the lights, the excitement, the gaiety, and all its subtler stimulating influences began to take effect upon me. My blood
ran quicker and I felt that I was just beginning to live. To
some natures this stimulant of life in a great city becomes
a thing as binding and necessary as opium is to one addicted
to the habit. It becomes their breath of life; they cannot exist
outside of it; rather than be deprived of it they are content to
suffer hunger, want, pain, and misery; they would not exchange
even a ragged and wretched condition among the great crowd
for a degree of comfort away from it."[37]) It may lead to physical and moral deterioration as it sucks the individual down
into the "gas-light life" of the underworld. Many are then
unable to summon the necessary will-power to withstand complete submission, and therefore become saddled with the habits
of drink, gambling, or other vices. But life is a game and he
who would play it must be willing to take his chances with
the rest in the thick of it, which means in the heart of this or
that city.

The complexity of urban life involves a complexity of human types. No longer is it possible to limit oneself to the Negro group when it is only one element in a mixed population,
or to any one class where class boundaries are eternally shifting and dissolving. In this novel one realizes anew that fluidity
in American conditions which allows quite naturally for rapid
transitions from the proletarian to the artistic world, from
the haunts of gamblers to the respectable middle-class homes of
white wage-earners. White school-children, Cuban factory
workers, Negro pullman porters, professional colored prize-
fighters and actors, German musicians, and New York clerks
all provide background at the proper moment. Variety is the
keynote and animation the tone. It may be in the "Club", the

---

37) Johnson, James W.: *The Autobiography of an Ex-Coloured Man.*
    p. 90.

centre of colored Bohemia, or in Berlin with a "party of men composed of artists, musicians, writers, and for aught I know, a count or two"[38]) evidently discussing "everything that ever entered man's mind", or in the Southern cigar factory where "arguments are many and frequent, ranging from the respective and relative merits of rival baseball clubs to the duration of the sun's light and energy".[39]) But in any case there persists that sense of vital and continuous activity given by the modern city in general and perpetuated by changing the specific scene and actors frequently.

There is tension at the heart of this milieu, but it is tension created by more factors than the race problem. The question of race relationships inevitably enters at times but it is a point for philosophizing and discussion rather than a practical issue. We become aware of hostility between white and black Southerners or of differences between the Northern and Southern attitude towards the Negro, not through a direct view of group action and feeling but through the arguments of two or three characters together or the ideas and meditations of an individual on the subject. While the small Southern town of earlier novels was described as directly impregnated with the views of race prejudice, to the exclusion of other elements, the present cosmopolitan and urban atmosphere escapes with a contact which seems not only indirect but often casual because of the presence of so many other absorbing interests. The world has become too sophisticated and too intricate to permit the dominance of any one thread in the pattern.

James Weldon Johnson opened the way for a series of novels in the decade between 1920 and 1930 equally flexible in the use of background. Writers had, in addition to his literary precedent, the experience of the northward and cityward expansion of Negroes we have already noted as a consequence of the boom in American industry during the World War. Walter White, in his story, "Flight", (1926) shifts his characters from the

---

38) Johnson, James W.: *The Autobiography of an Ex-Coloured Man.*
pp. 140—141.
39) Ibid. p. 97.

langour and grace of New Orleans to the progressive society life of Atlanta, then gradually northwards from Philadelphia to white New York and to the Negro centre of Harlem. And several times life in Paris is introduced providing the necessary cosmopolitan touch: "A big liner, Paris, the boulevards, the shops, the theatres, the restaurants, all the life of 'la plus belle ville du monde'."[40]) Paris serves a similar purpose in Jessie Fauset's "Plum Bun", (1929). Again we are taken from Philadelphia to both the white and colored worlds in New York, and again we find ourselves on French soil. Here is an atmosphere created by the Louvre and the Luxembourg, by the winding Seine crossed by its distinctive bridges, by the gay cafés, fashionable shops, and exotic restaurants. In the novel, "There is Confusion", (1924), there are also scenes laid in Philadelphia, Harlem, and in France during the War.

Quite apparent is the attraction which these recent Negro novelists feel for French surroundings, but their concern for Europe is not limited to this one direction. Nella Larsen turns to Copenhagen, for example, in "Quicksand". (1928) We are shown school life in Georgia, urban life in Chicago and Harlem, and finally artistic and fashionable life in the capital of Denmark where the presence of a Negro is a curiosity and a wonder, before we are obliged to sink back to the tame mediocrity of a small Alabama town. In addition to the social whirl of "dinners, coffees, theatres, pictures, music, clothes", we are told of "the charm of the old city itself, with its odd architectural mixture of medievalism and modernity, and of the general air of well-being which pervaded it."[41]) We are given opportunity to imagine ourselves "dodging successfully the innumerable bicycles like a true Copenhagener, — — — loitering on the long bridge which spanned the placid lakes, or watching the pageant of the blue-clad, sprucely tailored soldiers in the daily parade at Amalienborg Palace, or in the historic vicinity of the long low-lying Exchange, a picturesque

---

40) White, Walter F.: *Flight.* p. 233.
41) Larsen, Nella: *Quicksand.* pp. 205, 165.

structure in picturesque surroundings, skirting as it did the great canal, which always was alive with many small boats, flying broad white sails and pressing close on the huge ruined pile of the Palace of Christiansborg." Also of appeal is the Gammelstrand, "the congregation-place of the venders of fish, where daily was enacted a spirited and interesting scene betwcen sellers and buyers."[42])

But the climax of what might be called the urban-cosmopolitan tendency is presented in 1928 by Dr. Bois' novel, "Dark Princess". New York, Berlin, and Chicago form the setting at various times, with brief introductions of numerous other American cities, and constant reference to events which have occurred in India and England, Russia, and China. Urban civilization is seen in its extreme development amid the mad rush and noise and competition of Chicago: "Chicago is the epitome of America. New York is a province of England, Charleston, and New Orleans are memories, farming and industrial hinterlands. California is just beyond the world. Chicago is the American world, and the modern world, and the worst of it."[43]) The pastoral interlude among the fields and hills of Virginia, in the agricultural South, not only brings into relief through contrast the dominating urban color of the book, but serves as an attempt to connect all the widely scattered spots where the dark-skinned characters are struggling for recognition. For, as the princess claims, " here in Virginia you are at the edge of a black world. The black belt of the Congo, the Nile, and the Ganges reaches by way of Guiana, Haiti, and Jamaica, like a red arrow, up into the heart of white America. Thus I see a mighty synthesis: you can work in Africa and Asia right here in America if you work in the Black Belt ... I have been sore bewildered by this mighty America, this ruthless, terrible, intriguing Thing. My home and heart is India. Your heart of hearts is Africa. And now I see through the cloud. You may stand here ... halfway between Maine and Flo-

---

42) Ibid. p. 167.
43) Du Bois, W. E. B.: *Dark Princess*. p. 284.

rida, between the Atlantic and the Pacific, with Europe in your face and China at your back; with industry in your right hand and commerce in your left and the Farm beneath your steady feet; and yet be in the Land of the Blacks."[44])

In such a passage is suggested that true cosmopolitan spirit which manifests itself throughout the novel in a breadth not only of geography but of peoples. The milieu embraces many nations, classes, and races, not only whites and Negroes, but Indians, Chinese, Japanese, Arabians, Egyptians, not only aristocrats but workers and communists, politicians and Ku Klux Klan members, farmers and representatives of the middle class. The suave diplomacy at the distinguished dinner table in Berlin where the Oriental guests "talked art in French, literature in Italian, politics in German, and everything in clear English"[45]) is superseded by the fevered conferences of illiterate and scheming Chicago politicians, or the manual work of subway diggers who "perform vast surgical operations with insertions of lumber and steel and muscle."[46])

But this same passage also suggests a special concern for dark-skinned people, whether Negro or Oriental. Those of African, Asiatic, and American Negroid blood are suggested to have a common cause, a similar reason for working together against white supremacy. There is no one-group situation here, for the colored characters are unavoidably mixing with their white neighbors in every part of the world. The close proximity of city life and modern means of communication insure such a state of affairs. Yet we sense a tension in the "Dark Princess" between peoples of different skin color which is more of a serious reality than that in "The Autobiography of an Ex-Coloured Man". It is a milieu where the "problem of the color line" is widened to include far more than the American Negro, but where the sympathy is still placed on the dark side.

The other novels of this period already shown as using the same general type of milieu fall between Johnson's casual and

44) Ibid. p. 286.
45) Du Bois, W. E. B.: *Dark Princess*. p. 19.
46) Ibid. p. 266.

Du Bois' earnest treatment of race issues. None of them attempts to give a setting in which consciousness of race is not present, but there are varying forms and degrees of presentation. In no case is there the directness of treatment seen in the earlier propaganda novels of Chesnutt and Dunbar, or in "The Fire in the Flint". It is as an undercurrent, and often the problem is regarded either as more theoretical or as personal, applicable to the development of some particular individual, the further consideration of which therefore belongs within the sphere of the next chapter.

But there is another important aspect of this group of novels which must be stressed in a study of milieu. This is the question of the class of people presented within this cosmopolitan-urban atmosphere. We have already seen a flexibility on this score, both in "The Autobiography of an Ex-Coloured Man" of 1912 and in the "Dark Princess" of 1928. But the fact that their central characters, as we shall observe more closely in the following chapter, are not from the lower class is significant of a tendency which the remaining novels of this group bring to clear expression. This is a tendency to portray not the peasant type of "Folks From Dixie" and "The Conjure Woman", nor the ignorant and helpless masses of black people in the small Southern town, but the educated and respectable middle class. In earlier novels the educated Negro occasionally appeared, but as an exception and in the rôle of leader rather than as the average of a group. But now we find Negroes who, if not affluent, are at least in comfortable conditions and who take certain standards of social position and culture for granted. It is a long step from the crude cabins of plantation days to the "cream colored rooms" and exquisite furnishing mentioned in "Quicksand". Here are "beds with long, tapering posts to which tremendous age lent dignity and interest, bonneted old high-boys, tables that might be Duncan Phyfe, rare spindle-legged chairs, and others whose ladder backs gracefully climbed the delicate wall panels. These historic things mingled harmoniously and comfortably with brass-bound Chinese tea-chests, luxuriously deep chairs and davenports, tiny tables of

7

gay color, a lacquered jade-green settee with gleaming black satin cushions, lustrous Eastern rugs, ancient copper, Japanese prints, some fine etchings, a profusion of bric-a-brac, and endless shelves filled with books."[47])

The interior of such a Negro home suggests that sense of taste which is a mark both of refinement and sophistication. Notice the social gathering in "Passing", (1929): "There were the familiar little tinkling sounds of spoons striking against frail cups, the soft running sounds of inconsequential talk, punctuated now and then with laughter. In irregular small groups, disintegrating, coalescing, striking just the right note of disharmony, disorder in the big room, which Irene had furnished with a sparingness that was almost chaste, moved the guests with that slight familiarity that makes a party a success. On the floor and the walls the sinking sun threw long, fantastic shadows."[48]) The home of the Marshalls in "There is Confusion", with its "quiet dignity and atmosphere of presperity"[49]) is typical of that "better class of colored people" upon whom these novelists are specializing. It makes no difference whether it is Walter White's "Flight", Nella Larsen's "Quicksand" and "Passing", or Jessie Fauset's "There is Confusion" and "Plum Bun", we have introduced to us a self-contained and capable class of Negroes. They are not isolated from the white world but they are living and loving, suffering and achieving fairly much within their own group boundaries and our attention is focussed upon their doings regardless of how many white characters or characters from a lower social class may appear in the book. This is the colored, ambitious professional world, the world of writers and teachers, doctors, students, and artists, and society people even boasting a "leisure class" element.

The atmosphere is not only successful and respectable, but at times even snobbish so that we find prejudice within prejudice: "Negro society — — was as complicated and as

47) Larsen, Nella: *Quicksand.* pp. 97—98.
48) Larsen, Nella: *Passing.* pp. 166—167.
49) Fauset, Jessie R.: *There is Confusion.* p. 63.

rigid in its ramifications as the highest state of white society. If you couldn't prove your ancestry and connections you were tolerated, but you didn't belong. You could be queer, or even attractive, or bad or brilliant, or even love beauty and such nonsense if you were a Rankin, or a Leslie, or a Scoville; in other words if you had a family."[50]) And often we find a criterion more important than family, and that is complexion. The greatest asset for winning recognition within the Negro group is the possession of a light-brown skin color, the lighter the better: "And within the circle of those who were called Negroes she found duplications of the lines between the two major groups — — — there were churches attended in the main only by colored people who were mulattoes or quadroons, others only by those whose complexions were quite dark."[51])

The outstanding example of this prejudice is offered by a novel which has a new and different type of milieu but only because the heroine's black skin excludes her from that association with the respectable middle-class people she craves. Thus snobbishness is a major issue in "The Blacker the Berry", (1929), where the Negroes have their "blue vein circle" and their motto of "whiter and whiter every generation".[52]) "The people who, in Emma Lou's phrase, really mattered, the business men, the doctors, the lawyers, the dentists, the more moneyed pullman porters, hotel waiters, bank janitors, and majordomas, in fact all of the Negro leaders and members of the upper class, were either light-skinned themselves or else had light-skinned wives. A wife of dark complexion was considered a handicap unless she was particularly charming, wealthy, or beautiful."[53])

Urban-Proletarian; Rural-Peasant.

Consequently it is the other side of the picture which "The Blacker the Berry" shows, the contrast to the prosperous and

50) Larsen, Nella: *Quicksand.* p. 19.
51) White, Walter F.: *Flight.* pp. 54—55.
52) Thurman, Wallace: *The Blacker the Berry.* pp. 18—19.
53) Ibid. p. 59.

respectable mulatto group. This is one of the reasons why it may be considered as a point of transition to still a fourth type of milieu. Within the last three or four years have appeared several works of fiction differing in some important aspects from those already mentioned. We have passed from the plantation-slave background to the emancipated but ignorant Negro masses in the small Southern town to the cultured, successful middle class of the city, whether at home or abroad. And now we find a new realistic milieu which presents a challenge to respectability and believes in facing facts and people as they are. Often it continues to use the city, but in this case it concentrates upon some particular one and upon the life of the "lower class" of Negroes there. Again we come to a one-group treatment where the existence of white folk beyond the horizon is a fact of little immediate importance. Gone is the cosmopolitan and refined atmosphere of the preceding group. These present novelists are above all concerned with the Negro, the local scene, and the common people. The particular locality chosen is often Harlem as the centre of American Negro urban life, and the particular people are most often manual workers or idlers in touch with the "underworld".

Thus we observe in "The Blacker the Berry" the daily life of gamblers, drifters, and prostitutes in the heart of Harlem. It is true that the heroine has education and a middle class background, and that there are scenes laid in a little Rocky Mountain town and Los Angeles, but this is all preliminary to the important part of the book where she associates with those Harlemites beyond the pale.

But Wallace Thurman's preoccupation with Harlem and its lower class is, in a way, a forced issue, caused by the social ostracism from other spheres of a character who aspires higher. Therefore, in order to appreciate the purest treatment of this type of milieu, we must turn to Rudolph Fisher's "The Walls of Jericho" or Claude Mc Kay's "Home to Harlem" appearing in 1928. Both are frankly interested in proletarian types foremost and in Harlem as the most desirable spot on earth for Negroes. We move in a world inhabited by day laborers, piano

movers, maids and saloon keepers, dock workers, train men
and sailors, on the one hand, and bums, prostitutes, drunkards,
gamblers and vagabonds on the other. In "The Walls of Jericho" the business man, poet, lawyer, preacher, and social
worker are kept in a proper subordinate place and are in no
way allowed to interfere with the prevailing proletarian spirit.
Symbolic is the contrast between week day and Sunday on
Harlem's main street: "And so Seventh Avenue, most versatile
of thoroughfares, becomes Harlem's Broadway during the
week and its Fifth Avenue on Sunday; remains for six days, a
walk for deliberate shoppers, a lane for tumultuous traffic, the
avenue of a thousand enterprises and the scene of a thousand
hair-breadth escapes; remains for six nights a carnival, bright
with the lights of theatres and night clubs, alive with darting
cabs, with couples moving from house party to cabaret, with
loiterers idling and ogling on the curb, with music wafted from
mysterious sources, with gay talk and loud Afric laughter. Then
comes Sunday, and for a few hours Seventh Avenue becomes
the highway to heaven; reflects that air of quiet, satisfied self-
righteousness peculiar to chronic church goers."[54]) But Sunday
and respectability come only once a week and cannot destroy
the preponderance of the other mood. "Patmore's Pool Parlor"
holds more attractions than the Episcopal church for the majority of these Harlemites.

The very fact that Claude Mc Kay has named his book
"Home to Harlem" is indicative of the value placed upon it as
a Negro centre. Harlem has been utilized and even appreciated
by the preceding group of novelists, but they have a tendency
to regard it as only one of the increasing number of Negro
urban centres, to portray nothing questionable, and to give impressions rather objectively and soberly. Nowhere among them
is such a lyrical outburst as "Oh, to be in Harlem again after
two years away. The deep-dyed color, the thickness, the closeness of it. The noises of Harlem. The sugared laughter. The
honey-talk on its streets. And all night long, ragtimes and 'blues'

---

54) Fisher, Rudolph: *The Walls of Jericho.* p. 189.

playing somewhere, — — — singing somewhere, dancing somewhere! Oh, the contagious fever of Harlem. Burning everywhere in dark-eyed Harlem."[55]) Here is revealed not only a new concentration of a novelist upon this milieu, but a new treatment which is both idealization and realism. The vital attraction of this background is stressed without any attempt to hide what might be considered its improper aspects. We see that a primary interest of this world is in physical pleasure and its denizens satisfy their appetite for sex or food in an equally frank and natural manner, without thought of shame or convention. Harlem is glorified and at the same time Harlemites are stripped of protective clothing and shown as they are, loafers and jazzers and street girls, enjoying life in their own way, without claiming virtue and without consciousness of vice.

It is a society lacking traditional morals but pulsating with its own kind of love, devotion, and sympathy which, on the whole, seem to overbalance its hates, jealousies, and fears. Above all, it is an instinctive society where emotion rather than intellect holds sway. The drive of ambition and the struggle for career have no place in this group where it is enough to have a good dinner and congenial company to-day: "Jake went to Aunt Hattie's to feed. Billy Biasse was there and a gang of longshore men who had boozed and fed and were boozing again and, touched by the tender spring night, were swapping love stories and singing — 'Harlem has got the right stuff, boh, for all feelings'. 'Youse right enough', Jake agreed, and fell into a reverie of full brown mouth and mischievous brown eyes all composing a perfect whole for his dark-brown delight."[56])

The other outstanding works of fiction during recent years all preserve at the heart of their milieu the same opposition to the cosmopolitan — cultural atmosphere, to a greater or less degree. They may not choose Harlem as a point of concentration and they may differ in various other ways from

55) Mc Kay, Claude: *Home to Harlem.* p. 15.
56) Ibid. pp. 293—294.

McKay's and Fisher's novels, but the link in common which joins them all together within the borders of this fourth general type of milieu is their challenge to respectability, the tendency to "call a spade a spade", the assumption that after all, life is an instinctive and not a rational matter, whether for good or bad.

The background of George Schuyler's satirical book, "Black No More" (1931), might be described as "All American" since North, South and far West are all included with points as far apart as Atlanta, San Francisco, and Mississippi. Nevertheless, because of the fact that it is so thoroughly American, no matter what specific place is used, it strikes the local rather than the cosmopolitan note. There is a standardization of treatment so that we breathe the same air throughout. This effect is helped by the class of people described who, whether educated or uneducated, prosperous or poor, all alike reveal materialistic aims which are far distant from the lofty ideals and dreams of such novels as "There is Confusion", and "Dark Princess". George Schuyler is not dealing exclusively with Negroes, the very plot of his book would prevent that — nor is he dwelling upon proletarian or "underworld" life, and yet his middle-class characters are not the ideal and refined type we have seen previously. They are entirely opportunistic, self-centered, shrewd, practical, and scheming. Aeroplane travel, big business and graft are their bread and meat. What seems to be idealism is exposed as various forms of ego display and desire for power. Money-getting and not art is the chief interest. It is essentially an uncultivated world, from the patent ignorance of the uneducated mill-hands to the bluffs and pretensions of scientists, politicians and preachers. Even while keeping in mind the fact that "Black No More" is a satire and a farce, it is noteworthy that Schuyler chooses the realistic rather than the idealistic approach to the people of his milieu, carrying to an extreme point the insistence of Fisher and McKay upon things as they are.

Other books of this group attempt to show conditions and people as they are and the predominance of instinctive life without such extreme materialistic implications, as well as without sole reliance on urban background. Langston Hughes' "Not Without Laughter", (1930) and Jean Toomer's "Cane", (1923) are concerned once more with the humble class of Negroes in a local setting, but primarily in the town and country side, rather than in the large city. "Not Without Laughter" shows simple, unpretentious Negroes in the every day life of a small Western town, and "Cane" has the background of Southern peasant life. At the end of the former book the scene shifts to Chicago, and there is a section of the latter book devoted to the doings of the Negroes in Washington. But both have an unmistakable center of interest and concentration removed from the city. Either we have the close home town atmosphere or the spaces of the country-side: "New York? Impossible. It was a fiction —. He forces himself to narrow to a cabin silhouetted on a knoll about a mile away. Peace. Negroes within it are content. They farm. They sing. They love. They sleep."[57]) This is the Georgia of red mud and moonlight, fir trees and saw mills, where urban sophistication is replaced by country habits, superstitions, and primitive love. According to the stimulus received, people fear the "blood burning moon" or burst into spontaneous song: "Like purple tallow flames, songs jet up. They spread a ruddy haze over the heavens. The haze swings low. Now the whole countryside is a soft chorus", for "things are so immediate in Georgia".[58])

The little town of Stanton in Kansas brings us more complexity as inevitable with the greater collection of people in one centre, but it is not city sophistication. We become acquainted with the hard working servant class of Negroes who have simple interests and means of recreation: "The old Negroes went to the revival, and the young Negroes went to the carnival, and after sundown these August evenings the mourning songs of the Christians could be heard rising from the Hickory Woods while the profound syncopation of the minstrel band blared from Galoway's Lots, strangely intermingling their

---

57) Toomer, Jean: *Cane*. pp. 163—164.
58) Ibid. pp. 164, 192.

notes of praise and joy."[59]) There is something harmless even
about its "red-light district" called the "Bottoms": "It was
a gay place — people did what they wanted to, or what they
had to do, and didn't care — for in the Bottoms folk ceased
to struggle against the boundaries between good and bad, or
white and black, and surrendered amiably to immorality.
Beyond Pearl Street, across the tracks, people of all colors came
together for the sake of joy, the curtains being drawn only
between themselves and the opposite side of the railroad, where
the churches were and the big white Y. M. C. A." There is not
even the atmosphere of degradation and viciousness here which
exists in a comparable locality in the small town of "The Fire in
the Flint". The "underworld" section of "Not Without Laughter"
has much of the same a-moral attitude as that of "Home to
Harlem" and "Cane", to be attributed largely to the same
emphasis upon instinctive and natural living: "To those who
lived on the other side of the railroad and never realized the
utter stupidity of the word 'sin', the Bottoms was vile and
wicked. But to the girls who lived there, and the boys who
pimped and fought and sold licker there, 'sin' was a silly word
that did not enter their heads. They never looked at life through
the spectacles of the Sunday-school. The glasses good people
wore wouldn't have fitted their eyes, for they hung no curtain
of words between themselves and reality. To them things were
what they were."[60])

A similar attitude prevails in two more pieces of fiction
which might be classified as exotic literature. The scene of
"Banjo", (1929), is laid in the French seaport town of Marseilles, the scenes of "Tropic Death", (1926), in Central America
and the West Indies. We are far removed from the United
States and yet it is still the a-moral lower class of Negro we
find, rather than the middle class "nice" people, travelling
abroad for cultural purposes and study.

The very air of Marseilles is contrary to anything respect-

---

59) Hughes, Langston: *Not Without Laughter*. pp. 107—108.
60) Ibid. p. 232.

able, conventional, or stereotyped. Here is "the port that seamen talked about — the marvelous, dangerous, attractive, big, wide-open port"[61]) with its shifting and mixed population encouraging to a vagabond mode of life: "They were all on the beach, and there were many others besides them — white men, brown men, black men. Finns, Poles, Italians, Slavs, Maltese, Indians, Negroids, African Negroes, West Indian Negroes — deportées from America for violation of the United States immigration laws — afraid and ashamed to go back to their own lands, all dumped down in the great Provencal port, bumming a day's work, a meal, a drink, existing from hand to mouth, anyhow anyway, between box car, tramp ship, bistro, and bordel."[62]) The picturesque variety characterizing the place is especially marked among the Negro group on which interest is focussed: "Negroes speaking the civilized tongues, Negroes speaking all the African dialects, black Negroes, brown Negroes, yellow Negroes. It was as if every country in the world where Negroes lived had sent representatives drifting into Marseilles. A great vagabond host of jungle-like Negroes trying to scrape a temporary existence from the macadamized surface of this great Provencal port."[63])

Just as in his earlier book, Claude McKay here depicts a milieu where the chief rule of life is and must be through circumstances to live freely and frankly for the moment. In this Marseilles underworld where sailors, loafers, harlots, street musicians, taxi drivers, coal and harvest workers and policemen all rub shoulders, it is the black boys who know how to seize the greatest pleasure, "loafing after their labor long enough to laugh and love and jazz and fight." It is all a natural expression of their "loose, instinctive way of living" in such vivid contrast not alone to whites but to the "colored intelligensia" which "lived its life 'to have the white neighbors think well of us', so that it could move more peaceably into nice

61) McKay, Claude: *Banjo*. p. 12.

62) Ibid. p. 6.

63) Ibid. p. 68.

'white' streets."[64]) These dark-skinned beach boys of the "Ditch" have no more sense of shame in being themselves than the girls and boys in the "Bottoms". There is no feeling of inhibition or repression: "There were no dots and dashes in their conversation — nothing that could not be frankly said and therefore decently — no act or fact of life for which they could not find a simple passable word." The interest in food, drink, jazz music, and sex is quite obvious, as in "Home to Harlem", for in the physical and emotional side of life lie infinite resources of joy for them which they see no reason for not utilizing. Thus association with them was something like "participating in a common primitive birthright."[65])

Enhancing the sensuous and vagabond spirit is the "magic of the Mediterranean." It brings to the Marseilles docks the "great commerce of all continents". There at any time are "picturesque proletarians from waters whose names were warm with romance: the Caribbean, the Gulf of Guinea, the Persian gulf, the Bay of Bengal, the China Seas, the Indian Archipelago. And, oh, the earthy mingled smells of the docks! Grain from Canada, rice from India, rubber from the Congo, tea from China, brown sugar from Cuba, bananas from Guinea, lumber from the Soudan, coffee from Brazil, skins from Argentina, palm-oil from Nigeria, pimento from Jamaica, wool from Australia, oranges from Spain and oranges from Jerusalem. In piled-up boxes, bags, and barrels, some broken, dropping their stuff on the docks, reposing in the warm odor of their rich perfumes — the fine harvest of all the lands of the earth."[66])

Here is perhaps the truest sort of cosmopolitanism, yet it enters into this milieu only because it is characteristic of the local spot itself. Such a seaport as Marseilles is touched by the winds of so many countries that something international and cosmopolitan is inseparable from its very nature. In this way

---

64) Mc Kay, Claude: *Banjo*. pp. 319—320.

65) Ibid. p. 321.

66) Ibid. pp. 66—67.

one does not lose a feeling for a fundamental localization. The same is true of Walrond's "Tropic Death". Through the collection of stories the variety of scene and people only increases our insight into the nature of the whole region, that of the tropics lying below the Gulf Stream. The truth about this particular section is intimately connected with the exotic and cosmopolitan elements penetrating it. Thus both McKay and Walrond at their most exotic are painters of local color along with the majority of the other writers in this group.

Walrond's story, "The Wharf Rats", gives this impression at the very start: "Among the motley crew recruited to dig the Panama Canal were artisans from the four ends of the earth. Down in the Cut drifted hordes of Italians, Greeks, Chinese, Negroes — a hardy, sun-defying set of white, black, and yellow men. But the bulk of the actual brawn for the work was supplied by the dusky peons of those coral isles in the Caribbean ruled by Britain, France, and Holland."[67]) And in addition to the Panama Canal zone in Central America many of the scenes in this book are set in these "coral isles" of the West Indies, Trinidad, and Barbados with reference to St. Vincent, St. Lucian, Martinique, and others. Creole, Jamaican and Spanish girls are all to be found in the slums of Colon, "a city of sores" in Honduras, where a population of mixed blood is inevitable. Half breed yellow Cubans speaking Spanish, Jamaicans, and black American Negroes may be thrown together on the same ship, as is the case in "The Yellow One".

Such a mixed and varied motley of people could hardly be expected to uphold intellectual and conventional standards. They are regarded as from the bottom layers of society, West Indian peasants, black workers in stone quarries, mulatto prostitutes and sailors. Blood flows thickly and passion mounts high in this region of langorous heat. Life is held cheap and death is a commonplace where overcrowded conditions and the competitions of jealousies and fears thrust people into fierce and elemental struggles.

---

67) Walrond, Eric: *Tropic Death.* p. 89.

And it is an atmosphere in which individuals struggle not only against each other but against ominous natural and supernatural forces. Drought is an ever threatening enemy to man: "Throats parched, grim, sun-crazed blacks cutting stone on the white burning hill-side dropped with a clang the hot, dust-powdered drills and flew up over the rugged edges of the horizon to descend into a dry, waterless gut."[68]) Rain becomes a dire need after the sun had "wrung toll of the earth" in this way, "had robbed the land of its juice, squeezed it dry."[69]) Snakes, whales, and bats have unsavory power and fire hags and ghosts work mischief at night. The superstitions of this area centre not around such figures as Chesnutt's conjure woman, but around the obeah man: "Over smoking pots, on black, death-black nights, legends of the bloodiest were recited till they became the essence of a sort of a Negro Koran. One refuted them at the price of one's breath. And to question the verity of the obeah, to dismiss or reject it as the ungodly rite of some lurid, crack-brained Islander, was to be an accursed pale-face, dog of a white. And the obeah man, in fury of rage, would throw a machette at the heretic's head or — worse — burn on his doorstep at night a pyre of Maubé bark or green Ganja weed."[70]) As in "Cane", supernatural powers bring a brooding sense of disaster into this milieu which is lacking in an earlier book like "The Conjure Woman". Even though the same ignorance is basic to both, a different type of imagination is at work.

With the fiction of the last group we emerge into a type of milieu where race prejudice is no longer present as such a serious issue. It is a more or less accepted fact but the people have no time for concern with it. They are too occupied with their own intense living, their own experience of ecstasy and tragedy. They are too simple in make-up to theorize and analyze and the natural thing is to avoid race trouble if possible or

68) Ibid. p. 11.
69) Ibid. p. 18.
70) Ibid. p. 90.

otherwise to get through with it as quickly and easily as possible. Although we see here much of the same naiveté and instinctive qualities as in the characters of the first group, these Negroes have none of the same illusions. There is no assumption on their part that the white man is master and god and that their duty is to serve faithfully and then keep out of the way. Their only assumption is that the white man, mediocre as he is, nevertheless has the power, and that is a fact not to be disputed. It is bad fortune, but life has many outlets and the object is to concentrate on whatever riches are available. Luckily these are legion along with the sorrows.

With an analysis of this fourth group, our study of the milieu comes to an end. In regard to its bearing upon the development of race consciousness, there are certain conclusions towards which it leads us. In general we can trace a correspondence of these four milieus to those stages of race consciousness discussed in the first part: submission, defence, offence, and non-resistance, except that in these novels there is no certain line of demarcation between the defensive and offensive attitude. The preoccupation with the *plantation-slave* milieu and the idyllic nature of the scenes point to a certain acceptance of the status quo. The typical relationship between master and servant is a happy and a romantic one. The rôle of superior is assumed by the white man and the rôle of inferior taken for granted by the Negro. As a result there is little tension on this score. No spirit of competition or active antagonism between the races mars the harmony of Southern chivalrous times where the Negroes lead their humble and yet satisfying lives within their restricted sphere. The psychology is that of *submission*.

The next two presentations of milieu show a blending of defensive and offensive attitudes obvious and active in the one case, and hidden and dormant in the other case. In the *small Southern town* novel of Chesnutt and White this mixture of *defence and offence* corresponds to the widening and the complicating of the milieu. According to these novelists, the strong tension in the atmosphere is created by the white prejudice, and met by a helplessness and at the same time a growing sense of injustice which indicates the race consciousness of rebellion. This group of novels cannot be seen in any other light than as direct propaganda, as challenge, as exposé of the sins of the white man. The whole setting is presented in such a way as to produce this effect, to present the masses of ignorant free Negroes as suppressed and victimized by the forces of race prejudice at work.

With a still greater widening of the milieu in the *urban-cosmopolitan* group, the *defence-offence* element seems to be buried under the complexity of other issues. But its latent influence can be sensed. The effort to reveal largely the respectable or cultivated intelligent class of Negroes indicates a subtle form of defence on the part of the authors, giving a proof to the world that such Negroes with such superior capacities exist. Any propaganda is indirect and therefore perhaps all the more effective. The fact that these Negroes can occupy themselves with other than race problems, can endeavor, in spite of their sensitivity to the obvious injustices practiced on them, to place emphasis on certain positive values in life, on their pursuit of their careers and the fulfilment of their dreams in so far as the white world allows, all this may be regarded by readers as a mark of their superiority. The race consciousness present in this milieu is refined, neither the prejudice nor the rebellion against it is obvious in any crude display or direct form. Lynching and riots would be quite out of taste. And yet the spirit of independence and resistance is brooding always within.

The type of milieu which we find in the last group does not allow for suppressions and undercurrents. Whether *proletarian* or *peasant*, the people are what they are and their feelings and emotions are quite evident. Their race consciousness is neither offensive nor defensive, directly or indirectly. Their pride is in being themselves without apology. There is no need for idealization and stress upon their virtues. They are *non-resistant* because there is no reason why they shouldn't be and because they have the urge to use their energy in other directions. They are evidently a reflection of the non-resistant attitude of the authors who created them, who have no case to prove and therefore feel free to show their every-day actual life in all details.

————

Chapter 11. *THE INDIVIDUAL.*

In tracing the manifestations of race consciousness in American Negro fiction it is not enough to observe the broad lines. It is necessary to go from the general to the particular, from a sweeping survey of the milieu to a more detailed examination of its central figures. It is through the medium of the individual, his ways, doings, sayings, and views about the problems of life, that we can come into much more intimate touch with the force of race consciousness wherever present. Insight follows upon contact, and therefore acquaintance with the various characters of these books will naturally further our understanding of their basic attitudes towards racial questions.

Acquiescent—Virtuous—Naive.

In the earlier books by Negro authors where the plantation-slave milieu is prominent, the individual is not much more than an embodiment of group characteristics. The old-fashioned virtues and the harmless vices of the Negro community as a whole, whether slave or free, are reflected in this or that person who steps into the foreground. It is only that he or she as a rule contains an intensification of the simple emotions and attitudes and habits motivating the common life. One man may be a little more constant in love and devotion, one girl more attractive and vital, one woman more spiritual-minded or worldly ambitious than their fellows, and therefore they are marked out quite naturally to become the centre of attention.

Thus the belle of Mas' Rob's plantation, Anner 'Lizer, bears resemblance to the school mistress heroine of Miltonville. "Of all the girls of the Selfridge estate, black, brown, or yellow, Anner 'Lizer was, without dispute, conceded to be the belle. Her black eyes were like glowing coals in their sparkling brightness; her teeth were like twin rows of shining ivories; her brown skin was as smooth and soft as silk, and the full lips that enclosed her gay and flexible tongue were tempting enough to make the heart of any dusky swain throb and his mouth water."[1]) Similarly does Miss Callena ensnare. "When he came back, the eyes of all the town saw Miss Callena Johnson, beribboned and smiling, sitting on his right and chatting away vivaciously. As to her looks, the half had not been told. As to her manners, those smiles and head-tossings gave promise of unheard-of graces, and the hearts of all Miltonville throbbed as one — Miss Callena's smile was like an electric spark setting fire to a whole train of combustibles."[2]) It is interesting to note that Miss Callena, who lives outside the boundaries of slavery with all the supposed advantages thereupon, can match but not outstrip the slave girl in physical charm.

And where it is a question of inner qualities, we must accede Anner 'Lizer first place. She has an emotional depth, a sincerity, and a desire to do right which the more practical minded Miss Callena lacks. We see this first in her feeling for religion: "The weirdness of the scene and the touch of mysticism in the services — though, of course, she did not analyse it thus — reached her emotional nature and stirred her being to its depths."[3]) and second in her earnest effort to "get" it in spite of the distractions of her love-affair. She is perhaps romantic in the true sense of the word whereas Miss Callena's romanticism is more the sentimental type, vanishing like smoke when put to the test. We cannot blame her for her susceptibility to the suitor possessing "a nice cottage wif no encumbrances on it, a couple o' nice hosses, a cow an' ha'f a dozen of de fines' hogs in Miltonville," but the fact that "perhaps even the romantic Miss Callena had an eye to the main chance"[4]) indicates once more that tendency of a stronger worldly spirit to creep into the free Negro community. The implication for

1) Dunbar, P. L.: *Folks From Dixie*. p. 4.
2) Ibid. pp. 239—240.
3) Ibid. pp. 6—7.
4) Ibid. pp. 262, 263.

the character is the same as it was for the milieu: that it is far easier to remain pure of heart and single of purpose on the enslaved but protected plantation.

Removed from the plantation, temptations towards self-seeking are greater, as we see in the case of the dapper Mr. Alonzo Taft, "the black beau ideal and social mentor for all the town"[5]) who unscrupulously deceives and rivals the deliberate and conscientious Mr. Dunkin in his courtship of Miss Callena. The competitor of Anner 'Lizer in love has genuine jealousy but its expression is restricted mostly to spiteful remarks. She makes no cold-blooded, planned campaign to win the desirable Sam. She is undoubtedly not capable of the artfulness found in individuals either of Miltonville or of Bull-Skin Creek where there are two rival factions presenting candidates for a new church pastor, and where the scheming and plotting of Sister Williams and Brother Sneedon against each other's cause are endless.

The clever Negro will recognize the worldly competing with the spiritual side and play upon it with opportunity: "No more happy expedient for raising the revenues of the church could have been found than that which was evolved by the fecund brain of the Reverend Isaiah Johnson. Mr. Johnson was wise in his day and generation. He knew his people, their thoughts and their appetites, their loves and their prejudices. Also he knew the way to their hearts and their pocket-books."[6]) It is true that there was also a lack of pure spirituality on the plantation. Even Sam, "with his smooth but fearless ways, Sam, with his lightsome foot, so airy in the dance, Sam, handsome Sam",[7]) refused to attend church and preferred to play his banjo or hunt in the woods with his dog. But we must remember that although he was a sceptic, he was an unconscious one. There is something honest and wholesome about his instinctive and direct avoidance of religion which would point to a fun-

---

5) Ibid. p. 237.

6) Ibid. p. 125.

7) Ibid. p. 5.

damental quality certainly more spiritual than that of the supposedly pious church member, Brother Jabez, who surpasses even Pastor Johnson's anticipation of worldliness in his people by turning glutton.

On the ideal side, the naturally virtuous character of the slave is illustrated by the master-servant relationship. Aunt Emmeline is the devoted Mammy grown old in service who suffers together with her white family when it undergoes trials. It is as if her own individuality were lost in the force of her love and sympathy and impulse to help remove the troubles of her superiors. And the faithful black Peter reacts instinctively in this way, as we sense in his whimsical remark to his horse: "Bess, I 'spect you 'ca'se you got jedgment, an' you don' have to have a black man runnin' 'roun aftah you all de time plannin' his haid off jes' to keep you out o' trouble. Some folks dat's human-bein's does. Yet an' still, Bess, you ain't nuffin' but a dumb beas', so dey says. Now, what I gwine to do? Co'se dey wants to fight. But whah an' when an' how I gwine to stop hit?"[8]) Peter has the protective attitude of a father towards his reckless young master. In fact, devotion of slave to master is even more conspicuous in Dunbar's book than the devotion of Negroes to each other, with such important exceptions as those of Anner 'Lizer and Sam.

But in Chesnutt's collection of plantation tales, love and loyalty are on the whole confined to an exchange between Negro characters. The love of Tenie and Sandy, of Chloe and Jeff, of Dan and Mahaly, of Sis' Becky for her baby is absolute. "Sandy en' his noo wife got on mighty well tergedder, en' de niggers all 'mence' ter talk about how lovin' dey wuz. W'en Tenie wuz tuk sick oncet, Sandy useter set up all night wid 'er, en' den go ter wuk in de mawnin'des lac'; he had his reg'lar sleep; en Tenie would 'a' done anythin' in de worl' for her Sandy."[9]) Therefore when she does her best to help him and is cruelly thwarted by circumstances it is small wonder that she

8) Dunbar, P. L.: *Folks From Dixie.* p. 175.

9) Chesnutt, C. W.: *The Conjure Woman.* p. 43.

"'peared ter be out'n her min' fer a long time"[10]) with grief, as were Dan and Chloe on the loss of their sweethearts. Affection nourished often by personal charm strikes deep roots in the hearts of such characters, whether lovers or mother and child. "Dis yer little Mose wuz de cutes', blackes', shiny-eyedes' little nigger you eber laid eyes on, en he wuz ez fon' er his mammy ez his mammy wuz er him." A mother could never resist the appeal of a pickaninny like this, just as a lover could never resist that of a girl like Mahaly, "a monst'us lackly gal, — tall en soopl', wid big eyes, en a small foot, en a lively tongue",[11]) resembling Anner 'Lizer and Miss Callena in her healthy exuberance.

It is true that these are only ordinary human beings, and therefore we find plenty whose motives are mixed, prompted by self-interest as much as by devotion to another. Uncle Julius himself, the teller of these tales, is an excellent proof of this. He frequently has some hidden egoistic reason for narrating some particular story of slave life, which does not appear on the surface. Haunts in the swamp and "goophered" grape vines are described because he wishes to continue his clandestine enjoyment of honey in a bee-tree or of grapes from the vine. The gruesome fate of "po' Sandy" is pictured with the hope of diverting his master from tearing down the old school house, since Uncle Julius has his own designs on it. There is something clever and opportunistic about Uncle Julius which he projects especially into one of his characters, the conjure woman. It is repeatedly stressed that "Aun' Peggy neber lack ter wuk fer nobody fer nuffin'", and consequently she is always propitiated with offerings, whether substantial amounts of corn and peas or "a silber dollah en a silk han 'kercher".[12]) If they are insufficient she does not hesitate to say so: "'You'll hafter fetch me sump'n mo', sez Aun' Peggy, 'fer you can't 'spec' me ter was'e my time diggin' roots en wukin' cunj'ation fer nuffin'."[13])

---

10) Ibid. p. 56.
11) Ibid. p. 169.
12) Ibid. p. 207.
13) Ibid. p. 146.

However, we can see that even in the sly Uncle Julius and the mercenary Aunt Peggy, the instinct towards good predominates. When Uncle Julius wants lenient treatment for his grandson, or the recovery from illness of his mistress, or the reconciliation of two white lovers connected with his master's family, he tells stories accordingly, strikingly suitable to the occasion. And Uncle Julius' creation, Aunt Peggy, chooses to use her magic powers in constructive ways: to soften a harsh master, to reunite mother and child, to protect lovers against enemies or rivals. All the main characters of his tales embody the essential kind-heartedness of Uncle Julius himself. With the exception of one unscrupulous conjure man there are no bad individuals on this plantation he describes. One Negro steals a pig but he is amply punished for it, and besides, that is hardly to be ranked as a sin among these child-like people. The worst sins shown by most of the outstanding characters are carelessness and jealousy, so often leading to disaster.

And on the whole, whatever failings these simple-hearted Negroes have in both Dunbar's and Chesnutt's stories are glossed over with humour. One must smile at the duplicity practiced by Mr. Alonzo Taft, Sister Williams, and Uncle Julius. We sympathize with the weaknesses of characters which often make them all the more lovable. If we wish to find a serious treatment of sin, whether committed by Negro or white, we must turn to the next group and the first novels.

Rebellious—Active—Professional—Social Minded.

The deterioration of Negro character painted in "The Sport of the Gods" is made vivid by the contrast between older and younger generation, and between protected Southern and exposed Northern surroundings, as we have seen in the previous chapter. Fanny and Berry are the mother and father who have roots in the old order so that their religious faith and their ethical principles are not killed by the cruel and unjust forces working against them. The failure to save her children from demoralization in New York and the suffering of his unfair imprisonment shake both of their very natures but something reasserts itself at the last. When we see the change between the "simple, easy man" at the start who "went out cheerily to his work" for his master,[14]) and the man after five years in prison we can wonder all the more at his ultimate salvation. "He no longer looked to receive kindness from his fellows — — hard treatment had given his eyes a lowering look — — all the higher part of him he had left behind, dropping it off day after day through the wearisome years. He had put behind the Berry Hamilton that laughed and joked and sang and believed, for even his faith had become only a numbed fancy."[15]) With tragedy waiting for him also outside, it is natural that "the hope of revenge sustained him" for a while, until circumstances and Fanny's influence restore him to his better self. Her faith, which is described as "stalwart" at first, "still hung by a slender thread after every catastrophe had occurred.[16])

But such faith is incomprehensible to their children. From shame over his father's imprisonment and resentment at the attitude and treatment of the community because of it, Joe passes to indifference when safe in a new environment: "He forgot to feel the natural pity for his father toiling guiltless in the prison of his native State",[17]) in proportion to his absorption in the new life opening up to him. From the time that he is thrilled by the sophistication of New York and its "underworld" and fascinated by "the yellow skinned divinity who sat at a near table drinking whisky straight"[18]) his downfall is only a matter of time. Even his mother can no longer be blinded to the faults of this previously spoiled and adored boy: "Fannie looked at her son, and she seemed to see him more clearly than she had ever seen him before, — his foppery, his meanness, his cowardice."[19]) It is no surprise that under the influence of his new associates Joe discards all of his earlier training as false.

14) Dunbar, P L.: *The Sport of the Gods*. p. 35.
15) Ibid. p. 243.
16) Ibid. pp. 250, 252.
17) Ibid. p. 88.
18) Ibid. p. 125.
19) Ibid. p. 136.

"It was very plain to him now that to want a good reputation was the sign of unpardonable immaturity, and that dishonour was the only real thing worth while."[20]) Since there is no one around to administer "the corrective and clarifying" kick which Dunbar recommends for his character, it seems inevitable that these standards should project him into a situation where murder is the outcome. The mental apathy and paralysis following are the tragic signs of spiritual barrenness: "He was as one whose soul is dead, and perhaps it was; for all the little soul of him had been wrapped up in the body of this one woman and the stroke that took her life had killed him too."[21])

The daughter Kitty, does not have a character to lead her to such extremes. There was a "sound quality" in her make-up and a "certain self-respect" helping her to maintain a sense of balance. But even she is too young and inexperienced to withstand all the temptations around her. She begins to long for more freedom to participate in this city-life: "At first the girl grew wistful and then impatient and rebellious — — the quick poison of the unreal life about her had already begun to affect her character. She had grown secretive and sly."[22]) Her new ambition for success on the stage takes the place of her old one for pretty clothes. Both desires seem rather harmless placed beside those of Joe, but the parents feel an old-fashioned humiliation over having their daughter a public dancer and singer. There is something vulgar about it which they regard in the nature of a disgrace only quantitatively stronger in Joe's case.

If Dunbar is severe in exposing the weaknesses of his Negro characters in "The Sport of the Gods" he is even more so in dealing with those white characters whose attitudes are largely responsible for the downfall of this Negro family. Their race prejudice is presented as at the bottom of all the evil consequences. If Maurice Oakley had not been so quick to turn with-

---

20) Ibid. p. 151.
21) Ibid. p. 210.
22) Dunbar, P. L.: *The Sport of the Gods*. pp. 129—130.

out real evidence against his long trusted servant, circumstances could not have encouraged the deterioration of Berry and accomplished that of Joe and Kitty. But his latent prejudice makes him only too ready to believe the worst of any Negro, especially since Emancipation. '"We must remember that we are not in the old days now. The Negroes are becoming less faithful and less contented, and more's the pity, and a deal more ambitious — — as soon as a Negro like Hamilton learns the value of money and begins to earn it, at the same time he begins to covet some easy and rapid way of securing it'."[23]) That generalization alone is enough to convict Berry Hamilton of theft in the eyes of a man whose "conservatism was the quality that had been the foundation of his fortunes",[24]) and in the eyes of other outstanding citizens of the town who take his guilt for granted. Old Horace Talbot has an explanation coming from an attitude of pity and condescension. He feels that the Negroes are too irresponsible by nature even to be expected to assume the tasks of free men and the standards of white men, while Mr. Beachfield Davis regards the supposed crime as a sign of "total depravity": '"All niggers are alike, and there's no use trying to do anything with them'."[25])

Any injustice pertaining to such attitudes might be excusable on the grounds of being unconscious. But not so are we allowed to regard the conscious crimes of Francis Oakley whose "touch of weakness in his mouth"[26]) is portentous, and of Maurice Oakley who refuses to exonerate Berry even after he has conclusive evidence of his innocence. We have opportunity only to sense the deterioration of the delicate, artistic, cowardly Francis, but that of the once stern and strong-willed Maurice is made clear: "It would have been hard to recognize in the Oakley of the present the man of a few years before. The strong frame had gone away to bone, and nothing of his old power sat on either brow or chin. He was a man who trembled

23) Dunbar, P. L.: *The Sport of the Gods.* pp. 25—26.
24) Ibid. p. 8.
25) Ibid. pp. 53—54.
26) Ibid. p. 11.

on the brink of insanity. His guilty secret had been too much for him."[27]) When we set him beside Joe in his state of complete disintegration we are prompted to acclaim the white man as the greater criminal in that the power to do right is in his hands whereas the Negro boy, in spite of his more direct and brutal crime, is presented as the helpless puppet of many evil forces. Both of them receive punishment for their sins, but Joe's is imposed upon him by a society which has encouraged his fall, while Oakley's is the result solely of inner conflict causing mental sickness. The fact that Oakley is sensitive to his conscience to that extent may spare him from the rôle of a villain, but at the same time his opportunities for good were greater than the Negro's, and therefore his crimes are in proportion.

This tendency to portray the faults of Negro characters as the result of external forces and those of white characters as voluntary persists in the novels dealing with the Southern small town. In "The Marrow of Tradition", the figure of Josh, the desperate rebel filled with hatred and revenge against the whites, cannot even compete for the place of villain beside the degenerate and hypocritical Tom Delamere or the ruthless and brutal Mc Bane, one of them a young white man of aristocratic family and the other a "poor white" of common stock. There is something admirable about Josh, a certain Satanic strength in reacting against the old crime committed by the Ku Klux Klan against his parents. "Here was a Negro who could remember an injury, who could shape his life to a definite purpose, if not a high or holy one. When his race reached the point where they would resent a wrong, there was hope that they might soon attain the stage where they would try, and, if need be, die to defend a right."[28]) He has no illusions about white people. Bitterness has been stamped on his nature by that cruel childhood experience so that resentment rather than forgiveness is the outcome: "'De niggers is be'n train' ter fergiveniss; an' fer fear dey might fergit how ter fergive, de w'ite folks gives 'em some-

---

27) Ibid. pp. 229—230.
28) Chesnutt, C. W.: *The Marrow of Tradition*. p. 112.

thin' new ev'y now an' den, ter practice on'"[29]) A non compromise position always has an appeal, and we are led to respect
the spirit of courage behind Josh's conviction that "I'd ruther be
a dead nigger any day dan a live dog!"[30]) We sense the making
of a hero in such a nature, spoiled by the activity against him
and his of a race prejudice which has fostered the growth of
destructive in place of constructive forces. The evil in Josh is
shown as nothing more than a response to the evil in a society
dominated by Anglo-Saxons.

Tom Delamere, on the other hand, has wealth and social
position behind him, as well as the asset of good looks. He seems
to be a child of fortune and yet at the very outset the moral
weakness is indicated which leads him from one form of depravity to another, from deceit and idleness to drinking, gambling and murder. "No discrimating observer would have characterized his beauty as manly. It conveyed no impression of
strength, but did possess a certain element, feline rather than
feminine, which subtly negatived the idea of manliness."[31]) He
does not have the excuse for deterioration we have seen before
in the case of the weak Negro Joe, since Tom's circumstances
are so obviously favorable.

It is hard to say whether Tom or Captain McBane with
his "square-cut jaw, his coarse, firm mouth, and the single gray
eye" is the more despicable character. He is the antithesis of
Tom, without education or background and yet with tremendous
strength of will. Through sheer effort and determination, "this
broad-shouldered, burly white man" has climbed up the social
ladder to political and financial power.[32]) He and the Negro
Josh are two giants pitted against each other, but the difference
is that McBane has ruthlessly sacrificed others to gain his personal ends. The easiest object of exploitation was the masses of
Negroes, whether through his activity with convict labor or
with the Ku Klux Klan, and his race prejudice is therefore nec-

29) Ibid. p. 113.
30) Ibid. p. 284.
31) Ibid. p. 16.
32) Ibid. p. 53.

essary for his purposes. We are left to judge how crude his point of view is when we observe his conversation on the subject with the aristocratic General Belmont and the conservative editor, Carteret: "'I've handled niggers for ten years, and I know 'em from the ground up. They're all alike, — they're a scrub race, an affliction to the country, and the quicker we're rid of 'em all the better'. Carteret had nothing to say by way of dissent. McBane's sentiments, in their last analysis, were much the same as his, though he would have expressed them less brutally. 'The Negro', observed the general, daintily flicking the ash from his cigar, 'is all right in his place'".[33]) It is true that these other two white men are opposed to the Negroes and eager to influence public opinion towards their suppression, but their prejudices are described as at least having the merit of sincerity due to inherited attitudes whereas that of McBane is entirely opportunistic in origin and uncontrolled in practice. He is presented as the aggressor and Josh the victim at bay driven to desperate means.

McBane and Josh are duplicated in another novel of Chesnutt's in the characters of Fetters and Bud Johnson. Again Fetters is one of those many "poor whites" to whom the Civil War gave a chance to expand and make a way for themselves. "There had been a time when these old aristocrats could speak, and the earth trembled, but that day was over. In this age money talked, and he had known how to get money, and how to use it to get more," so that at the time of the story he is "mortgage shark, labour contractor and political boss."[34]) As in McBane's case, his unscrupulous tactics and brutality are displayed with people in general and Negroes in particular. Bud is a "short, powerfully built Negro seemingly of pure blood" who has fallen into Fetters' clutches for some minor offence and is receiving a punishment far out of proportion to it. The experience is filling him with much of Joe's bitterness: "The colonel observed that this Negro's face, when turned towards the white man in front of

33) Ibid. p. 88.
34) Chesnutt, C. W.: *The Colonel's Dream.* pp. 225, 158.

him, expressed a fierce hatred, as of some wild thing of the woods, which, finding itself trapped and betrayed, would go to any length to injure the captor."[35]) Once more the white character is the deliberate sinner and the Negro character the sinner forced by circumstances over which he has no control.

It must be remembered that there are other sorts of characters in these novels not dominated by the blacker emotions. For instance, we still find survivals of the old master-slave psychology appearing in individuals. The hero of "The Colonel's Dream" is a white business man, a "man of affairs", and yet with a Southern aristocratic background and tastes, and at the same time with "one of those rare natures of whom it may be truly said that they are men, and that they count nothing of what is human foreign to themselves".[36]) His career in the North presumably accounts to a great extent both for the development of his practical ability and for the growth of a spirit of tolerance in racial matters which makes the shiftlessness and the race prejudice in his old Southern home town to which he returns all the more distasteful. He is pictured as an idealist in the "full flow of philanthropic enthusiasm", with belief in human nature and thus in the possibilities in reform, and yet with a certain prudence and patience which made him "content to await the uplifting power of industry and enlightenment". A latent conservatism prompts him to take the middle way without arousing unnecessary antagonism. "His aim was to bring about by better laws and more liberal ideas, peace, harmony, and universal good-will", and he was satisfied to do the "work of sowing that others might reap".[37])

Both his conservative and liberal tendencies are manifested in his relationship to Uncle Peter, who used to be his Negro boy companion in pre-war days. On rediscovering him as a feeble old man he is the essence of kindness to him, but there is a paternalism and condescension which mirror the deep-buried

35) Ibid. pp. 63, 69.
36) Ibid. p. 27.
37) Ibid. pp. 188, 195, 247.

Southern belief in "the Negro in his place". The attitude is the result of much more conscious assumption on Uncle Peter's part, who, in contrast to the enlightened colonel, unqualifiedly regrets the passing of the old regime: „'De cullud folks don' was'e much time wid a ole man wa't ain' got nothin', an' dese hyuh new w'ite folks w'at is come up sence de wah, ain' got no use fer niggers now dat dey don' b'long ter nobody no mo!'"[38]) He welcomes the opportunity to give faithful service to a beloved white master again, just as Sandy does to old Mr. Delamere in "The Marrow of Tradition" where we see that "the old gentleman leaned on his servant's arm with frank dependence, and Sandy lifted him into the carriage with every mark of devotion".[39]) Such a relationship has a certain loyalty on both sides which stands testing, but is made possible only by the rôle of respectful submission continued by these ex-slave servants.

The attitude of submission loses its purity of motive and is carried to an extreme in the servility of Jerry from "The Marrow of Tradition". He is so anxious to please his white superiors that he makes himself ridiculous. Because of the obvious advantages, his greatest wish is to be white himself, and since he is disillusioned as to the efficacy of lotions to make kinky hair straight and dark skin light, the only alternative is to conform as far as possible with the race in power. His philosophy is opportunistic, his ethics expedient: "'I'm gwine ter keep my mouf shet an' stan' in wid de Angry-Saxon race, — ez dey calls deyse'ves nowadays, — an' keep on de right side er my bread an' meat. W'at nigger ever give me twenty cents in all my bawn days?'"[40]) Here we see the signs of the Negro clown stereotype, popularized by the vaudeville stage. Jerry stands as a sad example of the demoralizing influence of a tradition of superiority and inferiority surviving in a new industrial, economic, and social order.

Chesnutt has given us a variety of Negro characters emerg-

38) Chesnutt, Charles W.: *The Colonel's Dream.* p. 24.
39) Chesnutt, Charles W.: *The Marrow of Tradition.* p. 26.
40) Ibid. p. 90.

ing from the masses, adding to those who in temperament and outlook belong to plantation days, the rebel and the self-seeking opportunist, both products of the special conditions in the Southern small town. But there is also another kind of individual who foreshadows the next group of novels, that is, the educated and capable Negro, emancipated in the true sense of the word. We have glimpses of this quality in the deferential yet intelligent school-master, Taylor, of "The Colonel's Dream", in the efficient nurse of "The Marrow of Tradition„ who sold her time to white people for money without any question of love between them, and in the mulatto sister of the proud white woman, Mrs. Carteret. But the fullest expression is found in Dr. Miller of "The Marrow of Tradition", with his background of medical study and training in New York, Paris and Vienna: "The mulatto's erect form, broad shoulders, clear eyes, fine teeth, and pleasingly moulded features showed nowhere any sign of that degeneration which the pessimist so sadly maintains is the inevitable heritage of mixed races."[41]) He is obviously a man of intelligence and culture, used to association with cultivated people in the North and in Europe. And in spite of opportunity to escape from oppressive race prejudice by seeking a career elsewhere, he had chosen for idealistic reasons to return to his home in the South, start a practice, and found a hospital: "His people had needed him, and he had wished to help them, and had sought by means of this institution to contribute to their uplifting." He is not too confident of results: „'There are eight or nine millions of us, and it will take a great deal of learning of all kinds to leaven that lump.'"[42]) Also he is not a radical or rebel on race questions: "Miller was something of a philosopher. He had long ago had the conclusion forced upon him that an educated man of his race, in order to live comfortably in the United States, must be either a philosopher or a fool; and since he wished to be happy, and was not exactly a fool, he had cultivated philosophy."[43])

---

41) Chesnutt, Charles W.: *The Marrow of Tradition.* p. 49.
42) Ibid. p. 51.
43) Ibid. pp. 59—60.

Here we are introduced to an intelligent Negro, willing to compromise and coöperate if given a fair chance, and yet once more it is indicated that a hostile environment and unjust treatment thwart and finally embitter him. Even professional white people who are in a position to acknowledge and respect his capacity regard him as a "social misfit". They felt "there was something melancholy, to a cultivated mind, about a sensitive, educated man who happened to be off color".[44]) And if he could not hope for better coöperation from people of his stamp, there is still less chance of consideration for his rights at the hands of an illiterate mob whipped up to a white heat of prejudice and violence. When great personal tragedy comes to him he is completely disillusioned and yet his natural reaction of harshness towards the influential white family largely responsible for the disastrous race riot is miraculously mitigated by "the last appeal of poor humanity".[45]) He is moved to take compassion on the suffering of those who have caused his own. Here is a species of magnanimity seeming unconsciously to repeat the Christian virtues cultivated by Negroes in slave days. We have only to think of the mercy to an enemy shown by Nelse Hatton in Dunbar's story "Nelse Hatton's Vengeance". Dr. Miller has occasion to go the rebellious way of Josh, but something shown as innately fine in his nature restrains him and enables him to go on his more difficult and more creative way a sadder and a wiser man.

But after all Dr. Miller is a minor character. It is significant that in the early novels of this group there are no Negro heroes in spite of the fact that the stories fall under the category of propaganda. The colonel is a white man. The likeable and sterling yet rather mediocre Ellis is cast in a more important rôle than Dr. Miller in "The Marrow of Tradition". Dr. Miller has the makings of a hero, but if we wish to see his type playing a major part we must turn to that later book of this group, "The Fire in the Flint". Here we discover that Dr. Kenneth Harper is

---

44) Ibid. p. 75.
45) Ibid. p. 325.

a spiritual brother to him, and this time presented as the out-standing character of the novel.

Kenneth has also returned to the South after years of med-ical preparation, filled with eagerness and ambition to realize his professional dreams of the practice he is going to build up and the hospital he is going to found. He is disgusted with the sordid and vicious aspects of his environment, which seem to him so visible on the surface and so blatantly connected with racial antagonism, but at the same time something optimistic in his nature keeps him at first from discouragement and paralysis of effort: "'It was here long before I was born', he said to him-self philosophically, 'It'll probably be here long after I'm dead, and the best thing for me to do is to stick to my own business and let other people's morals alone.'"[46]) He is practical minded and naturally even of disposition, with no desire to stir up un-necessary trouble or take part in futile conflict. He has much of the Booker T. Washington philosophy of concentration on es-sentials and compromise on non-essentials, considering it his special task to combat prejudice through the evidence of his professional skill and through the winning of economic security: "'I'm going to solve my own problem, do as much good as I can, make as much money as I can. If every Negro in America did the same thing, there wouldn't be any race problem'".[47])

But his doubts cannot be repressed: "He was suddenly con-scious of a feeling that he had been thrust into a tiny boat and forced to embark on a limitless sea, with neither compass nor chart nor moon to guide him. Would he arrive? Or would he go down in some squall which arose from he knew not where or when? The whole situation seemed so vast, so sinister, so monstrous, that he shuddered involuntarily, as he had done as a child when left alone in a dark room at night."[48]) A further acquaintance with the conditions about him lead him to an in-escapable realization of how cruel and how hopeless they are not

---

46) White, Walter: *The Fire in the Flint.* p. 41.
47) Ibid. p. 28.
48) Ibid. pp. 71—72.

only for him but for all his people set apart by skin color. It comes as a new and keen revelation to him, returning to the scene of his boyhood with the outlook of a mature man who has minimized in absence the complexity of the problem: "As he saw each day more and more of the evasions, the repressions, the choking back of natural impulses the Negro practised to avoid trouble, Kenneth often thought of the coloured man as a chip of wood floating on the surface of a choppy sea, tossed this way and that by every wind that blew upon the waters."[49]) — — "Yes, the Negro in the South had many things in common with the chameleon — he had to be able to change his colour figuratively to suit the environment of the South in order to be allowed to stay alive."[50]) It seems clear to him that his people are being kept in ignorance because of the economic advantage to the white South, and therefore that all Negroes who protest against the injustices practiced on their group will be branded as radicals and dangerous characters seeking "social equality". Knowledge of the motives behind prejudice only tends to push him all the more into an active part of the evolving struggle against it: "He had determined to stay out of reach of the long arms of the octopus they called the race problem — but he felt himself slowly being drawn into its insidious embrace."[51])

The psychological interest of "The Fire in the Flint" centers around the hero's conflict between rebellion and compromise and the gradual transformation of his nature under the pressure of the environment. The strain of his effort to keep to his original position in spite of the increasing difficulty begins to tell on him: "He had been almost morose, his mind divided between his work and the effort to keep to a 'middle-of-the-road' course in his relations to the whites. The inevitable conflict within himself, the lack of decisiveness in his daily life that he consciously developed and which was so diametrically opposite to that he used in his profession, had begun to create a complex

---

49) White, Walter: *The Fire in the Flint*. p. 73.

50) Ibid. p. 109.

51) Ibid. p. 98.

personality that was far from pleasing."[52]) According to the
author, it is only fair to Kenneth to point out that much of his
spirit of compromise arose from honest conviction of its wisdom.
He believed that the time had not yet come when a Negro could
champion complete freedom in the South, that the half-century
since Emancipation had witnessed gradual improvement which
only needed more time to approximate solution. Yet his personal
ambition at odds with his surroundings tends to make him more
of a conscious opportunist: "In a freer atmosphere Kenneth
would have been a direct, straightforward character, swift to
decision and quick of action. One cannot, however, compromise
principles constantly and consciously without bearing the marks
of such conflicts."[53])

We are not surprised to find him breaking under the strain
and swinging over to an extreme when, as in Dr. Miller's case,
family misfortune of the worst kind occurs. At the moment of
crisis he is seized by a spirit of violent rebellion: "He sprang
to his feet. A fierce, unrelenting, ungovernable hatred blazed
in his eyes. He had passed through the most bitter five minutes
of his life. Denuded of all the superficial trappings of civilization, he stood there — the primal man — the wild beast,
cornered, wounded, determined to fight — fight — fight! The
fire that lay concealed in the flint until struck, now leaped up
in a devastating flame at the blows it had received! All the art
of the casuist with which he had carefully built his faith and a
code of conduct was cast aside and forgotten! He would demand
and take the last ounce of flesh — he would exact the last drop
of blood from his enemies with all the cruelty he could
invent!"[54]) The saturation point of bitterness for any Negro
character in fiction is reached by Kenneth in this experience
and the thoughts it brings. Bitterness combined with fury
against the white perpetrators of the evil goad him into un-
restrained expression: "'Superior race'! 'Preservers of civiliz-

52) Ibid. p. 148.
53) Ibid. p. 148.
54) Ibid. p. 269.

ation'! 'Superior', indeed! They called Africans inferior! They, with smirking hypocrisy, ruled the Turks! They went to war against the 'Huns' because of Belgium! None of these had ever done a thing so bestial as these 'preservers of civilization' in Georgia! civilization! Hell! The damned hypocrites! The liars! The fiends! 'White civilization'! Paugh! Black and brown and yellow hands had built it! The white fed like carrion on the rotting flesh of the darker peoples! And called their toil their own! And burned those on whose bodies their vile civilization was built!"[55])

As before, we are given a character whose spirit of revenge is called into being not by any inherent evil in his nature but by the remorseless evil imposed on him from the outside. Like Dr. Miller, he is pictured as having done all that was humanly possible and consistent with his self-respect to adjust peaceably to white dominance. There is again acute suffering in the face of the tragic failure: "It was his Gethsemane. He felt as though some giant hand was twisting his very soul until it bled."[56]) And again, in the midst of his agony, there is a basic feeling of humanity which prompts him to respond to the plea for medical aid made by a prominent white family in town.

This modern Negro has no conscious Christian beliefs in his life: "Religion, which had been the guide and stay of his father in like circumstances, offered him no solace."[57]) He sees the church as a "vast money machine" and the emotional type of religion about him as a "theatric performance", and yet he has a feeling for the underlying sincerity and genuineness of his people's faith. Although as an educated man he feels superior to the ignorance and credulity characterizing the masses of Negroes about him, he realized that, just as in slavery times, perhaps this primitive religion is a necessary refuge for them from the hardships of their lot in a white and prejudiced world. He considers that it has resulted in the cultivation of certain ethical and constructive forces in the group, by virtue of

55) White, Walter: *The Fire in the Flint.* p. 271.
56) Ibid. p. 272.
57) Ibid. p. 72.

which he regards his own race as morally ahead of the whites: "He was much more contented as a member of a race that was struggling upward than he would have been as one of that race that expended most of its time and thought and energy in exploiting and oppressing others."[58]) He himself can find no consolation in what appears to him an illusion, and nevertheless, while discarding Christianity intellectually, there seems to be an indication that a certain Christian behavior is inseparable from his life when he relinquishes the opportunity to commit an act of revenge against his enemy at large, the white race. However, the underlying assumption is that the spirit of hate and vengeance is too foreign to his nature quite apart from Christian influence, to predominate, even in the bitterness of crisis, over his better instincts.

Minor characters offer variations while contributing to one theme. While Kenneth is "the natural pacifist" who is forced out of his position, his younger brother, Bob, is "the natural rebel, revolt was a part of his creed."[59]) He hates the white people with an intense hate. His resentment first causes moodiness and brooding until it is directed into a new channel expressed in the idealistic and fervent desire of becoming a "powerful champion of his race".[60]) The sister, Mamie, is a buoyant and lively girl who seems "happy because of the sheer joy of living" but who nevertheless feels "as though they were living on the top of a volcano".[61]) Kenneth's fiancée, Jane, is a capable, intelligent, and courageous person, fully aware of the precarious position of Negroes in the small Southern town and with the ambition to take concrete steps towards improvement. All these characters possess different temperaments and yet are united not only in their wish to serve the race but in the underlying race pride which prompts it. These educated individuals stand out from the ignorant and exploited masses of Negroes filling the background, because of their critical faculties, their indep-

58) White, Walter: *The Fire in the Flint.* p. 163.
59) Ibid. p. 24.
60) Ibid. p. 193.
61) Ibid. pp. 30, 31.

endence and sense of personal and racial worth combatting old assumptions of inferiority. The new pride of race springing into consciousness finds its most intense expression in Jane, representative of the Negro woman grown clear-eyed through suffering and long thought: "'I am sick and tired of hearing all this prating about the 'superior race'. Superior — humph! Kenneth, what you and all the rest of Negroes need is to learn that you belong to a race that was centuries old when the first white man came into the world. You've got to learn that a large part of this thing they call 'white civilization' was made by black hands, too, besides what white hands have created. You've got to learn that the Negro today is contributing as much of the work that makes this civilization possible as the white race, if not more'."[62]) Here is the voice of the patriot eager for the doing of noble deeds in the cause.

The devotion to ideals and the strength to fight against obstacles revealed by such outstanding Negroes are made all the more evident when placed in juxtaposition to the vices of most of the white characters. Opportunism and moral weakness are common among them. Roy Ewing, a leading white citizen, owner of a big store, deacon in the church, and president of the Chamber of Commerce is exposed as a man having illicit sex relations underneath a mask of respectability and fearing to go against public opinion even when he is persuaded of an injustice. He is actually surprised at the suggestion that he should take a stand against lynching: "'Why, it would ruin my business, my wife would begin to be dropped by all the other folks of the town, and it wouldn't be long before they'd begin calling me a 'nigger-lover'. No, sir-ee! I'll just let things rock along and let well enough alone'."[63]) Likewise the fineness of fibre in the Negro characters is emphasized by the contrasting viciousness and coarseness of such people as the sheriff or the profane and illiterate County Commissioner of Health, "long, lanky, a two days' growth of red beard on his face". The villainy of these men

---

62) Ibid. p. 139.
63) Ibid. p. 70.

and their group is analogous to that of a Captain McBane or a Fetters, and is likewise portrayed as flourishing in the soil of a violent and grasping race prejudice.

Restless-Passive-Sophisticated-Individualistic.

When we study the individuals in the urban-cosmopolitan group of novels, we discover that the sheep and the goats are not so easily separable. The Negro hero and the white villain are no longer in evidence. We pass beyond a preoccupation with morals. Good on one side and evil on the other are not accepted as a commonplace any more than is the introduction of occasional evil elements into the good characters only explainable in terms of the hostile activity of external causes. Now it becomes a question not of virtues, such as loyalty, honesty, industry, and courage, but of cleverness, beauty, variety of feeling. It is not the simplicity of strong character but the complexity of vivid personality which attracts these novelists. The big sweeping lines with which the preceding novelists draw their characters so as often to give the impression of types rather than of individuals seem to be replaced by minute strokes and lines here and there, creating an effect of subtlety and personal differences. The heroes and heroines are studied from the inside rather than from the outside, and thus we have glimpses into an intricacy of mood and feeling that makes it impossible to classify and catalogue them so definitely and so conclusively.

These tendencies find an initial expression in James Weldon Johnson's fictional autobiography. The very fact that an autobiographical form is chosen indicates this new emphasis on the subjective side and on the complexity of human nature thus revealed. We see life through the eyes of a hero who is all too human. There is no attempt to endow him with virtues any more than to convict him of vice. He is a mixture of many conflicting impulses and varied characteristics evincing both strength and weakness. By his own confession he was something of a spoiled boy, subject to "fits of sentimental hysteria" and "temperamental excess", which were fostered by a preoccupation with his books and music.[64]) But while childhood conditions encouraged him in habits of introspection and partial isolation from the world about him, his susceptibility to the opinions and judgments of that world is evident in his career as a man. He admits to "a certain sense of vanity of which I have not been able to rid myself"[65]) which means that he is not adverse to participating in situations likely to feed it. Often we discover mixed motives at work: "I began to analyze my own motives and found that they, too, were very largely mixed with selfishness. Was it more a desire to help those I considered my people, or more a desire to distinguish myself, which was leading me back to the United States?"[66]) He is somewhat of a drifter and when he decides that he is wasting time and finds that "the desire to begin work grew stronger each day"[67]) we tend to feel that he is rather easily diverted from his formulated goal, his ambition to help his own people by means of his musical gifts. He has independence and courage enough not to beg for help from the university authorities when his money was stolen, and to confess the secret of his racial identity to the white girl whom he loved and who was accepting him without question as a white man, and yet his opportunism is revealed by his "passing" as a white man. He is not a particularly admirable character but a very interesting one.

Claim for respectability rests upon social and cultural status rather than upon the moral code of a man who was at one period a confirmed gambler and participator in the Bohemian night life of New York. He is aristocratic in his outlook both through his training and through choice: "My mother dressed me very neatly, and I developed that pride which well-dressed boys generally have. She was careful about my associates, and I myself was quite particular. As I look back now I can see

64) Johnson, James W.: *The Autobiography of an Ex-Coloured Man.* p. 27.
65) Ibid. p. 94.
66) Ibid. p. 147.
67) Ibid. p. 142.

that I was a perfect little aristocrat."[68]) The result is a marked
snobbishness in the adult manifested in his reaction to the lower
class of Negroes in the South: "The unkempt appearance, the
shambling, slouching gait and loud talk and laughter of these
people aroused in me a feeling of almost repulsion."[69]) Undoubtedly the fact that his father was of an old and exclusive
Southern white family and that he himself is a mulatto so light
in skin color as to be indistinguishable from a white person
tends to increase a certain sense of superiority to his own race.
His decision to free himself from it springs from a feeling of
"shame at being identified with a people that could with impu-
nity be treated worse than animals."[70]) This hero has a natural
affinity for artistic and select circles, for the refinements of
manners and culture, for poised and gracious human beings
animated by vivid yet elusive fire: "Indeed, she seemed to me
the most dazzlingly white thing I had ever seen. But it was not
her delicate beauty which attracted me most; it was her voice, a
voice which made one wonder how tones of such passionate
colour could come from so fragile a body."[71]) There is no room
for any touch of vulgarity here. Sophistication is allowable and
often desirable in his associates, but never vulgarity.

These preferences do not seem to exclude the capacity for
deep feeling. In fact, the very sensitivity which makes him
draw back in repulsion from coarseness exhibits his openness
to emotional experience. Much of this is associated with his
status as a colored man in the United States and with the
ensuing conflicts. The two greatest causes for suffering are
connected with this fact, coming as a result of his first identity
as a boy with his race and later of his escape from it. The "fate-
ful day" in school when his teacher forbade his rising with the
white pupils and thus singled him out as a Negro and an inferior left an indelible mark on him: "There did come a radical

---

68) Johnson, James W.: *The Autobiography of an Ex-Coloured Man.*
    p. 7.
69) Ibid. p. 56.
70) Ibid. p. 191.
71) Ibid. p. 198.

change, and, young as I was, I felt fully conscious of it, though I did not fully comprehend it. Like my first spanking, it is one of the few incidents in my life that I can remember clearly. In the life of everyone there is a limited number of unhappy experiences which are not written upon the memory, but stamped there with a die; and in long years after, they can be called up in detail, and every emotion that was stirred by them can be lived through anew; these are the tragedies of life. We may grow to include some of them among the trivial incidents of childhood — a broken toy, a promise made to us which was not kept, a harsh, heart-piercing word — but these, too, as well as the bitter experiences and disappointments of mature years, are the tragedies of life."[72]) And it is doubly a tragedy when it marks the beginning of a race complex which handicaps him greatly in his boyhood associations by conditioning his own attitude towards them: "I now think that this change which came into my life was at first more subjective than objective. I do not think my friends at school changed so much toward me as I did toward them. I grew reserved, I might say suspicious. I grew constantly more and more afraid of laying myself open to some injury to my feelings or my pride. I frequently saw or fancied some slight where, I am sure, none was intended. On the other hand, my friends and teachers were, if anything, different, more considerate of me; but I can remember it was against this very attitude in particular that my sensitiveness revolted."[73])

Here is a character who becomes more and more possessed by race consciousness, but it is not an aggressive or resentful race consciousness, or one stimulating to social reform and ambition. It is rather a factor taken for granted, the main importance of which lies in its influence upon the mood and feeling of the individual. We find ourselves again on the subjective note: *my* reaction to being a Negro: "And so I have often

---

72) Johnson, James W.: *The Autobiography of an Ex-Coloured Man.* p. 20.

73) Ibid. p. 22.

lived through that hour, that day, that week, in which was wrought the miracle of my transition from one world into another, for I did indeed pass into another world. From that time I looked out through other eyes, my thoughts were coloured, my words dictated, my actions limited by one dominating, all-pervading idea which constantly increased in force and weight until I finally realized in it a great, tangible fact."[74])

It is to be expected that a man who is so sensitive to "the dwarfing, warping, distorting influence" of race prejudice, who has no powerful urge towards the reform and betterment of a race in which he has no real belief, and who possesses the same white complexion as that of the dominant group, should not feel hindered from changing races, when circumstances fostered the desire. And yet to such a person as we have here happiness is not found by any mere change in external conditions. It is not so simple to pacify his needs as it would have been to pacify those of a Dr. Miller or a Dr. Kenneth Harper. As a white man he is freed from economic troubles, from flagrant persecution, insults, and curtailed rights, but he is not freed from internal suffering, "a vague feeling of unsatisfaction, of regret, of almost remorse".[75]) A latent conscience seems to develop signs of activity at the time when he falls in love with a white girl and must make the decision as to whether to confide to her the whole truth about himself. "Up to this time I had assumed and played my rôle as a white man with a certain degree of nonchalance, a carelessness as to the outcome, which made the whole thing more amusing to me than serious; but now I ceased to regard 'being a white man' as a sort of practical joke."[76]) But the unrest is buried far deeper than this, for even after he has achieved the joy of a happy marriage and two charming children while continuing to live as a white man, he often feels that "I have been a coward, a deserter, and I am

74) Ibid. pp. 19—20.
75) Ibid. p. 3.
76) Ibid. p. 199.

possessed by a strange longing for my mother's people".[77])
Seemingly in opposition to his laissez-faire attitude towards
life is a spark of self-sacrificing idealism fanned into flame by
his admiration of the bravely struggling and aspiring Negro
leaders: "Beside them I feel small and selfish. I am an ordinarily successful white man who has made a little money. They
are making history and a race. I, too, might have taken part in
a work so glorious."[78])

Such alternation between repulsion and attraction is bound
to cause a chronic restlessness. On one side is the shame, feeling
of superiority, and individualism which drive him from his
race, on the other is the strange feeling of affinity and desire
to help which pull him back so strongly that when reminded
of "a vanished dream, a dead ambition, a sacrificed talent, I
cannot repress the thought that after all, I have chosen the
lesser part, that I have sold my birth-right for a mess of pot-
tage."[79]) This is the sort of burden borne by the mulatto who
is identified with both races and with neither, who is torn
between two poles with no hope for complete solution at either
end. But as we become acquainted with his temperament we
recognize his restlessness as a fundamental part of it, as accen-
tuated and not caused by his race consciousness. He is revealed
to us as the sort of complex organism that would always find
the attainment of inner peace a difficult thing. Life demands
too many various often contradictory responses, and inner
peace is a condition which rests to a large extent upon a sim-
plification of which a sophisticated and richly developed mind
seems incapable. A driving moral purpose or a whole hearted
consecration to an ideal can bring about that singleness of purpose and concentration of energy necessary to harmony but
denied to the modern educated Negro in the complex urban-
cosmopolitan atmosphere.

77.) Ibid. p. 210.
78) Ibid. p. 211.
79) Ibid. p. 211.

With the introduction of such a central figure, James Weldon Johnson, just as in the case of the milieu, breaks the way for a new treatment. In a succession of novels we find individuals whose main attraction originates not from strong character but from rich personality, whose tastes are discriminating and whose mode of response is subjective. We find the sensitive and refined mulatto in quest of personal happiness endangered more by inner than outer factors. We leave the rebel for the seeker, the social reformer for the individualist, the dynamic extravert for the dreaming introvert. Significant of the change is the new preoccupation with heroines in place of heroes. The outstanding characters of "Flight", "Quicksand", "Passing", "Plum Bun", and "There is Confusion" are all attractive mulatto girls eager to seize life fully, and confused as to ways and means. The complexity of personality possessed by the hero of "The Autobiography of an Ex-Coloured Man" can perhaps find its most adequate expression in the feminine temperament, traditionally more emotionally sensitized and more subtle than the masculine.

An elusive charm may add to this impression as in the case of auburn-haired Mimi in "Flight". She seems to capture something of the colourfulness of purple and jade green waters, the grace of langorous waves and the luxuriousness of tropic plants from her New Orleans home, and "in combination with these reminders of tropic warmth and colour was Mimi's air piquant, vaguely mysterious and seductive".[80]) We think of Clare in "Passing" as "stepping always on the edge of danger" with the "odd dreaming look in her hypnotic eyes".[81]) Her "tempting mouth" which is "sweet and sensitive and a little obstinate" and the "peculiar soft lustre" of her "ivory skin" are appealing, but it is especially her eyes, "dark, sometimes absolutely black, always luminous, and set in long, black lashes. Arresting eyes, slow and mesmeric, and with, for all their warmth, something withdrawn and secret about them. — — —

80) White, Walter F.: *Flight.* p. 59.
81) Larsen, Nella: *Passing.* pp. 4, 146.

Ah! Surely! They were Negro eyes! Mysterious and concealing. And set in that ivory face under that bright hair, there was about them something exotic."[82]) There is something indefinable and intangible about her which people sense. "And, no matter how often she came among them, she still remained someone apart, a little mysterious and strange, someone to wonder about and to admire and pity."[83])

A similar combination of vividness is found in Helga Crane, the heroine of "Quicksand": "In vivid green and gold negligee and glistening brocaded mules, deep sunk in the big highbacked chair, against whose dark tapestry her sharply cut face, with skin like yellow satin, was distinctly outlined, she was — to use a hackneyed word — attractive."[84]) Her instinct for gorgeousness, her conviction that "dark-complexioned people should wear yellow, green, and red" to bring out "luminous tones"[85]) has ample opportunity for expression in Copenhagen where she is urged to wear bright colors and luxurious jewelry to the point where she herself feels "like a veritable savage" but evokes admiration and creates the impression of someone "attractive, unusual, exotic", "'superb eyes — color — neck, column — yellow — hair — alive — wonderful'."[86]) This is aided by her general bearing, "that air of remoteness" which was "a little mysterious and added another clinging wisp of charm."[87])

Likewise we find Angela of "Plum Bun" with "vitality beneath her pallor", giving "the effect of a flame herself; intense and opaque at the heart where her dress gleamed and shone, transparent and fragile where her white warm neck and face rose into the tenuous shadow of her hair". The effect on even a worldly and rich white man is tantalizing: "She was young, she was, when lighted from within by some indescribable mechanism, even beautiful; she had charm and, what was for him even

82) Larsen, Nella: *Passing*. pp. 45—46.
83) Ibid. p. 147.
84) Larsen, Nella: *Quicksand*. p. 3.
85) Ibid. p. 38.
86) Ibid. pp. 152, 155, 157.
87) Ibid. p. 163.

more important, she was puzzling. In repose, he noticed, studying her closely, her quiet look took on the resemblance of an arrested movement, a composure on tip-toe so to speak, as though
she had been stopped in the swift transition from one mood to
another."[88]) There is "an exquisite perfection" and a radiant,
unattainable quality about Johanna with her "slender flaming
body" which intrigues and arrests the attention of Peter in
"There is Confusion".

But it is Matthew in "Dark Princess" who receives the deepest influence from this type of personality. The heroine is an
Indian princess, but she has a mulatto skin color and the same
kind of fascination as the mulatto heroines: "First and above
all came that sense of color; into this world of pale yellowish
and pinkish parchment, that absence or negation of color, came
suddenly, a glow of golden brown skin. It called for no light and
suffered no shadow, but glowed softly of its own inner radiance
— — she was looking with eyes that were pools of night —
liquid, translucent, haunting depths — whose brilliance made
her face a glory and a dream."[89]) There are many details of
exquisite feature and dress helping the impression, but "above
and beyond and much more than the sum of them all was the
luminous radiance of her complete beauty, her glow of youth
and strength behind that screen of a grand yet gracious manner." Such a person also seems as a being apart, in spite of her
warm sympathy: "With all her gentle manner and thought-
fulness, she had a certain faint air of haughtiness and was ever
slightly remote."[90]) We would expect this of a princess, but we
only find an intensification in her of a quality common to all
these heroines.

External appearances are often important in reflecting some
inner quality of personality. Manner of dress, for example, can
be a witness to refinement of taste. The fact that the princess
"was carefully groomed from her purple hair to her slim toe-

---

88) Fauset, Jessie R.: *Plum Bun.* p. 122.
89) Du Bois, W. E. B.: *Dark Princess.* p. 8.
90) Ibid. p. 14.

tips"[91]) and had "the faultlessness of her dress"[92]) which gives
the effect of expensive simplicity only reveal the innate aristocrat just as in the case of the well-dressed Johanna and the hero
of James Weldon Johnson's novel. Applied further, an interest
in beautiful objects, and a desire for their possession are signs
of a true aesthetic appreciation and a discriminating sense of
value. "All her life Helga Crane had loved and longed for nice
things" showing her "urge for beauty".[93]) "Always she had
wanted, not money, but the things which money could give,
leisure, attention, beautiful surroundings. Things. Things.
Things."[94]) There is even something sensuous in her response
to a luxurious and artistic environment when it is opened to her,
whether in Harlem or Copenhagen. It comes as the fulfilment
of the sort of dreams which Angela also had: "Somewhere in
the world were paths which lead to broad thoroughfares, large
bright houses, delicate niceties of existence. Those paths Angela
meant to find and frequent."[95])

Such delight in physical beauty, sensations of color and
warmth, and material comforts is characteristic of individuals
who place personal happiness ahead of any form of service.
Most of the heroines are avowedly concerned with the things
of this world even at the expense of character development or
the realization of supposedly higher ambitions. Angela may feel
ashamed, "for she knew that for the varieties and gewgaws of
a leisurely and irresponsible existence she would sacrifice her
own talent, the integrity of her ability to interpret life, to write
down a history with her brush",[96]) yet she rejoices in the present. Helga Crane goes so far as to feel contemptuous of all
attempts towards „uplift", while absorbed in her pursuit of
happiness, seemingly answered by the "new and delightful pattern of her life" in Harlem with financial independence, books,

91) Ibid. p. 14.
92) Ibid. p. 8.
93) Larsen, Nella: *Quicksand.* p. 14.
94) Ibid. p. 147.
95) Fauset, Jessie R.: *Plum Bun.* p. 12.
96) Ibid. p. 112.

theatres, parties, beautiful homes and gracious soft-mannered people.[97]) Clare Kendrick has no feeling for doing "the right thing". She has no social conscience. "Why, to get the things I want badly enough, I'd do anything, hurt anybody, throw anything away."[98])

With such a-moral tendencies, characters whose skin is light enough to allow it will not hesitate to "pass" as white any longer than did James Weldon Johnson's character. Mimi, Clare, and Angela take the decisive step. As Angela expresses it in direct terms, "'I am both white and Negro and look white. Why shouldn't I declare for the one that will bring me the greatest happiness, prosperity, and respect?'"[99]) There is something of the rebel in these natures making freedom from restraint a prerequisite of happiness for them, and therefore each is led to think of the "possibilities for joy and freedom which seemed to her inherent in mere whiteness."[100]) A white skin becomes an asset to be regarded as a kind of golden key to Paradise where one can escape from all the petty restrictions and more serious burdens entailed by classification as a Negro. In avoiding this classification and crossing the border line between the races, there is always a possible danger of discovery often adding a certain piquancy to the situation. To be able to deceive the white world so completely is not only playing a very good joke on it over which one can laugh in secret, but also it is playing an absorbing game in its own right: "she was swimming in the flood of excitement created by her unique position. Stolen waters are the sweetest. — — The realization, the secret fun bubbling back in some hidden recess of her heart, brought colour to her cheeks, a certain temerity to her manner — — If the thing to do were to play a game she would play one."[101]) Difficulties which in theory seem unsurmountable become minimized when the break is made. To take a chance in a strange and

97) Larsen, Nella: *Quicksand.* p. 99.
98) Larsen, Nella: *Passing.* p. 149.
99) Fauset, Jessie R.: *Plum Bun.* p. 80.
100) Ibid. p. 14.
101) Ibid. pp. 123, 146.

unfamiliar environment where one must always think of ways to account for one's background would be more than enough to dampen the less venturesome spirits, but to those who have the gift, obstacles are soon circumvented, and dangers even become commonplaces: "'It's such a frightfully easy thing to do. If one's the type, all that's needed is a little nerve',"[102]) in the opinion of the unconventional and irrepressible Clare with the "having way".

But to risk and to dare for the sake of happiness is not necessarily to achieve. The sweetness of stolen fruits may disappear through the satiation time brings. The typical restlessness of these characters is evident in their final reaction to "passing". They fail to find either permanent or complete happiness in this separation from their own race. The rosy dreams appear more and more an illusion. After the first excitement has worn off or new conveniences and pleasures have been enjoyed for a while, being white proves to be a tasteless or a boring or even a sickening affair to them. After contacts with various groups in white New York Angela finds herself critical of them. The intellectual and bohemian atmosphere of Greenwich Village encourages serious talk among journalists, artists, and students of various kinds but the topics under discussion, "peaks of civilization superimposed upon peaks, she found, even though interesting, utterly futile".[103]) She feels herself in sympathy with a point of view which would say to them "'how far you are away from the things that really matter, birth and death and hard, hard work'."[104]) A bourgeois and sophisticated society group at first appears more attractive to her, with their gaiety, their frank desire for money and the "goods of this world", for "fine apartments, beautiful raiment, delicate viands and trips to Paris and Vienna".[105]) But still something is lacking. It is not her world: "for years she had craved such a milieu, only to find herself, when once launched into it, outwardly

---

102) Larsen, Nella: *Passing*. p. 37.
103) Fauset, Jessie R.: *Plum Bun*. p. 117.
104) Ibid. p. 115.
105) Ibid. p. 268.

perfectly at ease, inwardly perturbed and dismayed."[106])

The trouble as analyzed by Mimi lies in the temperament of white people in general. She sees "morose, worried faces" everywhere among them and such an "obsession with material things" that all naturalness is crowded out of life.[107]) Mechanization is the result: "There was always that strained, unhappy expression on the countenances of these people who, like scurrying insects, rushed madly here and there, each as though upon his efforts depended the future of civilization and life and everything else. Like cogs in a machine, she said of them one day, and thereafter she always thought of them as cogs. Here they have created a machine of which they are intensely proud and of which they think they are the masters. Instead, ironically enough, the machine has mastered them and they must do its bidding."[108]) Mimi is not portrayed as a sentimentalist. She sees the good and bad in both whites and Negroes, and even condemns certain attitudes in her own race which were primary in forcing her desertion, but in spite of this she misses something vital that she feels only those dark people can supply.

Such realizations bring new appreciations for old and discarded values. Even the self-willed Clare who has learned so well how to get the things she wants out of life is tormented by the knowledge of what she has left behind her: "'You can't know how in this pale life of mine I am all the time seeing the bright pictures of that other that I once thought I was glad to be free of — — It's like an ache, a pain that never ceases."[109]) Her contrast of "pale" and "bright" provides the key to the problem. These young heroines are described as filled with a longing for the vividness and warmth of their group, for the originality, spontaneity and ready laughter, for a "primitive note" and freedom from inhibitions. Values are sensed which are intangible but with a "vibrant, warming quality".[110]) So

---

106) Ibid. p. 271.
107) White, Walter: *Flight*. p. 212.
108) Ibid. pp. 267—268.
109) Larsen, Nella: *Passing*. p. 8.
110) White, Walter: *Flight*. p. 97.

important are these values to them that these sophisticated "white" New Yorkers cannot resist the temptation to return and visit the Negro centre. Harlem serves as a magnet so that they all find themselves irresistibly drawn back. Again Angela senses "that fullness, richness, even thickness of life"[111]) in Harlem making it a thing unique. Both Clare and Mimi slip away from unsuspecting husbands to breathe its invigorating atmosphere: "It was a new Harlem she now saw, or rather, though she did not realize it, it was a new Mimi through whose eyes she saw it. Gone were the morose, the worried, the unhappy, the untranquil faces she had been seeing down town for years. Here there was life and spontaneous laughter, here there was real joyfulness in voices and eyes. Here was leisureliness, none of the hectic dashing after material things which brought little happiness when gained."[112]) These elements are indicative in their opinion of a rich and varied group temperament emphasized by such an external thing as variety of skin color: "There were faces of a mahogany brownness which shaded into the blackness of crisply curled hair. There were some of a blackness that shone like rich bits of velvet. There were others whose skins seemed as though made of expertly tanned leather with the creaminess of old vellum, topped by shining hair, blacker than 'a thousand midnights, down in a cypress swamp'. And there were those with ivory white complexions, rare old ivory that time had mellowed with gentle touch."[113])

There can be situations analogous to "passing" arousing similar reactions. Helga Crane in "Quicksand" is not sufficiently light in complexion to pass as white, and yet her opportunity to live permanently in Europe with her white relatives and in an exclusively white world offers itself also as an escape from the handicaps of race in a place where there are "no Negroes, no problems, no prejudice."[114]) She idealizes the pleasures and material advantage. this new life can bring to her and finds

---

111) Fauset Jessie R.: *Plum Bun*. p. 216.
112) White, Walter: *Flight*. p. 244.
113) Ibid. p. 199.
114) Larsen, Nella: *Quicksand*. p. 123.

solace for a time in the delights of Copenhagen. But the experience of "meeting only pale serious faces when she longed for brown laughing ones"[115]) discloses that restlessness which draws her back to Harlem likewise: "Again she had had that strange transforming experience — that magic sense of having come home — *These* were her people. Nothing, she had come to understand now, could ever change that. Strange that she had never truly valued this kinship until distance had shown her its worth." There is some firm connection which binds her forever "to these mysterious, these terrible, these fascinating, these lovable dark hordes".[116]) Like Angela she is struck by the gradations of color and type adding to the richness of effect: "A dozen shades slid by. There was sooty black, shiny black, taupe, mahogany, bronze, copper, gold, orange, yellow, peach, ivory, pinky white, pastry white. There was yellow hair, brown hair, black hair, woolly hair. She saw black eyes in brown faces, blue eyes in tan faces."[117]) How much more interest can these surroundings provide than the stately and pretentious life of Danish society.

With such attitudes it is natural that these characters should experience loneliness and suffering caused by isolation from Negroes and that they should regard a return to them as a possible remedy. In their search for happiness, Angela, Mimi, Clare, and Helga Crane all escape from the Negro group and later make the decision to return to it. Material well-being, social opportunity, and freedom from race prejudice are still not enough to satisfy. The real freedom comes to be regarded as something deeper. The possession of luxuries is undoubtedly desirable but not worth the price of separation. Mimi, for example, is no ascetic: "She loved the comforts of her home, from the shiny brass knocker on the snowy white front door to the full-length mirrors," and yet "'Free! Free! Free!' she whispered exultantly as with firm tread she went down the

115) Ibid. pp. 207—208.
116) Ibid. pp. 213, 94.
117) Ibid. p. 131.

steps". Her aim is to find "'my own people — and happiness'!"[118]) The conclusion left for us to draw is that James Weldon Johnson's hero might have resolved his tension and unrest by declaring likewise for the dark instead of the white side.

But the suggestion is that their tendency to feel loneliness and suffering is not provoked only by the problem of their racial status. It seems to form a basic part of their natures, to be a prerequisite of complex and sensitive organisms as we have already found in "The Autobiography of an Ex-Coloured Man". Clare had an unfortunate childhood making her "belligerently sensitive"[119]) and all the more susceptible to the pains of adult life no matter how gallantly she meets them. The pain is after all an inextricable part of life itself. Not all of it by any means can be blamed on race, according to Angela and Mimi who feel that much of the cause for unhappiness lies in their own incapacity to adjust, initiate, or accept: "Why was I given this restless spirit, this ceaseless inability to be content with what life has brought me? Why cannot I be like other women, able to content myself with whatever comes, refusing to let the tiny mice of search for the unattainable gnaw at my restless heart?"[120])

In the case of Helga Crane it is even more noticeable that no single external situation can soothe her discontent. She is comparable to the wandering Jew in her ceaseless motion and change from one group and place to another, from Negroes to white, America to Europe, and back again. While it is true that she becomes dissatisfied with the white group, she finds herself equally so with the reverse situation at times: "With the waning summer the acute sensitiveness of Helga Crane's frayed nerves grew keener. There were days where the mere sight of the serene tan and brown faces about her stung her like a personal insult — — It was as if she were shut up, boxed up, with hundreds of her race, closed up with that something in the racial

118) White, Walter: *Flight.* pp. 295, 300.
119) Larsen, Nella: *Passing.* p. 24.
120) White, Walter: *Flight.* p. 285.

character which had always been, to her, inexplicable, alien. Why, she demanded in fierce rebellion, should she be yoked to these despised black folk?"[121]) Such a reaction is to be expected from a mulatto who from childhood has not been able to fit completely into either racial group and suggests the age-old tragedy of the individual of mixed blood who is "neither — nor", "both — and". But except on the basis of a deep temperamental set, her fluctuation between Europe and America would not be so easily explainable. Even in the heat of her resolve to return to the United States she recognizes the quality of impermanency about her decision: "Not that she intended to remain. No. Helga Crane couldn't, she told herself and others, live in America — — Nor, she saw now, could she remain away. Leaving, she would have to come back — — mentally she caricatured herself moving shuttle-like from continent to continent."[122]) Knowing this, she is prompted like Mimi to turn inwards for an explanation of her "indefinite discontent", "growing restlessness", "oppression of loneliness", "overwhelming anguish", "urgent longings" and "chaotic turmoil". "Frankly the question came to this: what was the matter with her? Was there, without her knowing it, some peculiar lack in her? — — Why couldn't she be happy, content, somewhere? Other people managed, somehow, to be. To put it plainly, didn't she know how? Was she incapable of it? — — She became a little frightened, and then shocked to discover that, for some unknown reason, it was of herself she was afraid."[123])

In the climax of suffering reached by this heroine we find a contrast to that of Kenneth Harper in "The Fire in the Flint", which illustrates an important difference between the treatment of character in the two groups of novels. Kenneth's problems are social, Helga Crane's personal, Kenneth's causes for suffering could presumably by removed by abolishment of an active and thwarting prejudice, Helga Crane's are largely within her own nature. In his intensest suffering he is rather healthily

121) Larsen, Nella: *Quicksand*. pp. 117, 120—121.
122) Ibid. pp. 214—215.
123) Ibid. pp. 104, 179—180.

extraverted while she is abnormally introspective and subjective. In a last attempt to find happiness and peace she turns to sex in its physical aspects alone and religion in its crudest evangelical form presenting themselves as a possible escape from conflict and doubt. This leads to the blackest moment of all as she learns "what passion and credulity could do to one": "In her was born angry bitterness and an enormous disgust. The cruel, unrelieved suffering had beaten down her protective wall of artificial faith in the infinite wisdom, in the mercy of God. For had she not called in her agony on Him? And He had not heard. Why? Because, she knew now, He wasn't there. Didn't exist. Into that yawning gap of unspeakable brutality had gone, too, her belief in the miracle and wonder of life. Only scorn, resentment, and hate remained — and ridicule — —Everything in her mind was hot and cold, beating and swirling about. Within her emaciated body raged disillusion. — — She couldn't, she thought ironically, even blame God for it, now that she knew that He didn't exist. — — Her suffering and shrinking loathing were too great. Not to be borne."[124]) The Gethsemane experience of Kenneth Harper was centered definitely around the race problem. To this mulatto heroine, race is only one of many problems and whether race, sex, or religion they are of interest to her only in so far as they affect her private emotional life.

But the depth and subtlety of their emotions do not seem to exclude the use of mental processes in these heroines. In fact, presence of critical and analytical powers would be a necessary concomitant of such intelligent and highly developed human beings. Although they are eager to feel deeply those emotions aroused by happiness, they are not on the naive level of the folk characters. Their response is far from instinctive and that is obviously one reason why their achievement of happiness is so precarious or so doubtful. Skepticism is the expression of restlessness in their intellectual life. A certain paralysis of action is often the result of an introspective state of mind encouraged by the habit of analysis and comparison, by the ability to

124) Larsen, Nella: *Quicksand*. pp. 290—291, 298.

view situations from many angles. Thus we see not so much solving as searching, asserting as questioning. This tendency, added to their sophistication and knowledge of life, leads them to ask "what is wrong with the world" as well as "what is wrong with me". The first question may have interest only in its bearing upon the second and yet in their rôle as critics we have opportunity to observe another resource of these complicated natures. They have a keenness to enable them to point out flaws in the existing order of things even though they have not the inclination to remove them. Sensitivity of organization allows primarily for an amazing awareness which is a compound of heart and brain.

The greater their awareness the greater their radicalism. The more they search the more they realize that they are fundamentally out of sympathy with many of the established mores either forced upon them or voluntarily accepted by them. White civilization, for example, has assigned them to an inferior status, but they have no illusions on the subject even though they choose to "pass" instead of to fight for fair treatment. Skepticism about the whole question of Anglo-Saxon superiority has already been initiated by the calm and ironic observation of James Weldon Johnson's hero. His comparison of Paris and London is a case in point: "How these two cities typify the two peoples who built them! Even the sound of their names expresses a certain racial difference. Paris is the concrete expression of the gaiety, regard for symmetry, love of art, and, I might well add, of the morality of the French people. London stands for the conservatism, the solidarity, the utilitarianism, and, I might well add, the hypocrisy of the Anglo-Saxon. It may sound odd to speak of the morality of the French, if not of the hypocrisy of the English; but this seeming paradox impresses me as a deep truth — — There is a sort of frankness about the evils of Paris which robs them of much of the seductiveness of things forbidden, and with that frankness goes a certain cleanliness of thought belonging to things not hidden — — The difference may be summed up in this: Paris practises its sins as lightly as it does its religion, while London practises both very seriously."[125])

This critical-minded hero makes an even more severe attack indirectly, through reporting the conversation of a liberal and unprejudiced white man. He obviously expresses the hero's own thought on the subject, but more effectively since he is a member of the privileged group: "'Can you name a single one of the great fundamental and original intellectual achievements which have raised men in the scale of civilization that may be credited to the Anglo-Saxon? The art of letters, of poetry, of music, of sculpture, of painting, of the drama, of architecture, the science of mathematics, of astronomy, of philosophy, of logic, of physics, of chemistry, the use of the metals, and the principles of mechanics, were invented or discovered by darker and what we now call inferior races and nations. We have carried many of these to their highest point of perfection, but the foundation was laid by others. Do you know the only original contribution to civilization we can claim is what we have done in steam and electricity and in making implements of war more deadly? — — Why, we didn't even originate the religion we use — — After all, racial supremacy is merely a matter of dates in history.'"[126])

In a similar way does the heroine of "Flight" find her views about white civilization expressed by a young iconoclastic white professor: "'Our gods are steam and electricity and steel -— we have combated plagues and disease, we have greater material comfort, we can travel farther and faster than ever before — — We've developed the printing-press and the telephone and telegraph and the radio; but what has been the result? We've made it possible to spread faster and more easily bigotry and hatred and intolerance and give more power to the mob — — and we call ourselves free men, boast of it — — we are all of us petty little creatures who are slaves to the newspaper and radio, to

125) Johnson, James W.: *The Autobiography of an Ex-Coloured Man.* pp. 137—139.
126) Ibid. pp. 162—163.

politicians and mouthy preachers, to our own employers and the movies, to the telephone and every other regimented idea or thing.'" The mention of Anglo-Saxon art and literature calls forth another outburst which gladdens Mimi as a confirmation and concretion of "some of her own vague dissatisfaction": "'As if other civilizations didn't have art and literature, ethics and philosophies of life and codes of conduct many of them much better than anything we, busy as we are with material things, have created. Through luck and abundant natural resources we've become immensely wealthy — not through any particular effort on our own part yet we pat ourselves on the back and think we're God's elect'."[127])

The religion of this white civilization does not escape judgement. Continuing along the revolutionary line of thought, Mimi goes so far as to question the white Christianity which uses warfare as a method and which is divided into a thousand rival denominations and sects spending most of their time "arguing over what they believe and what the other fellow does not believe".[128]) None of the main characters in these novels are what could be called Christians. They are too aware of what they name a contradiction between the Christian theory of white people and their practice. It appears to them as a system for exploitation based on hypocrisy. They are too sophisticated to hold the simple faith of their Negro forefathers, and their skepticism is all the more increased by their estimate of the harm it has done their race to believe in this way: "And this, Helga decided, was what ailed the whole Negro race in America, this fatuous belief in the white man's God, this childlike trust in full compensation for all woes and privations in 'Kingdom come'. — — How the white man's God must laugh at the great joke he had played on them! Bound them to slavery, then to poverty and insult, and made them bear it unresistingly, uncomplainingly almost, by sweet promise of mansions in the sky by and by."[129])

127) White, Walter: *Flight.* pp. 270—271.
128) Ibid. pp. 269—270.
129) Larsen, Nella: *Quicksand.* p. 297.

In their contrast to the materialization, standardization, hypocrisy and mechanization of Western white civilization, we would expect Oriental values to hold attraction for the critical and searching minds of these Negro characters. Thus we find Mimi impressed by the personality of the quiet and reserved Chinese who seems to possess "the wisdom and the dignity of a bronze Buddha" and in agreement with his belief that "'the great nation or people or civilization is not that one which has the greatest brute strength but the one which can serve mankind best'" and that "'the search for truth in life and life in truth is after all, the perfect religion, for in seeking truth we attain that which we can never find in formal creeds.'"[130]) This affinity between Negro and Oriental is shown in its furthest development in "Dark Princess" where the mulatto hero, Matthew Towns, and the Indian princess in spite of vastly different backgrounds can unite in their fundamental conceptions of life. The assumption is that the West has many spiritual lessons to learn not only from the East but even from the despised American Negroes whose spiritual resources are suggested by the very fact that the sensitive ones find it so difficult to adjust and to receive nourishment for their inner life in occidental white America.

For the longer we study this group of characters the more evident becomes the fact that in spite of their apparent worldliness and interest in material pleasures, in spite of their apparent egocentrism and individualism, they have unexplored capacities for spiritual depth and sacrificial living. And even in the midst of their most frantic and selfish attempts to gain personal happiness, they themselves seem dimly conscious of this fact. Their emotional unrest and their critical thinking can be interpreted as a form of „divine discontent" without which change and growth are impossible. They are presented as a sort of "leaven in the lump", as the kind of spiritual ferment which is sorely needed to stir the conscience and the imagination of a material minded white America towards a freer and more beautiful world. The more alive these young mulatto people be-

130) White, Walter: *Flight*. pp. 280, 282.

come to the truth of the situation the more proud they grow of the dark race which is felt to have these creative possibilities and the more inclined finally to declare for their black rather than for their white blood even with some sacrifice as a possible result. We discover, then, the existence of a race-consciousness founded on pride and a feeling of individual worth even though it is subordinated and treated as only one of many factors in their lives. Undoubtedly it is sometimes more than a satisfying sense of kinship which pulls some of these individuals back to the Negro group. There is also a desire to help and to identify with a race possessing to them a certain set of values and certain characteristics promising for a rich future.

However, we have no direct and militant expression of this type of consciousness as we do in such a novel as "The Fire in the Flint". These characters do not seem to feel the need of defending themselves on racial issues or of righting wrongs by any particular word and deed. Their very passivity is open to the interpretation of an even greater assurance on their part of racial worth. They have no great conceit on a personal score and, along with their poise and self-confidence, are still obliged to combat plenty of feelings of inferiority, but that is as human beings and not as Negroes. They are striving first of all to emerge as personalities who are too rich and varied to concentrate too much on the race-problem.

This explains the fact that it is in only two or three instances that we can see race pride asserting itself clearly and unhesitatingly. The heroines of "Quicksand" and "Passing" are avowedly too individualistic even to speculate in terms of service or to consider the possibilities of personal sacrifice for the sake of the good of the group in which they have no particular faith. The steps they take to return to the group are motivated by entirely personal reasons and stimulated by the congenial atmosphere it happens to radiate. But Angela adds to her demand for happiness a desire for something real and permanent her own race may have better chances of giving her. This points to a little more seriousness which is further seen in her instinctive response to the earnest words of a Negro leader: "He urged

the deliberate introduction of beauty and pleasure into the difficult life of the American Negro — — yet for a time, for a long
time, there would have to be sacrifices, many sacrifices made
for the good of the whole. 'Our case is unique', the beautiful,
cultured voice intoned; 'those of us who have forged forward,
who have gained the front ranks in money and training, will
not, are not able as yet to go our separate ways apart from the
unwashed, untutored herd. We must still look back and render
service to our less fortunate, weaker brethren. And the first
step toward making this a workable attitude is the acquisition
not so much of a racial love as a racial pride. A pride that enables us to find our own beautiful and praiseworthy, an intense
chauvinism that is content with its own types, that finds com-
pleteness within its own group; that loves its own as the French
love their country, because it is their own. Such a pride can
accomplish the impossible.'[131]) Angela who at that time is
"passing" as white, is stirred by this purposefulness very much
as was the main character in "The Autobiography of an Ex-
Coloured Man" when he senses the idealism of race leaders. But
it is not until she falls in love with a Negro that she feels com-
pelled to cross the bridge again, proving again the need for the
subjective note.

Johanna and the princess, Kautilya, are made of sterner
stuff. It may be partly due to the fact that their darker complexions exclude the possibility of escaping from the darker
peoples even if they had so wished. With any such temptation
removed and with a surplus of energy and ability it is natural
that much of it should find outlet in more powerful forms than
mere personal happiness and contentment. Johanna with her
"fluff of thick, black hair, and solemn, earnest eyes and an indefinite capacity for spending long moments in thought" expresses her strength through her all-consuming ambition and
her willingness to work for its fulfillment. She wants to become
great and considers her color not as a handicap but as an incentive to success. Her race pride expresses itself triumphantly

131) Fauset, Jessie R.: *Plum Bun.* pp. 218—219.

and repeatedly, even in childhood: "'Colored people — — can do everything that anybody else can do. They've already done it. Some one colored person somewhere in the world does as good a job as anyone else, — perhaps a better one. They've been kings and queens and poets and teachers and doctors and everything. I'm going to be the one colored person who sings best in these days, and I never, never, never mean to let color interfere with anything I really want to do.'"[132]) The beginning of her career gives signs of justifying this faith, but gradually the restrictions forced upon her and her friends by prejudice have their disillusioning effect and she also is forced to admit that "nothing in the world is so hard to face as this problem of being colored in America". She sees her friends "passing" or escaping from America, her fiancée checked in his career as a promising surgeon, and herself, whom the critics regard as a "really great artist", driven to "consider ordinary vaudeville". After a gallant struggle to achieve she is finally also brought to the point of seeking personal happiness first of all. "'But now that we have love, Peter, we have a pattern to guide us out of the confusion'" is the modified conclusion of this fiery and determined girl who at one time was willing to forego love for the sake of fame but who has been chastened through suffering.[133])

There remains, then, only the "dark princess" from these heroines who has any consistency in her strength of purpose and who has not only faith in the "dark-skinned" people of the world, but the sustaining power to act and guide her life on this basis. We have seen that in the case of the other heroines who show intimations of race pride the conscousness is evidently not dominating enough to inspire a consecration of their lives to it. Even the strong-willed Johanna renounces the struggle to elevate her race through her own success. But the princess is the embodiment of courage, self-sacrifice, and true nobility. Others have theorized but she is not content with anything but a strenuous application. She seeks to identify herself as an industrial

132) Fauset, Jessie R.: *There is Confusion.* p. 45.
133) Ibid. p. 283.

worker with the lowest and poorest of American city dwellers, and her attempt at democracy is all the more startling because she must descend from the highest rank of aristocracy. There is something of the snob about all these other heroines in spite of the emotional sympathy some of them experience for the masses of their people. But Kautilya not only believes in "the divinity of labor" but toils with her own hands among workers, thus making it necessary to consider her as a person somewhat apart and different from the rest of the outstanding characters in this group of novels we have been considering.

But we must remember that this princess is already set apart by more than her individual traits. After all, she is not a Negro. The fact that she is dark-complexioned, of a delicate and refined nature, and in close sympathy with American Negroes tends to associate her in our minds with these mulatto heroines. But although she belongs to this group in many essential points both external and internal, she has come from another racial stock. This may partly account for the fact that she is able as none of them to preserve that faith and optimism about the future for oppressed people which is often a prerequisite for activity in a cause. Her suffering in America is vicarious, voluntarily entered into since her rank as an Indian princess would ordinarily exempt her from the proscriptions of race prejudice. We are given the impression that her very position as an outsider who chooses to participate in the struggles of a mistreated class and race in America allows her to maintain a certain perspective and objectivity and to escape from that enervating hopelessness more inevitable for those by birth unavoidably connected with the problem.

The contrast between her and the mulatto hero of the book strengthens such an interpretation. While he is also sensitive and responsive to the fine things of life, he has at the same time his doubts, his periods of indifference and despair paralyzing to action: "Matthew brooded: 'Are we getting on so far? Aren't the gates slowly, silently closing in our faces? Isn't there widespread, deep, powerful determination to make this a white world?"[134]) Circumstances have been hard to Matthew Towns and have tended to crush his spirit: "It seemed somehow that he was always passive — always waiting — always receptive. He could never get to doing. There was no performance or activity that promised a shining goal. There was no goal. There was no will to create one. Within him, years ago, something — something essential — had died."[135])

This character has much in common with the "ex-coloured man" in his human imperfections and in the variety of his life from would-be doctor to pullman porter, politician, prisoner, laborer, and prospective husband of a princess. In addition, there is his restlessness, identifying him also with the heroines. There is the sensitivity to maladjustment and criticism of injustice in America. Finally there is his race pride prompting him to claim the Negroes as "the bravest people fighting for justice to-day"[136]) and to emphasize his black rather than his white blood. When it is suggested that after all he is not black, his reply comes quickly: "'My grand-father was, and my soul is. Black blood with us in America is a matter of spirit and not simply of flesh.'"[137]) But once more the evidence points to the fact that Matthew, in spite of the fact that he is perhaps the most admirable of all these Negro characters, would have remained a theorist in the beginning but for the personal stimulus of the princess, and later would have turned into a cynic or a self-seeking individualist after experiences of disillusionment and failure but for her continued faith and love.

From "The Autobiography of an Ex-Coloured Man" to the "Dark Princess" then, we are introduced to a series of Negro characters bearing a decided family resemblance even while striving to express their individuality. It is significant that most of them are young girls, that all of them are mulattoes living in cities, with education, social status, refinement, and pleasing personalities. None of them have economic problems. Their

---

134) Du Bois, W. E. B.: *Dark Princess*. p. 66.
135) Ibid. p. 148.
136) Ibid. p. 30.
137) Ibid. p. 19.

problems are primarily psychological. They are well supplied with the things of this world and, while frankly enjoying them, still can not find peace. They are seekers of intangible values even though their life energy in some way seems checked from functioning and flowing into achievement. Their longings alone are sufficient to raise them above the minor characters, whether white or colored. And often these minor characters serve the purpose of stressing their uniqueness. We see Mimi in harmony with her inefficient, dreamy, temperamental father but fundamentally at odds with both her practical, worldly, ambitious step-mother and her narrowminded, conventional, money-making white husband. We find Clare unable to feel kinship with her ignorant and rather vulgar white husband or even with Irene, the mulatto friend who believes in loyalty, duty, and permanence. It is to the adventure-loving, security-hating husband of Irene that her nature responds. Matthew Towns revolts against the dominance of his level-headed, clever and cold-blooded mulatto wife. There is no attempt, then, to portray all minor Negro characters as having this capacity for feeling and for dreaming and for desiring the unknown. Our heroes and heroines are not only more sensitively organized than their white neighbors but also than the majority of their own people. They are the exceptional individuals, not the raw materials but the refined products of their race.

Vital—Uneducated—Instinctive.

For the raw materials we must search the next group of novels where individuals are simple in character, in personal tastes, and in social status. Once more the nature of the transition can be sensed by the fact that Wallace Thurman's heroine in "The Blacker the Berry" is coal black, and that she has little acquaintance with those soft and luxurious regions where our mulatto heroines moved. Emma Lou knows all too well about what economic struggle means and is not only directly conscious of but expressive about the cruelties of a special form of race prejudice. Against her will she is forced down to the level of the lowest class in Harlem, cut off from the companionship she

desires with suave and educated mulatto men, from participation
in college life, from good positions and living accommodations,
embittered by her realization that it is all on account of her
black color: "Not that she minded being black, being a Negro
necessitated having a colored skin, but she did mind being too
black—There was no place in the world for a dark girl."[138]) Her
race consciousness is extreme in its resentment of the injustice
practised against her and leads to a hyper-sensitivity: "Emma
Lou was burning up with indignation. So color-conscious had
she become that any time some one mentioned or joked about
skin color she imagined they were referring to her."[139]) This
complex has been in the process of development since childhood
and has been caused by prejudice within prejudice, by that
interracial attitude of snobbery on the part of exclusive mulattoes. Emma Lou thinks to escape it by geographical flight but
finally faces defeat, and continues "to go down, down down,
until she had little respect left for herself."[140]) She is comparable to the mulatto heroines in experiencing loneliness — "it
was terrible to be so alone"[141]) — — but the causes are quite
different. After all, Emma Lou is shown to be a rather mediocre
person who feels the only way to happiness is the possession of
a lighter skin color. She is concentrated on one point and all her
troubles arise from one problem. Her discontent over social
ostracism encourages an introspective state of mind, but her
thoughts run repeatedly in the same channel and therefore
we could never recognize her as a complex personality.

But the transition is not completed until we turn to the other
books of this last group where we can find characters who are
not only dark and living on a very low social plane but who are
presented to us as quite contented with that state of affairs.
They wish to take life as it comes and have neither inclination
nor ability to bother themselves over theoretical possibilities. It
is interesting to observe that the loss of complexity and rest-

---

138) Thurman, Wallace: *The Blacker the Berry.* pp. 9, 60.
139) Ibid. p. 205.
140) Ibid. p. 223.
141) Ibid. p. 147.

lessness and the abandonment of the use of heroines go together. All the remaining novels present heroes, most of them with the typical masculine characteristics of simplicity, objectivity, and strength tempered by gentleness.

There is a strong resemblance between Shine in "The Walls of Jericho", Jake in "Home to Harlem", and Banjo in "Banjo". Shine is "a supremely tranquil young Titan, with a face of bronze, hard, metallic, lustrous, profoundly serene"[142]) whose "hardness" is an instinctive protective covering for a simple, loving disposition. He is quite unable to analyze and dissect himself, and acts without any attempt to ascertain the true nature of his motives. It is necessary for his more sophisticated mulatto fiancée to reveal him to himself: '"There's a wall round you. A thick stone wall. You're outside, looking. You think you see yourself. You don't. You only see the wall. Hard guy — that's the wall. Never give in, never turn loose. Always get the other guy. That's the wall. — — You're not hard — — I don't believe you'd ever do anything really cruel. Don't believe it's in you.'"[143])

This shows him as far removed from the introspective type of person. The call which changing situations make for adjustment are met by him as directly and actively as possible and if one course fails he has recourse to another. When he is rebuffed in love, instead of reacting with brooding moods he "worked harder and played harder and knew that nothing ailed him". He knows no other way to meet entangled emotional situations than through action. His emotions are strong but his anger is short-lived and his contentment with what life offers is habitual. His occupation of piano moving is a source of real joy to him and the truck he drives is like a personal friend from whom he can in times of stress derive a sort of "unconfessed consolation".[144])

Jake and Banjo are equally natural and equally glad to be alive. The "tall, brawny, and black" Jake had not been disillusioned or toughened in any inner sense by the rough life he

---

142) Fisher, Rudolph: *The Walls of Jericho.* p. 13.
143) Ibid pp. 255—257.
144) Ibid. p. 216.

has led. He has wandered far and wide and made his living in a variety of ways from vagabonding to working on the railroad; he has known stark hunger and cold and other physical discomforts, but the keen edge has not been removed from his zest for life. Walking along the street on a spring day is enough to bring him joy: "Oh, sweet to be alive in that sun beneath that sky! And to be in love — even for one hour of such rare hours! One day! One night! Somebody with spring charm, like a dandelion, seasonal and haunting like a lovely dream that never repeats itself — — There are hours, there are days, and nights whose sheer beauty overwhelm us with happiness."[145]) Their happiness is closely connected with the vitality flowing from physical health. All three Negroes have vigorous bodies which enable them to partake in a carefree and natural mode of existence: "Banjo lived entirely on his strength and was scared of contacts with any Negro that had lost the one thing a vagabond black had to live by."[146]) Shine's strength is utilized in moving pianos, Jake's and Banjo's in the adjustment to eternally new and changing situations.

For the life of a vagabond is revealed as not always easy. The will and the strength to survive have certainly been necessary in Banjo's case: "Banjo was a great vagabond of lowly life. He was a child of the Cotton Belt, but he had wandered all over America. His life was a dream of vagabondage that he was perpetually pursuing and realizing in odd ways, always incomplete but never unsatisfactory. He had worked at all the easily-picked-up jobs — longshoreman, porter, factory worker, farm hand, seaman".[147]) And often one must have courage to pay the price of such unconventional living. When hard times come it is part of the game. In his sickness, for example, Banjo "bore his punishment bravely like a man — one who knows that he must take the consequences of spurning the sheltered, cramp-

---

145) McKay, Claude: *Home to Harlem.* p. 280.
146) McKay, Claude: *Banjo.* p. 186.
147) Ibid. p. 11.

ing ways of respectability to live like a reckless vagabond, who burns up his numbered days gloriously and dies blazing."[148])

Escape from "ways of respectability" is essential to the well-being of these characters. They have to breathe free and bracing air not found within the confines of respectable society. Their lack of education alone is enough to exempt them and is displayed by much more than their habits of speech, their frank use of dialect: "Jake's life had never before touched any of the educated of the ten dark millions."[149]) Banjo's reply to serious question is, "'I ain't edjucated, buddy'".[150]) He is not defensive on the point because it is a fact he accepts without shame or desire to change. That Shine is uneducated and uncultured is apparent in all he does and says, and often expresses itself in an utter naiveté when he is placed in a social situation for which his background has given him no key of understanding. He is completely out of his element in the fashionable Episcopal church where the mulatto Linda takes him, and his reactions are typical of an unpolished manual worker: "While he couldn't compare it with the Lafayette Theatre of course, still Joshua Jones considered it a pretty good show. — — The singing came nearer and entered in the rear, and Shine obeyed the impulse to turn and look; but before he could determine what the trick in it was, Linda pinched his arm sharply and brought him about, puzzled and resentful, to see her shaking her bowed head with ill-concealed vigor, Thereupon he noticed that everyone else stood like Linda, motionless, with lowered head as if it wasn't proper to look; and he wondered what manner of performance this was, which one might attend but on which one might not gaze."[151])

Patently "unrespectable", these individuals do not presume to have ethical attitudes such as ambition for personal or social betterment. Their conscious philosophy of life only supports their loose and instinctive habits. To them it is of little avail

---

148) Ibid. p. 244.
149) McKay, Claude: *Home to Harlem*. p. 164.
150) McKay, Claude: *Banjo*. p. 102.
151) Fisher, Rudolph: *The Walls of Jericho*. p. 178.

to plan one's conduct. To Banjo "whatever happened, happened. Life for him was just one different thing of a sort following the other".[152]) "Jake took what he wanted of whatever he fancied and kept going."[153]) The only solution is to take what comes as easily as possible: "It was a new world for Jake and he took it easily. That was his natural way, wherever he went, whatever new people he met. It had helped him over many a bad crossing at Brest, at Havre and in London — — take it easy — — take life easy."[154]) There is no use trying to reform and to stir up unnecessary trouble. There is no escaping undesirable conditions in an imperfect world filled with imperfect people. One must just seize the maximum amount of pleasure out of life as one goes along. Banjo views the World War as a catastrophe in which "'one half of it done murdered the other half to death'". But it is better to forget than to mourn: "'The wul' is just keeping right on with that nacheral sweet jazzing of life — — The wul' goes round and round and I keeps right on gwine round with it — — And I guess that if evah I went down in the bushes in the Congo, even the cannibals them would wanta mess with mah moon if I leave me careless, and if I runned away to the Nothanmost Pole, the icebugs would squash me frozen stiff if I couldn't prohtect mahself — — Ise a true-blue travelling-bohn nigger and I know life, and I knows how to take it nacheral. I fight when I got to and I works when I must and I lays off when I feel lazy, and I loves all the time becausen the honey-pot a life is mah middle name'."[155])

To them actualities are better than ideals. They reason that one cannot be sure of the future, but one can be sure of the sensuous pleasure of the moment. There is bound to be change, "the grand rhythm of life rolled on everlastingly without beginning or end in human comprehension",[156]) but there are always men and women and therefore always love. Love is more subtle

152) McKay, Claude: *Banjo*. p. 27.
153) McKay, Claude: *Home to Harlem*. p. 269.
154) Ibid. p. 105.
155) McKay, Claude: *Banjo*. pp. 304—305.
156) Ibid. p. 235.

to them than food and drink, and equally necessary, equally capable of direct and immediate assimilation: "A little brown girl aimed the arrow of her eye at him as he entered. Jake was wearing a steel-gray English suit. It fitted him loosely and well, perfectly suited his presence. She knew at once that Jake had just landed. She rested her chin on the back of her hands and smiled at him. There was something in his attitude, in his hungry wolf's eyes, that went warmly to her — — Her shaft hit home."[157]) Love is an instinct to be satisfied as such, and not to be limited in its expression according to the prudish codes of a professedly monogamous society. This does not mean having a type of love which is unrelievably promiscuous. Shine and Jake are both held by one woman, but it is because of the functioning of a natural instinct uncorrupted by any sense of morals or duty. It is no effort for them. They cannot help themselves. Likewise they cannot help responding to qualities in women above and beyond mere physical attraction. No matter how much society would accuse these men of immorality and of existence on an animal plane, they show an unfailing sincerity of feeling and capacity to sense and appreciate fineness in people, but fineness which is innate and not artifically created by culture: "Mystery again. A little stray girl. Finer than the finest. She was not elegant and educated, but she was nice"[158]) and Jake finds his thoughts repeatedly returning to that "little brown girl" who had appealed to his spirit as well as his body: "The mulattress was charged with tireless activity and Jake was her big, good slave. But her spirit lacked the charm and verve, the infectious joy, of his little lost brown. He sometimes felt that she had no spirit at all — that strange, elusive something that he felt in himself, sometimes here, sometimes there, roaming away from him — — caught a moment by some romantic rhythm, color, face, passing through cabarets, saloons, speakeasies, and returning to him — — the little brown had something of that in her, too. That night he had felt a reaching out

157) McKay, Claude: *Home to Harlem.* p. 11.
158) Ibid. p. 212.

and marriage of spirits — — But the mulattress was all a wonderful tissue of throbbing flesh. He had never once felt in her
any tenderness or timidity or aloofness."[159])

Love is a direct road to happiness: "Love should be joy lifting man out of the humdrum ways life,"[160]) according to Jake
with his "generous and warm" nature. It is one of the most
important ways of winning that happiness "respectable" people
also desire but lose because they are afraid of obeying their truest instincts. In the mulatto heroines we are aware of an intellectual activity at times inimical to their emotional natures.
Doubts and skepticism would keep them from the enjoyment
of certain pleasures which Banjo and Jake would seize in-
stantaneously. Jake is able to consider the body and spirit as
one and inseparable in a sort of Walt Whitman-like way impossible to the restless Helga Crane who fights against the recognition of passion as a legitimate force in life or as compatible with
the rest of her highly cultivated and refined personality. If life
is approached from an instinctive rather than from an analytical point of view, then conflicts vanish into thin air. This is
possible for characters without complexity and thus without a
variety of interests and tastes. Certainly Shine, Jake, and Banjo
do not demand much of life. It is enough for Jake to find his
"little lost brown" and for Banjo to have the money for a meal
today and the freedom to take the open road tomorrow. It is
perhaps a case with them of seeing life simply and seeing it
whole.

The issue of whites versus Negroes is then fitted into the
whole in proper proportion. Being black is a fact one neither
denies nor laments. When Banjo declared himself as a "true-
blue travelling-bohn nigger" it is with a sense of gladness. Jake
admits that "things ain't none at all lovely between white and
black in this heah Gawd's own country",[161]) but that cannot
dampen his exuberance. It may be partly because of a recogni-

---

159) Ibid. pp. 41—42.

160) Ibid. p. 328.

161) Ibid. p. 46.

tion that all the good is not on one side and all the bad on another which keeps them from that type of thwarted resentment felt by former characters. As Banjo points out: "'I know that theah's a mighty mountain a white divilment on this heah Gawd's big ball. And niggers will find that mountain on every foot a land that the white man done step on. But we niggers am no angels, neither.'"[162]) He will give money to "a poah hungry white kid" while claiming that "'I ain't nevah yet fohget that Ise cullud and that cullud is cullud and white is some'n else.'"[163]) Here is revealed a consciousness of uniqueness and a certain pride in that uniqueness that can evidently afford to deal tolerantly with the members of another race which has sought instead to present that uniqueness as a cause for shame and justification for unfair treatment. If a white man offers him a personal insult Banjo is ready for a fight on the spot, but so is he also if another Negro is the aggressor. It is not that Banjo loves white people. It is just that "he simply would not see life in division of sharp primary colors. In that sense he was color-blind. The colors were always getting him mixed up, shading off, fading out, running into one another so that it was difficult to perceive which was which. Any pleasing color of the moment's fancy might turn Banjo crazy for awhile."[164]) Naturally, then, he would be scornful of "race uplift" talk, not merely because he feels it is wasted breath encouraging to futile effort better spent in pleasurable ways, but because life is after all more important than color.

Whether proletarian or peasant, in the city or in the country, other Negro characters in this group are similarly in a position to feel life instead of color because they come from the lower ranks of Negroes where "respectability" is no aim and where instinctive living is allowable. When they can find satisfaction on an instinctive plane and when they are free to do so, then race is no problem. Race prejudice becomes a factor to be taken

---

162) McKay, Claude: *Banjo*. p. 305.

163) Ibid. p. 255.

164) Ibid. p. 170.

into account only when the aspirations of the individual Negro bring him up against the stone wall built to check him in any such attempt. The characters not only in the novels but in the collection of sketches contained in "Cane" and "Tropic Death" do not as a rule come within striking distance of this wall any more than did Shine, Jake, and Banjo, all of them centered within their particular dark group. The daily facts of existence are their eternal realities and the horizon does not have to be wide for these.

In these sketches again vitality is treasured more than virtue. The vital man attracts the woman and the vital woman attracts the man. Among the peasant characters in Georgia there is no conflict about responding to this attraction. Response is inevitable. We can imagine Karintha as a child of twelve, "a wild flash that told the other folks just what it was to live", and understand that "men had always wanted her, this Karintha, even as a child, Karintha carrying beauty perfect as dusk, when the sun goes down."[165]) She is irresistible from the start and easily senses her power: "At sunset, when there was no wind, and the pine-smoke from over by the saw-mill hugged the earth, and you couldn't see more than a few feet in front, her sudden darting past you was a bit of vivid color, like a black bird that flashes in light. With other children one could hear, some distance off, their feet flopping in the two-inch dust. Karintha's running was a whir. It had the sound of the red dust that sometimes makes a spiral in the road. At dusk, during the hush just after the sawmill had closed down, and before any of the women had started their supper-getting-ready songs, her voice, high-pitched, shrill, would put one's ears to itching. But no one ever thought to make her stop because of that. She stoned the cows, and beat her dog, and fought the other children — — Even the preacher, who caught her at mischief, told himself that she was as innocently lovely as a November cotton flower."[166])

---

165) Toomer, Jean: *Cane.* p. 1.
166) Ibid. p. 2.

Or there is Carma, primitive and powerful: "Carma, in overalls, and strong as any man, stands behind the old brown mule, driving the wagon home. It bumps and groans and shakes as it crosses the railroad track. She, riding it easy. I leave the men around the stove to follow her with my eyes down the red dust road."[167]) Esther with her "chalk-white face" is weak and timid herself and therefore worships the strength of Barlo, "a clean-muscled, magnificent, black-skinned Negro — — Black. Magnetically so. Best cotton picker in the county, in the state, in the whole world for that matter. Best man with his fists, best man with dice, with a razor — — Lover of all the women for miles and miles around. Esther decides that she loves him." She is a stranger to this vigorous figure and has nothing in common with him, and yet "he became the starting point of the only living patterns that her mind was to know."[168])

Passion kindles the atmosphere between Muriel and Dan, Bona and Paul, but they are in the city where public opinion works against it: "Dan looks at her, directly. Her animalism, still unconquered by zoo-restrictions and keeper taboos, stirs him. Passion tilts upward, bringing with it the elements of an old desire. Muriel's lips become the flesh-notes of a futile, plaintive longing. Dan's impulse to direct her is its fresh life."[169]) But Mrs. Pribby is reading the newspaper in the next room and she represents the town to Muriel, and the opinion of the town is more important to her than the attraction she feels for this virile Dan who scorns her timidity: "Do what you're bid, you she-slave. Look at her. Sweet, tame woman in a brass box seat. Clap, smile, fawn, clap. Do what you're bid."[170]) The school girl, Bona, on the contrary, is ready to take any steps in defiance of convention to win the attraction of the athletic Paul, from the moment "the dance of his blue-trousered limbs thrills her",[171]) and yet she, too, fails to meet the crisis.

167) Ibid. p. 16.
168) Ibid. pp. 36, 40, 42—43.
169) Ibid. p. 11 .
170) Ibid. p. 121.
171) Ibid. p. 134.

In some cases these individuals can make a complete and unhesitating response to vitality, in other cases there are barriers. This points to the existence of a struggle between the primitive and the civilized in their natures which at first glance seems more in keeping with what we sensed in the mulatto heroines than in Shine, Jake, and Banjo. But the difference now is that whenever instinctive living cannot predominate unchallenged it at least is recognized as the greater value. Our mulatto heroines in their involved thinking would not have granted the point so simply. Their own type of vitality was frailer and compounded of charm and subtle fascination, and this present more primitive form of it would have repelled or have been quite incomprehensible to them. Now it is true that little Carrie Kate in "Cane" experiences an inhibition, a fear of the condemnation of "respectable" people that spoils her naturalness with Lewis: "Their meeting is a swift sunburst — — He stretches forth his hands to hers. They feel like warm cheeks against his palms. The sun-burst from her eyes floods up and haloes him. Christ-eyes, his eyes look to her. Fearlessly she loves into them. And then something happens. Her face blanches. Awkwardly she draws away. The sin-bogies of respectable southern colored folks clamor at her: 'Look out! Be a *good* girl. A good girl. Look out!' She gropes for the basket that has fallen to the floor."[172]) However, the change is not due to her uncertainty as to her own preferences. If entirely free to choose or if courageous enough to flout group opinion then there seems little room for doubt that her natural impulses would have triumphed through her own wish.

Instinctive—Intellectual.

Just as we would have expected an emphasis on the world of ideas or on derived emotions in the more sophisticated middle class characters of the last group, so we are not surprised to discover this emphasis on simple and primary emotions in these lower class often illiterate characters. But the significant feat-

172) Toomer, Jean: *Cane.* p. 205.

ure is that this last emphasis continues even when we have
presented to us in this group of novels individuals once more
with an active intellectual life. The boy, Sandy, in "Not Without
Laughter", the mysterious figure of Lewis in "Cane", and the
student worker Ray in "Banjo" and "Home to Harlem" are
proletarian in sympathy while cultivating their mental sides.
They all have had education, but it has not formed a barrier
between them and those of their race who in many cases have
lacked the opportunity. Nor has it destroyed in them the
capacity to appreciate the vital qualities in their cruder associates, by furnishing them an artificial set of values. They
indicate that they are well able to separate the gold from the
dross which is a part of any system of education.

Sandy has aspirations. There is something about this little
Negro boy, "the shade of a nicely browned piece of toast",[173]
which reminds us of what Ray may have been in childhood. The
grandson of a wash-woman, the son of a cook and a vagabond
father, he dreams of becoming great and struggles to keep on
with what he considers necessary education for this goal even
when forces work against him. While delivering clothes for his
grandmother, working in a barber shop or hotel or running an
elevator in order to earn money, Sandy wrestles with his
problem: "Sandy wondered how people got to be great as, one
by one, he made the spittoons bright and beautiful."[174]) As he
lies in bed at night he thinks, "'I want to learn! — — I want to
go to college. I want to go to Europe and study.'"[175]) It is such
a wish that encourages his initiative in taking the first big step
from the small town of Stanton to Chicago "where the buildings
were like towers, the trains ran overhead, and the lake was like
a sea"[176]) in the glorified picture he has constructed. And it is
such a wish that keeps him to his purpose through the hot days
of a Chicago summer, "standing straight in his sweltering red

---

173) Hughes, Langston: *Not Without Laughter*. p. 17.
174) Ibid. p. 226.
175) Ibid. p. 279.
176) Ibid. p. 287.

suit in the cage of the hotel elevator — — 'I'm going back to my classes in September — — I'm through with elevators.'"[177])

But the source of Sandy's inspiration has not come from cultured but from humble people. It is his simple and faithful-hearted, hard-working grandmother, Hager, who is able to stir his ambition, while his "respectable" well-to-do Aunt Tempy with her talk of money-making, industry and success leaves him unmoved. He reacts instinctively from Tempy's snobbishness and airs of superiority from the day he rejected in favor of his cheaper homemade presents the expensive Christmas gift she had condescended to bring him. Tempy's conception of the road to success is to imitate the habits of white people and to discard all "nigger" ways and connections. She is a shallow, unattractive type with no warm blood in her veins, a faithful member of the Episcopal church because of the social prestige conveyed. Not only is Sandy uninterested in becoming "proper" and successful in her sense of the words, but he is also actively interested in those very "nigger" ways she frowns upon, dance and song and carefree laughter. He adores his amiable, irresponsible, roving father and his vivacious unconventional Aunt Harriett who represent the gay side of life to him. When Jimboy plays jazz on his beloved guitar and Harriett rocks and sways and moves to its rhythm, Sandy is enchanted. Harriett is a creature of rhythm and joy and passion, immoral if necessary to fulfil her desires, defiant against the restraints of religion, society, and race. But her magnetism and vital, positive attitudes towards life leave a great impression on Sandy. He embodies something of Harriett's rebellious, free spirit in addition to that intellectual and serious motive which, ironically, he gets from the illiterate Hager rather than from the would-be refined Tempy. In both Harriett and Hager he senses genuineness, in Tempy, pretension: '"I want to do something for myself, by myself — — Free — — I want a house to live in, too, when I'm older — like Tempy's and Mr. Silas's — — But I wouldn't want to be like

---

177) Hughes, Langston: *Not Without Laughter.* pp. 312, 314.

Tempy's friends or her husband, dull and colorless, putting all his money away in a white bank, ashamed of colored people.'"[178])

In a flash Sandy's views are clarified. In protesting against the conclusions of the snobbish Tempy and her husband he comes to realize that the two approaches to life he values, that is, the instinctive and the intellectual, are not only possible to combine and possess simultaneously, but also possible to attain through association with his own misunderstood race: "'A lot of minstrels — that's all niggers are!' Mr. Silas had said once. 'Clowns, jazzers, just a band of dancers — that's why they never have anything. Never be anything but servants to the white people'. Sandy wonders and searches deeper for the truth of the matter. Clowns! Jazzers! Band of dancers! — — — Harriett! Jímboy! Aunt Hager! — — — A band of dancers! — — — Sandy remembered his grandmother whirling around in front of the altar at revival meetings in the midst of the other sisters, her face shining with light, arms out-stretched as though all the cares of the world had been cast away; Harriett in the back yard under the apple tree, eagle-rocking in the summer evenings to the tunes of the guitar; Jimboy singing — — — But was that why Negroes were poor, because they were dancers, jazzers, clowns? — — — The other way round would be better; dancers because of their poverty; singers because they suffered; laughing all the time because they must forget — — — It's more like that, thought Sandy." He also feels a need for this capacity for joy and for spon-taneous direct emotional experience defying and defeating ob-stacles, if for no other reason but to give him the impetus to fulfil the more ambitious side of his nature. „A band of dan-cers — — — Black dancers — — — captured in a white world — — — Dancers of the spirit, too. Each black dreamer a captured dancer of the spirit — — — Aunt Hager's dreams for Sandy dancing far beyond the limitations of their poverty, of their humble station in life, of their dark skins."[179])

---

178) Hughes, Langston: *Not Without Laughter*. p. 313.
179) Ibid. p. 313.

Sandy is necessarily more aware of race prejudice than
Shine, Jake, or Banjo because he is not purely instinctive, because he has aims and ideals which white society threatens to
crush, because his mind and imagination spur him to wonder
and to question conditions about him. Even in early childhood
we see this tendency to wonder and usually the relationship
of the two races intrudes into his musings in some form or
other: "He wondered sometimes whether if he washed and
washed his face and hands, he would ever be white. Someone
had told him once that blackness was only skin-deep — — —
And would he ever have a big house with electric lights in it,
like his Aunt Tempy — — — But it was mostly white people
who had such fine things, and they were mean to colored —
— — And when he got big, he wanted to travel like Jimboy.
He wanted to be a railroad engineer, but Harriett had said
there weren't any colored engineers on trains — — — And
Reverend Braswell was as black as ink, but he knew God —
— — God didn't care if people were black, did He? — — —
What was God? Was he a man or a lamb or what?"[180]) As
he grows to adolescence the questionings increase in urgency
as they become less abstract and more applicable to his immediate problems. His boy friends are obviously able to act
without perplexity, "but to Sandy himself nothing ever seemed
quite clear. Why was his country going stupidly to war? —
— — Why were white people and colored people so far apart?
Why was it wrong to desire the bodies of women? — — —
With his mind a maelstrom of thoughts as he lay in bed night
after night unable to go to sleep quickly, Sandy wondered many
things and asked himself many questions — — — Maybe school
didn't matter. —Yet to get a good job you had to be smart —
and white, too. That was the trouble, you had to be white! —
— — He understood then why many old Negroes said: 'Take
all this world and give me Jesus!' It was because they couldn't
get this world anyway — it belonged to the white folks. They
alone had the power to give or withhold at their back doors."[181])

180) Hughes, Langston: *Not Without Laughter*. pp. 183—185.
181) Ibid. pp. 276—280.

But awareness of the prejudice only seems to increase Sandy's loyalty to and pride in his own racial group. The assets of being a Negro outweigh the liabilities on the whole. The assumption is that to achieve intellectually he will have to struggle all the harder but it will be more meaningful then, when coming through the process of suffering, and of laughter in spite of suffering, which his race has learned so well. "Not Without Laughter" can be regarded as the watch cry of a group which is concerned with wresting inner victory from outer defeat, which believes in counteracting hate with joy rather than with sorrow and despair. Instead of towards active resentment or passive endurance or disillusionment or escape, the fact of prejudice stimulates Sandy towards an attitude of emergence, emergence through suffering, recognizing the evil but rising above it.

As suggested, the character of Ray has much in common with this serious, fun-loving boy. He seems to carry Sandy's traits and thoughts into adult life, giving them the ripeness of maturity. The first situation in which we see this Haytian Negro, "of average size, slim, a smooth pure ebony",[182]) is reading, even while he is employed as waiter on a train. He has had to stop his university education in order to make money, but he gives his spare moments to study and considers it a habit acquired for life. His ambition is to become a writer. "Ray had always dreamed of writing words some day" and had brooded over great books from childhood, from the pictures created by "Les Miserables", "Nana", and "David Copperfield", to the thoughts of "the great scintillating satirists of the age — Bernard Shaw, Ibsen, Anatole France, and the popular problemist, H. G. Wells", and of modern writers like James Joyce, Sherwood Anderson, and D. H. Lawrence, and above all, to the works of the Russians: "Only the Russians of the late era seemed to stand up like giants in the new. Gogol, Dostoievski, Tolstoy, Chekhov, Turgeniev. When he read them now he thought: Here were elements that the grand carnage

---

182) McKay, Claude: *Home to Harlem.* p. 127.

swept over and touched not. The soil of life saved their roots from the fire. They were so saturated, so deep-down rooted in it."[183]) What attracts him to the Russians is not their ideals but their temperament, their "restless searching within and without", their "energetic living", their feeling for reality.

His own dream of self-expression is linked up with his appreciation of the instinctive side of his race: "And literature, story-telling, had little interest for him now if thought and feeling did not wrestle and sprawl with appetite and dark desire over all the pages."[184]) He feels the impulse to "create out of the fertile reality around him" and this explains his statement in Marseilles that "'how the black boys live is the most interesting thing in the Ditch'" and therefore should be written about. When challenged by one of the beach boys, he defends his position:

"'But what do you find good in the Ditch to write about?'

'Plenty. I'm here, and mean to make a practical thing of the white proverb, "Let down your buckets where you are."

'You might bring up a lot of dirt.' Goosey turned up his nose in a tickling, funny, disdainful way.

'Many fine things come out of dirt — steel and gold, pearls and all the rare stones that your nice women must have to be happy.'"[185])

To recognize the gold in the dirt is more than a problem of literature to him. It is a problem of life hampered by the "dead stuff" of stereotyped education, the "false moralities" of Christianity, the "poisonous seed" of patriotism, and the "rottenness" in general of modern civilization. He is not blind to what he judges is the real destructive nature of so-called civilization with its "civilized world of nations, all keeping their tiger's claws sharp and strong under the thin cloak of international amity and awaiting the first favorable opportunity to spring. During his passage through Europe it had

---

183) Ibid. pp. 225, 228.

184) Ibid. p. 228.

185) McKay, Claude: *Banjo*. pp. 115—116.

been an illuminating experience for him to come in contact
with the mind of the average white man. A few words would
usually take him to the centre of a guarded, ancient treasure
of national hates".[186]) But his greatest indignation is aroused
by its refusal to recognize the gold in the dirt, its insistence
instead on cold "Anglo-Saxon standards", and the enervating
effect on his race and its best characteristics: "He hated civilization because the general attitude towards the colored
man was such as to rob him of his warm human instincts and
make him inhuman." The whole white world conspired to make
the Negro, as soon as he leaves his own group, so race conscious
and color conscious that it is no longer possible for him to respond to life spontaneously and naturally. He cannot act
without being mindful of his complexion and of the deprecia-
ting attitude which this white world would assume if he did
follow his emotions. In Ray's opinion, "it was easy enough for
Banjo, who in all matters acted instinctively. But it is not easy
for a Negro with an intellect standing watch over his native
instincts to take his own way in this white man's civilization."[187])

The difficulty comes in trying to reconcile these two sides:
"Ray wanted to hold on to his intellectual acquirements without
losing his instinctive gifts — the black gifts of laughter and
melody and simple sensuous feelings and responses."[188]) He
is more complex in nature than both Banjo and Jake: "Life
burned in Ray perhaps more intensely than in Jake. Ray felt
more and his range was wider and he could not be satisfied
with the easy, simple things that sufficed for Jake. Sometimes
he felt like a tree with roots in the soil and sap flowing out
and whispering leaves drinking in the air. But he drank in
more of life than he could distill into active animal living.
Maybe that was why he felt he had to write."[189]) He is con-

---

186) McKay, Claude: *Banjo*. p. 135.
187) Ibid. pp. 163—164.
188) Ibid. pp. 322—323.
189) McKay, C. aude: *Home to Harlem*. p. 265.

vinced that "from these boys he could learn to how to live — how to exist as a black boy in a white world and rid his conscience of the used-up hussy of white morality" but at the same time that "he could not scrap his intellectual life and be entirely like them".[190])

From Ray's point of view the crime of white civilization against the intelligent and sensitive Negro is in forcing him to face such a dilemma. But, like Sandy, Ray keeps his sense of values clear. Instead of giving way to bitterness or hopelessness he takes a firm stand. If it comes to a question of choosing between the two sides he feels certain as to where he would place his emphasis. For "of one thing he was resolved: civilization would not take the love of color, joy, beauty, vitality, and nobility out of his life and make him like one of the poor mass of its pale creatures. — — — Could he not see what Anglo-Saxon standards were doing to some of the world's most interesting peoples? Some Jews ashamed of being Jews. Changing their names and their religion ...... for the Jesus of the Christians. The Irish objecting to the artistic use of their own rich idioms. Inferiority bile of non-Nordic minorities. Educated Negroes ashamed of their race's intuitive love of color, wrapping themselves up in respectable gray, ashamed of Congo-sounding laughter, ashamed of their complexion (bleaching out), ashamed of their strong appetites. No being ashamed for Ray. Rather than lose his soul, let intellect go to hell and live instinct!"[191])

Furthermore, the crime of white civilization against the simple and uneducated Negro is in imposing standardizing and mechanizing patterns upon him. As a student he has had hopes for the adjustment in the world order of the dark masses, and "with the growth of international feelings and ideas he had dreamed of the association of his race with the social movements of civilization milling through the civilized machine". But his travels and observations had awakened his "fine intellectual prerogative of doubt".[192]) He has a growing con-

190) McKay, Claude: *Banjo*. p. 322.
191) Ibid. pp. 164—165.
192) Ibid. p. 324.

viction that a machine age and the type of progress it brings will not make his people happier but will only tend to rob them of many beautiful qualities. He finds little room for encouragement even in the theory of outstanding, supposedly idealistic, Nordic thinkers: "He did not think the blacks would come very happily under the super-mechanical Anglo-Saxon-controlled world society of Mr. H. G. Wells. They might shuffle along, but without much happiness in the world of Bernard Shaw. Perhaps they would have their best chance in a world influenced by the thought of a Bertrand Russell, where brakes were clamped on the machine with a few screws loose and some nuts fallen off. But in this great age of science and super-invention was there any possibility of arresting the thing unless it stopped of its own exhaustion?"[193])

But the saving of the situation both for the individual and the group is felt to lie in the power of those very qualities to which civilization is opposed. Developing Sandy's dim intuitions further, Ray reaches the conclusion that Negroes who wish it may be successful in attaining a harmonious union of their instinctive and intellectual life by their access to the racial stores of vitality and primitivity which have enabled the race to suffer and survive and triumph. For "a black man, even though uneducated, was in closer biological kinship to the swell of primitive earth life",[194] and this in turn endows him with a remarkable survival quality. Ray's belief in the potentialities of his race has been tested by his experience. A mulatto heroine like Mimi we have seen could be very critical of civilization and its effect on Negroes, and very appreciative of the primitive and instinctive values in her race, and yet her knowledge of the true nature of these values is confined to theory. She returns to her race but to its middle class group where these characteristics are more suppressed and tame. But Ray, like Sandy, knows what it is to live with the ignorant, poor, natural type of Negroes and to receive nourishment from them:

193) Ibid. p. 325.
194) Ibid. p. 323.

"The more Ray mixed in the rude anarchy of the lives of the black boys — loafing, singing, bumming, playing, dancing, loving, working — and came to a realization of how close-linked he was to them in spirit, the more he felt that they represented more than he or the cultured minority the irrepressible exuberance and legendary vitality of the black race — — — and that their loose, instinctive way of living was more deeply related to his own self-preservation than all the principles, or social-morality lessons with which he had been inculcated by the wiseacres of the civilized machine."[195])

With Sandy, Ray claims to understand what lies beneath this laughter and joy and spontaneous living. He senses a deep suffering from which these people have emerged and learns thereby to value them the more and to regard them as the most admirable and creative response to harsh experience: "He loved their natural gusto for living down the past and lifting their kinky heads out of the hot, suffocating ashes, the shadow, the terror of real sorrow to go on gaily grinning in the present. Never had Ray guessed from Banjo's general manner that he had known any deep sorrow. Yet when he heard him tell Goosey that he had seen his only brother lynched, he was not surprised, he understood, because right there he had revealed the depth of his soul and the soul of his race — the true tropical African Negro. No Victorian-long period of featured grief and sable mourning, no mechanical-pale graveside face, but a luxuriant living up from it, like the great jungles growing perennially beautiful and green in the yellow blaze of the sun over the long life-breaking tragedy of Africa."[196]) He understands also how puzzling all this is to white people, "that strange, childlike capacity for wistfulness - and-laughter" — — — "No wonder the whites, after five centuries of contact, could not understand his race. How could they when the instinct of comprehension had been cultivated out of them? No wonder they hated them, when out of their melancholy envi-

---

195) Ibid. pp. 324, 319.
196) Ibid. pp. 321—322.

ronment the blacks could create mad, contagious music and high laughter."[197])

Interpreted through Ray's eyes, the ability of individuals like Jake and Banjo to live joyfully and freely without any apparent recognition of the importance of racial issues is not the result of an ignorance about evil and pain and injustice but the result of a voluntarily chosen attitude of reaction towards a full knowledge. Here is a non-resistant attitude, the refusal to consider themselves in the light of a "problem" and therefore in the light of participators in a pitched battle between the races. The educated Negro who is more able to analyze and see fine points and thus complicate the issue, who tends to be more ambitious and proud and therefore more wounded on a personal score by racial discriminations, must learn from the uneducated Negroes, the sophisticated mulattoes must learn from the unpolished blacks, the professional people from the workers and peasants, the upper and middle classes of Negroes from the lower class. Instead of feeling that shame which has come from their assimilation of white standards and values they will grow to feel a pride which comes from an assimilation of Negro standards and values. Their answer to charges of inferiority will be full and triumphant living rather than futile arguing.

This tendency to glorify the instinctive life and its creative and regenerating possibilities is disclosed strikingly from a somewhat different angle in the character of Lewis. Lewis is the intelligent Negro not in touch with the city proletarians, but in touch with the simple and ignorant peasant folk in the rural districts of the South. It must be remembered that observation of the lower class living in urban conditions can not give us a complete picture of this instinctive behaviour in Negroes. We must turn from the city to the countryside and from the North of the United States to the South, as in "Cane", to find still other aspects dependent on closeness to the soil and nature. The implication seems to be that after all there is no better place for becoming acquainted with the emotional po-

---

197) McKay, Claude: *Home to Harlem.* pp. 266—267.

tentialities of the American Negro than in his original home in America, in the rural South where the masses of illiterate black folk still live and toil and sing.

Although the character of Lewis in the story "Kabnis", has no clear contours, it seems plausible that he has sensed a lack in an educated and confined life and has therefore come to the South to absorb refreshing food. The previous interpretation of the characters in the plantation-slave milieu would not be satisfying to Lewis who is not taking these simple types at their face value. He is searching and probing underneath for the meaning of these humble lives and of their primitive surroundings. Father John is far more to him than a helpless and infirm old man, an outworn preacher from superstitious slave days. To him, "he is like a bust in black walnut. Gray-bearded. Gray-haired. Prophetic. Immobile. Lewis' eyes are sunk in him. The others, unconcerned, are about to pass on". His imagination is captured by "that forehead. Great woolly beard. Those eyes. A mute John the Baptist of a new religion — or a tongue-tied shadow of an old."[198] He regards him as a "dead blind father of a muted folk who feel their way upward to a life that crushes or absorbs them."[199] Through this one figure he is able to establish contact with the whole emotional depth of the Negro-teeming South: "Lewis, seated now so that his eyes rest upon the old man, merges with his source and lets the pain and beauty of the South meet him there. White faces, pain-pollen, settle downwards through a cane-sweet mist and touch the ovaries of yellow flowers. Cotton bolls bloom, droop. Black roots twist in a parched red soil beneath a blazing sky. Magnolias, fragrant, a trifle futile, lovely, far off — — — — His eyelids close. A force begins to heave and rise."[200] It is this force which Lewis wants to realize. In him and in other shadowy characters of Jean Toomer's book we sense a new quality in the instinctive way of life, the opening of a door to mystic experience and strange spiritual depths.

198) Toomer, Jean: *Cane*. p. 211.
199) Ibid. p. 212.
200) Ibid. pp. 214—215.

Through his characters the author makes us feel that he who is responsive to this forces will know pain but grow strong while he who is afraid of it and resists will be a weak and ineffectual creature suffering from the futile pain of emptiness and thwarted urges. This is illustrated by the difference between Lewis and Kabnis. Both of them are educated Negroes of aesthetic temperament who have come from the North to the South in search of elusive meanings in life. But Lewis has been able to tap the source from which Kabnis shuts himself off: "His mouth and eyes suggest purpose guided by an adequate intelligence. He is what a stronger Kabnis might have been, and in an odd faint way resembles him."[201]) He has the courage to be himself and go his own way in spite of an inimical or misinterpreting public opinion, whereas Kabnis is lacking in will-power and is the prey of many fears and jealousies obstructing the passage for positive emotions and for receptivity to Lewis' type of experience: "If I, the dream (not what is weak and afraid in me) could become the face of the South. How my lips would sing for it, my songs being the lips of its soul."[202]) Lewis becomes aware of both the pathetic lack and the potentiality in this school-teacher and longs to be a medium through which he can find help: "His eyes turn to Kabnis. In the instant of their shifting, a vision of the life they are to meet. Kabnis, a promise of a soil-soaked beauty; uprooted, thinning out. Suspended a few feet above the soil whose touch would resurrect him. Arm's length removed from him whose will to help — — — There is a swift intuitive interchange of consciousness. Kabnis has a sudden need to rush into the arms of this man. His eyes call, 'Brother'. And then a savage, cynical twist-about within him mocks his impulse and strengthens him to repulse Lewis. His lips curl cruelly. His eyes laugh. They are glittering needles, stitching. With a throbbing ache they draw Lewis to."[203])

When Lewis is repulsed in this way by such people as Kab-

---

201) Ibid. p. 189.
202) Ibid. p. 158.
203) Ibid. p. 192.

nis and Carrie Kate it gives him a feeling for the "impotent pain" in so much of the life about him. To him the possibility of "triumphant living" is threatened by the fight of individuals against their instincts. Although his interpretation of "triumphant living" would allow more room for the subtle and intangible and poignant elements of human experience in addition to the abandoned, spontaneous, and immediately pleasurable elements stressed by Ray, both are at one in their conviction that the truest life values are to be discovered in the lowly places and among the lowly people. Ray is more the thinker with many theories and definite ideas, Lewis is more the aesthete with intuitions and hidden half-thoughts, but the one is grasping gold contained in the dirt, the other is absorbing those elements for sap contained in the soil.

An observation of the outstanding characters presented by Negro fiction from 1900 to 1930 shows that they fall into several distinct groups corresponding to the different treatments of milieu. The more we study the groups the more we tend to regard each not as a collection of individuals but as the expression of a type of character; to a greater or less degree. Within each group the single members bear a strong family resemblance to each other. Likewise we find that each type represents one of the stages in race consciousness which is a possible reason why instead of individuals we have types, lending themselves more readily to the illustration of social attitudes. Thus we see four clear-cut types: The acquiescent — virtuous — naive type, the rebellious — active — professional — social minded type, the restless — passive — sophisticated — individualistic type, and the vital—uneducated—instinctive type. Finally we see the beginning of a fifth type related to both the third and fourth: the instinctive — intellectual type, rejoicing in the senses and aesthetic experience as well as in the mind and mental experience, regarding spirit and body as inseparable parts of a whole, seeking and finding, restless and satisfied, suffering and happy, embodiment of an eternal paradox.

It is only in the books where the instinctive side of life is stressed, that is, in those embodying either submissive or non-resistant psychology, that there is an exclusive concentration on Negro characters, and often the blacker-skinned and more Negroid the better. In the second and third groups possessing the offensive-defensive psychology, the main characters are either white or more frequently mulatto. The first and fourth types have no shame, the first because it has no standards and is humble before its master and god, the fourth because its standards are self-contained and independent from those of the white world. Neither type is trying to prove or convince in relation to white civilization. The second and third types have a more or less consciously developed pride and superiority complex with either a recognized or unrecognized desire to prove their worth, either to a cruel or to a stupid white world.

The plantation characters seem to have no sense of injustice. The place assigned them in the social scale is evidently not disagreeable and permits of much happiness and interest within the daily round of events. Seeds of discontent have not begun to grow. Dreams of expansion and achievement in the outside world do not trouble their sleep or the peaceful course of their little experiences in their protected and paternalized environment. They contrast strongly to the small town emancipated characters who are burning with a sense of injustice and an ambition to earn a suitable place for themselves under the sun. The race consciousness of the latter is not slumbering but in agitated motion. There is a great gap between a pair of lovers like Dr. Kenneth Harper and Jane in "The Fire in the Flint" and Sam and Anner 'Lizer in "Folks From Dixie", the very title of the books being symbolic of the difference in character. The resentment of the Kenneths and Janes plunges them into activity — something must be attempted and initiated against unfair and stifling white dominance even if the odds are too great. A losing battle is more honorable than surrender, and there is always the chance of a turning tide. We gain the impression that their troubles would be soothed and eliminated and the outcome of the battle favorable if the white world would allow them freedom from interference and freedom of opportunity for the establishment of their economic security and the enjoyment of certain external and material advantages.

Yet we find these insufficient for the third group. The Northern mulattoes described in these novels have advantages and none of the crude forms of race prejudice practised against them, and nevertheless their sensitive spirits chafe just as much under the refined forms, as well as under a multitude of other conditions having no direct connection with race but depending rather on the unavoidable pains of living itself. In spite of the fact that a certain amount of success is in their grasp they seem to have no roots with which to settle down and find contentment. Various inferences can be drawn: that because they are Negroes the existence of race prejudice has given them definite if unrecognized complexes in childhood preventing the integration of their personalities and the capacity under any conditions for harmonious living in adult life, that because they are Negroes a hostile world discourages and hinders them from attaining to that kind of complete happiness their many-sided natures desire, or that because they are Negroes they are possessed of a higher set of values and higher spiritual aspirations than can be fed by the materialistic and crude standards of white civilization. All three inferences are interconnected and if true would form an indictment of the dominant white group. They point to the existence of an offensive-defensive type of race consciousness in these individuals throwing doubt on the validity of the traditional positions assigned to superiority and inferiority. Yet the very fact that they must remain inferences only confirms the point that their race consciousness is reserved and subtle in expression, the very element of control possibly being regarded both as a mark of superiority and a more effective means of proving its reality.

Control is not present in the fourth type, and at the same time not necessary. The immediacy of their reactions to life and to race as a part of life spares them from deep-buried complexes coming as the result of those conscious suppressions transformed with time to repressions. Without inhibitions there is no damning up of life energy, no thwarting of self-feeling bringing resentment or causing sensitivity as a soil for all kinds of conflicts. Characters like Sandy, Ray, and Lewis serve as a connecting link between the third and fourth type of character, possessing elements of both and yet suggesting that the complex restlessness of the one could be assuaged in the simple harmony of the other. Their criticism of "the colored intelligensia" offers another explanation of the failure on the part of this third type to escape conflict and become integrated: its failure to understand fully and to utilize those instinctive racial values embodied in the fourth type. The implication is that the responsibility for such failure cannot be laid entirely on forces outside the group, set in motion by a hostile white world, but depends also on that blindness and insensitivity within the Negro group itself which prevents it from drawing on its own inner resources. The boy, Sandy, the thinker, Ray, the dreamer, Lewis, are precursors of a possible new type in American Negro fiction, a type that is the parallel in literature to the "New Negro" in life, blending thought with feeling, courage with sensitivity, pain with joy. The implication of these writers seems to be that it is this well-balanced type which will reveal the greatest capacity to turn outer defeat into inner victory without the use of weapons.

———

Reference to the emotional tones and colors of these works of fiction can put the finishing touches to our comprehension of the type of race consciousness present in each case. This is because race consciousness is, after all, a growth from deep feelings of some kind. These can so permeate the whole mood of any literary production that we are able to sense their nature through an observation of these moods and in this way to reach the core of the race consciousness. It is thus the spirit of these books we must finally attempt to capture. We are now concerned with the irrational elements which are their very heartbeats and therefore the nearest we can hope to come to the inner emotional lives of their creators. The intellectual opinions expressed through the medium of characters or the critical point of view revealed through selection and treatment of milieu have importance in this chapter not for ther own sakes but for the part they play, along with other factors such as style and technique, in establishing the mood.

Pastoral Calm.

The nature of the milieu and the individuals within it and the relationship between the two will often largely determine the nature of the mood created by the book. If the character is organized on a simple and harmonious plan and if the environment is comparatively peaceful and stable it follows that his adjustment will be made with such quietness as to impregnate the whole atmosphere and emotional effect of the story with that quality. This is indeed the case with the plantation stories where the stream of life flows smoothly. There are no great rocks to obstruct or divert the water — no major catastrophies to cause trouble — but only the small pebbles of every day event to ripple the surface occasionally. Where the Negroes are actually on the plantation or in their isolated post-war communities carrying over the plantation customs and habits of mind, their adaptability to their surroundings without any apparent sense of limitation or frustration can only result in an optimistic mood. We gain the impression of a sunny and pleasant landscape with mild breezes, before the heat of an advancing day and the noise of marching armies have disturbed its idyllic quality.

This impression is enhanced by the episodal nature of the stories. There is no strain and stress of dramatic action leading to breathless suspense and climax. Single characters seem to form an integral part of their milieu and to move along inevitably with it, and the opposition of individual to individual caused by some local situation is never more than enough to arouse that type of comfortable suspense which one knows will be resolved by a happy ending. We cannot take the trials of Anner 'Lizer or Mr. Dunkin or Uncle Peter seriously because we are aware that all will be well with them and their problems dissolved in thin air by the sunshine of a virtue which is destined in the nature of things to win. When we see that "somehow, Sam had dropped the axe and was holding her in his arms"[1]) and that the scheming Alonzo was checked in his machinations "leaving Mr. Dunkin in undisputed possession of the field"[2]) it is as if the breeze had stopped tossing the heads of the meadow flowers and playing among the long grasses.

The calm of plantation life in "The Conjure Woman" is conditioned by a strain of pathos. Lovers are not always reunited and the virtuous do not always find happiness. The gruesome fate of Sandy, accidentally chopped down and sawed up for lumber when he is "goophered" temporarily as a tree, affects the atmosphere with the burden of human grief it brings. We can feel for the distracted Teenie as she "went 'roun' moanin', en groanin', en shakin' her head", and when we learn that the

---

1) Dunbar, Paul L.: *Folks From Dixie*. p. 26.
2) Ibid. p. 262.

Negroes "could hear sump'n moanin' en groanin' 'bout de kit-
chen in de night-time, en w'en de win' would blow dey hear
sump'n a-hollerin' en sweekin' lack it wuz in great pain en suf-
ferin'", we suffer with the spirit of Sandy imprisoned in the
timbers of the room.[3]) Again the dilemma of the devoted slaves,
Dan and Mahaly, thwarted by the malice of an unscrupulous
conjure man, creates a mournful mood: "W'en po' Dan sta'ted
to'ds her, ez any man nach'ly would, it des made her holler
wuss en wuss; fer she didn' knowed dis yer wolf wuz her Dan.
En Dan des had ter hide in de weeds, en grit his teef en hol'
hisse'f in, 'tel she passed out'n her mis'ry, callin' fer Dan ter de
las', en wond'rin' w'y he didn' come en he'p her".[4]) After such
a rending experience it is to be expected that in the vicinity of
her grave "de niggers useter heah him howlin' en howlin' doun
dere, des fittin' ter break his hea't".[5]) Perhaps the greatest
poignancy of mood is aroused by the experience of Chloe when
the full measure of her irremediable loneliness breaks upon her.
"De sun mought shine by day, de moon by night, the flowers
mought bloom, en de mawkin'-birds mought sing, but po' Jeff
wuz done los' ter her fereber en fereber."[6])

But we must recognize the fact that not only does the happy
ending persist in such stories of Chesnutt's as "Sis' Becky's
Pickaninny" and "Mars Jeems's Night-mare" but that pathos
where it does exist is not deep-seated or depressing. It is tempered externally by our knowledge of the ulterior motives of the
sly old narrator, shaping the record of events to his own purposes, and internally by the decisive part played by magic powers. When we realize, for instance, that the misfortunes of
Sandy, Mahaly and Dan rest upon their transformations into
a tree, a black cat and a gray wolf respectively, our scientific
minds spare too great a drain upon our tender emotions! When
the air of magic tends to lighten in this way the burden of any

3) Chesnutt, Charles W.: *The Conjure Woman*. p. 57.
4) Ibid. p. 187.
5) Ibid. p. 192.
6) Ibid. p. 222.

possible tragedy, we are left free to enjoy the exquisite blending of the humorous and the pathetic. The mood may be pensive or even melancholy at times, but it remains tranquil as if the soft early morning sunshine had turned for the moment into haze. The very fact that suffering is introduced into this little world not by anything actual and vicious inherent in milieu or individual but by something imaginative like superstition and sorcery only increases the gentle glow of unreality clinging to these tales. It is as if we viewed the characters moving about within an enclosed sphere of delicately colored glass, and the spectacle of their little joys and sorrows, protected so securely from contact with the real world as we know it, can stir and convince us not through any appeal to our sense of the actual but only through a soft and haunting call to our fancy.

Storm and Stress.

But glass is fragile and as it is shattered the dream world which we have sensed as a kind of escape, together with the lovely mood it has evoked, disappears. The novels of the next group with its changing milieu and changing set of characters provide a striking antithesis to the prevailing tone of the plantation episodes. The contentment of an isolated and patronized Negro community is replaced by the misery of a forcedly segregated and exploited Negro section. The more or less benevolent white masters revolving on a higher and removed sphere are replaced by a competing, unfriendly, and interfering white population in the closest proximity. The masses of the illiterate and simple-natured Negroes are not fitted to meet the exigencies of this new and intricate environment, nor equally are the few intelligent Negro characters. The desires of the one are too simple, the desires of the other too complex. From the white point of view, the standards of the one are too low and the standards of the other too high to be tolerated. The representative of the mass is regarded as a beast, the outstanding individual as a dangerous upstart. The result is in one case a despair in the face of helplessness, in the other case a rebellion against that helplessness. In both cases the hour bringing to the Negroes the knowledge and experience of race prejudice has arrived and the marshalling of forces proceeds rapidly under a blazing noon-day sun. There is a fundamental disharmony described at the heart of this milieu, due to an incompatibility of its racial groups which excludes the possibility of any coolnes or serenity of mood arising.

The tendency at last is to meet blow with blow. On the one side is shown the violent type of race prejudice which will not even stop with the dead. In "The Colonel's Dream" it commits the brutality of removing the coffin of a faithful Negro servant from the place assigned him by his appreciative and idealistic white master in his own burial ground: "Conspicuously nailed to the coffin lid was a sheet of white paper, upon which were some lines rudely scrawled in a handwriting that matched the spelling:

"'Kurnell French: Take notis. Berry yore ole nigger somewhar else. He can't stay in Oak Semitury. The majority of the white people of this town, who dident tend yore nigger funarl, woant have him there. Niggers by there selves, white peepul by there selves, and them that lives in our town must bide by our rules. By order of Cumitty.'"[7])

Or more destructive in result is when it leads to attack on the living, as witnessed in the race riot of "The Marrow of Tradition" or the lynching scene of "The Fire in the Flint".

But characters like Josh Green and Bob Harper do not allow themselves to be killed without first striking back. Josh gets his just revenge on the "poor white" villain, Mc Bane: "Armed with a huge bowie-knife, a relic of the civil war, which he had carried on his person for many years for a definite purpose, and which he had kept sharpened to a razor edge, he reached the line of the crowd. — — — A pistol-flame flashed in his face, but he went on, and raising his powerful right arm, buried his knife to the hilt in the heart of his enemy. When the crowd dashed forward to wreak vengeance on his dead body,

7) Chesnutt, Charles W.: *The Colonel's Dream.* p. 281.

they found him with a smile still on his face."[8]) Bob shoots
the white boy who has attacked his sister, as well as several
of the lynching mob which has pursued him, before his own
death. We have seen that in contrast to Josh and Bob, Dr. Miller and Dr. Kenneth Harper do not resort to violence or take
advantage of their golden opportunities for retaliation. Nevertheless their control only serves to prove the fineness of their
characters and does not lessen the tension in the air. We are
made to realize that if they are pushed an inch further the
control must snap and there will be battle to death. Even the
would-be temperate Kenneth is driven to this extreme of
feeling: "'I've tried — God knows I have — to keep away frcm
trouble with these white people in Central City. If they bother
me, I'm going to fight — you hear me — I'm going to fight
— and fight like hell! They'll get me in the end — I know
that — but before I go I'm going to take a few along with
me!'"[9]) Whether the attitude on the part of the whites in these
books is hatred, or fear or jealousy, on the part of the Negroes
bitterness, resentment, or despair, the component mood is a
black and powerful one.

There is nothing subtle about the mood of these propaganda
novels. It can be immediately sensed and has the strength of
simplicity and directness. All details of setting and incident,
all traits of character contribute to the one effect. This may be
done through the piling up of details and the complications
of plot in the earlier stories or in the economy of detail and
the concentration of plot in "The Fire in the Flint". In both
cases material superfluous or irrelevant to the creation of this
one effect is lacking, but in one case the lines are intricate and
winding, in the other they are straight and vigorous. They are
alike in their dependence on action and external event for the
creation of mood. Attitudes on the part of racial groups or individuals do not persist merely as mental states but express
themselves actively. It is the deed which counts. The assumption

---

8) Chesnutt, Charles W.: *The Marrow of Tradition.* p. 309.
9) White, Walter: *The Fire in the Flint.* p. 295.

is that the Negro inhabitants of Wellington might have survived an inimical attitude but not the race riot instigated by it. As a doctor, Miller might have more or less cheerfully worked against the distrustful attitude of white citizens by the persuasion of skilful work, but the burning down of his cherished hospital and the killing of his only child change the face of things. The ruin of his sister and the lynching of his brother have more effect on Kenneth than any amount of latent hate.

Thus when we examine the structure of these novels we find that the thought and feeling of Negro characters are conditioned by the swift movement of painful events, and that plots and subplots are well developed so as to convey that sense of injustice burning at the very heart of the dominant mood. Negroes feel that the white man is the aggressor, but that once the flint is struck the fire may leap out and destroy him. Injustices cannot be indefinitely borne especially when they are massed together so formidably. In "The Marrow of Tradition" alone a well-to-do and distinguished white woman refuses for years to recognize her deserving mulatto sister or even to give her the legal portion of the family property, a degenerate white "Southern gentleman" commits a gross crime and very cleverly manages to have the blame placed on an innocent and virtuous Negro servant, in addition to the already mentioned atrocities of Captain Mc Bane, expressed through the penal system and the Ku Klux Klan, and of politicians expressed through the race riot. The odds are overwhelmingly against the Negroes but the consequent sense of depression ordinarily to be expected is somewhat counteracted by the vigor they inject into the situation, fed by the courage born of despair.

The white heat of a summer's day brings a thunder storm to clear and cool the atmosphere, but in these books we see no further than the gathering, the breaking, and the raging of the storm. There is little choice between the discomfort caused by the intense heat and the strained and ominous atmosphere and that caused by the actual unleashing of the furious elements. The soft sunlight which was inseparable from the "peace before the storm" in the plantation stories is entirely a thing of the past, and now that storm eclipses even the powerful and steady rays of the noon-day sun, there is no light to relieve the gloom, no optimism or humour to lessen the tragedy. These novels are of serious intent and purpose. Instead of the "ignorance of bliss" there is a stern facing of the knowledge of evil. Instead of light touch and pastoral interlude there is heavy blow and tense melodrama. For the Negroes, fancy gives way to fact. Flirtations, feasts, and revival meetings give way to imprisonment on incomplete or false evidence, starvation due to economic exploitation and peonage, murder at the hands of a blood-thirsty mob. There is no time for Negro characters to go hunting or courting or dancing or to stop for leisurely chats with neighbors. The increased tempo of life and the pressure of hostile forces necessitate their conservation of energy in direct and purposeful ways whether it be positively, as in founding a hospital or organizing a coöperative farming society for their own dark group, or negatively, as in their various efforts to strike back at the other white group. There is a sense of urgency and struggle, of strife and force which strains and deafens and bruises.

Undercurrents.

With "The Autobiography of an Ex-Coloured Man" and its urban-cosmopolitan instead of small town setting, its worldly and individualistic instead of its idealistic and social minded characters, is introduced into the Negro novel a corresponding change of mood. Evidently the din of battle has died down and the storm is over. Yet we find no bright sunshine returning to flood a green and peaceful landscape. The afternoon is cloudy and at times slightly chilly as we hurry along crowded city streets, just enough to make us draw our silk mantles about us. It is time for musicales, art-exhibits, afternoon teas and other social gatherings and we are exposed to the suave and gracious atmosphere of social intercourse. Velvet gowns in place of rags and tatters, dinner parties with gleaming glass and silver ware in place of church suppers with thick mugs and plates, remind us of how far we have progressed from the plantation life, while the presence of leisurely soft-voiced ladies and of calm, controlled gentlemen remove us equally from the loud tones and the excited denunciations rife in the Southern small town.

The mores of this mulatto society group demand a certain restraint at least on the surface. It is not considered to be in good taste to reveal signs of strong emotions before others. It is better to keep a gay and lively or even a bored and indifferent exterior than one indicative of any passionate or violent feeling: "Philadelphians were not as a rule as strikingly dressed as the folks, say, from Washington, but they had a better time" while the Baltimore people "were a cross between the Philadelphians and the gay Washingtonians who played about in very distinct groups, superb in their fashionable clothes and their deep assurance."[10]) The resulting atmosphere is matter-of-fact rather than melodramatic and this impression is conveyed even by the style of this group of novels. The flow of words describing social life is smooth and even, often prosaic, not chaotic or striving after effect: "We walked a short distance up the Champs Elysées and sat for a while in chairs along the sidewalk, watching the passing crowds on foot and in carriages. It was with reluctance that I went back to the hotel for dinner. After dinner we went to one of the summer theatres, and after the performance my friend took me to a large café on one of the Grands Boulevards. Here it was that I had the first glimpse of the French life of popular literature, so different from real French life. There were several hundred people, men and women, in the place drinking, smoking, talking, and listening to the music. My millionaire friend and I took seats at a table where we sat smoking and watching the crowd."[11])

Here we have the mulatto in the midst of white European society but there are the same standards of pleasant and gracious living as those being adopted by the well-bred upper circles of Negroes in Harlem, Philadelphia, Baltimore, Washing-

---

10) Fauset, Jessie R.: *There is Confusion.* p. 116.
11) Johnson, James W.: *The Autobiography of an Ex-Coloured Man.* p. 129.

ton, the same casual, leisurely, and moderate mood enlivened by artistic and intellectual interests and by the interplay of witty and animated conversation. According to the hero of "The Autobiography of an Ex-Coloured Man", this parallel between the upper group of both races is little realized, especially since the very existence of such a group among the Negroes has been seldom recognized in life and even less in literature: "His character has been established as a happy-go-lucky, laughing, shuffling, banjo-picking being, and the reading public has not yet been prevailed upon to take him seriously. His efforts to elevate himself socially are looked upon as a sort of absurd caricature of 'white civilization'. A novel dealing with coloured people who lived in respectable homes and amidst a fair degree of culture and who naturally acted 'just like white folks' would be taken in a comic-opera sense",[12]) and yet in Harlem "there sat the most advanced coloured Americans, beautifully dressed, beautifully trained".[13]) It has evidently become a function of these novels to make known the habits and thoughts of this class of Negroes, thus fulfilling "the opportunity of the future Negro novelist and poet to give the country something new and unknown"[14]) foreseen by the hero of "The Autobiography of an Ex-Coloured Man" in 1912.

The mood is of necessity tempered not only by this modulation of style and by this new purpose replacing the heavy or the short, staccato style and the direct propaganda purpose of the last group of novels, but also by a decrease of action and plot. This decrease is to be expected, for, as the sense for the need of propagandizing is lost, in proportion will be lost the stress on the story. When it is no longer necessary to prove a point through dramatic action to inflame the emotions of the readers, the novelist can subordinate the use of sustained and detailed and climactic action to other factors. In this case it does not

12) Johnson, James W.: *The Autobiography of an Ex-Coloured Man.* p. 168.
13) Fauset, Jessie R.: *Plum Bun.* p. 216.
14) Ibid. p. 168.

mean a return to the particular form of the plantation stories. We are taken from these earlier short stories and from the plot novels constructed on the more traditional lines to what might well be considered the psychological novel. This is quite in keeping with the new milieu and its new type of individual, for the way to the understanding of a more subtle, sophisticated and complex type which has been trained to control will not be through an observation of what they do, which may often be deceiving, but through insight into what they feel and think. It is only the psychological method that can take us below the surface of this polished group to establish contact with undercurrents. A milieu characterized by refinement and culture cannot be adequately treated by the comparatively simple and direct technique of narration. It requires the sharp-edged yet finely tempered weapon of analysis and introspection.

The moment this weapon is used, the moment we come to feel that our afternoon mood has nuances, that it is more than what it seems to be on its lovely and placid surface. We come to understand that control can hide wounds beneath, that attitudes of gaiety, satisfaction, or boredom can be various masques for discontentment. Our realization does not spring from casual study of the background but from acquaintance with the motives and moods and inner experiences of the individuals placed against it, and it is at this point we must admit the presence of disharmony. Our mulatto heroines have no tendency to idealize and adapt unquestioningly even to such pleasant surroundings as theirs. While depending on and participating in it, they are nevertheless aware of its superficialities: "The tea to which she had so suddenly made up her mind to go she found boring beyond endurance, insipid drinks, dull conversation, stupid men."[15]) There is no especial indictment against Negro society for being this way but rather a dissatisfaction with the type of civilization which encourages and sets the standards for it, of which it is after all only an imitation, modelled on the same lines. The immediate cause for discon-

---

15) Larsen, Nella: *Quicksand*. p. 114.

tent, then, must be traced back to the original source in the white world, and we have seen in the previous chapter the restlessness which association in its upper circles brought to those mulattoes „passing" as white. The complaint of Mimi, ‘"I really am sick of the same old routine, there's never anything new and it all seems so futile, wasting so much time'", is dealt with summarily by her white husband — ‘"that comes from reading these stories by fellows like Dreiser and Sinclair Lewis — I told you they'd make you unhappy. That's why I leave those birds alone — they're always picking flaws in the best civilization the world's ever seen'", and ironically reënforced by her, ‘"bathtubs and radio and big business, eh' Mimi murmured softly, perhaps a shade too softly."[16])

We have already analyzed more in detail the various reasons for the incompatibility of such characters with their environment, connected with race prejudice and consciousness, and sometimes we recognized that it was only a preoccupation with personal troubles which created a tension. This is plain in the triangular situation of „Passing". Irene naturally belongs to this social world but the strain she is undergoing in relation to her husband and Clare makes its usually agreeable pastimes unbearable to her: "Hideous. A great weariness came over her. Even the small exertion of pouring golden tea into thin old cups seemed almost too much for her. She went on pouring. Made repetitions of her smile. Answered questions. Manufactured conversation. She thought: 'I feel like the oldest person in the world with the longest stretch of life before me' — — Chatter, chatter, chatter. Someone asked her a question. She glanced up with what she felt was a rigid smile — — Yes, life went on precisely as before. It was only she that had changed. Knowing, stumbling on this thing had changed her. It was as if in a house long dim, a match had been struck, showing ghastly shapes where had been only blurred shadows."[17]) Equally we know that the thoughts of Clare and Brian are far removed, and quite foreign to this tea party and to the other social functions they attend at

---

16) White, Walter: *Flight.* p. 265.
17) Larsen, Nella: *Passing.* pp. 165—166.

this period. We see into the private emotional lives of these three people so hidden to those about them. Irene has "an almost uncontrollable impulse to laugh, to scream, to hurl things about, to shock people, to hurt them, to make them notice her, to be aware of her suffering."[18]) But the significant feature is that she does not succumb to the impulse, and no one suspects it.

Thus we are led to feel, through the course of these novels, a strong undertone of unhappiness, whether for personal or social, racial or more distinctly human causes, which at the same time remains an undertone. The individuals are products of their environment and regulated largely by its laws and customs whether they wish it or no. In spite of all sorts of disturbing passions, radical ideas, and disrupting conflicts within, they do not as a rule openly defy and actively oppose themselves to the proscriptions of an irrational race prejudice or the conventions of their own "respectable" Negro group. They may escape from one city to another, one country to another, or even one race to another, but the causes of their unhappiness are too deep-rooted to be removed by geographical flight and consequently the mood created by an acquaintance with their lives is tinged with the weariness of futility and baffled hopes. The paralysis of doubt and disillusionment to which finely organized minds are prone seems to have fastened on their limbs and incapacitated them from running a race to victory. There is no fresh blood, no animating vigour here. Secret complexes, hidden sources of conflict and maladjustment have sapped away vital energy. We cannot lay our finger on the exact spot generating the trouble, for the introspective process which we are allowed to share with the characters is too involved and vague. At the same time we cannot demonstrate clearly the manifestations of the trouble, so smoothed over are they by habit patterns of calm and control. For example, there are no such tragic and dramatic endings here as in "The Fire in the Flint". The endings are what might be called modified happy ones with a certain measure of satisfaction awaiting individuals, arising from a state of mind

18) Ibid. p. 167.

and not from an external event. Nella Larsen's two novels could be considered exceptions but even in these cases the real nature of the tragedy lies in the deep psychological suffering, on quite another plane from the "battle, murder, sudden death" type of situation. Therefore we are left finally with the experience of a mood revealing neither happiness nor unhappiness sharply, containing both in a mild form due to their mutual process of modification. The air is temperate on this summer afternoon which is cloudy, without extremes of sunshine or rain.

Abandon.

But with the coming of night the clouds give way before the brilliance of the mood. Any vagueness or monotony is dispelled by the presence of vivid, strong contrasts, by moonlight and black shadows. In our last group of proletarian novels we find the mood dependent once more on the existence of direct, powerful, simple emotions as in the propaganda novels. The uncertainties and futilities of the preceding group are cast aside together with the repressions or suppressions which fed them. The hour has struck for living intensely and freely and for following with abandon the path indicated by one's instinctive nature. Yet the particular emotions which spring into force are not again those earlier ones of anger or hate, but rather the two extremes of joy and sorrow. Also, there is not a mixture of happiness and unhappiness resulting in something luke-warm. The joy and the pain are keen, distinct entities accelerating each other rather than modifying to form a third entity. The positive is enhanced by the negative and the negative by the positive and both are integral parts of rich, full-blooded living: "Here are none of the well-patterned, well-made emotions of the respectable world. A laugh might finish in a sob, a moan end in hilarity. — — — — Simple, raw emotions and real. They may frighten and repel refined souls, because they are too intensely real, just as a simple savage stands dismayed before nice emotions that he instantly perceives are false."[19])

19) McKay, Claude: *Home to Harlem.* pp. 337—338.

A light-hearted spontaneous mood is overflowing from books like "Banjo", "Home to Harlem", and "The Walls of Jericho". The characters have escaped from the bondage of respectability and are tending to make rather than to be made by their environment. It is as if discontent, doubt, and passivity were discarded along with the conventions and habits of a middle-class educated society, and a new harmony between individual and surroundings created through a positive will-to-live. The policy of adaptation or of rebellion is adopted instinctively according to its expediency in the immediate situation and its bearing upon the whole question of enjoyment. We have already observed that to the beach boys and to the manual workers or loafers in Harlem happiness is not something to be longed for but to be achieved by direct and unreflecting means. We sense their astonishing success and see it as a survival quality closely connected with their boundless vitality in turn closely connected with their primitive and natural approach to life and its would-be problems. Banjo is the embodiment of this approach: "That this primitive child, this kinky-headed, big-laughing black boy of the world, did not go down and disappear under the serried crush of trampling white feet; that he managed to remain on the scene, not wordly-wise, not 'getting there', yet not machine-made, nor poor-in-spirit like the regimented creatures of civilization was baffling to civilized understanding. Before the grim, pale rider-down of souls he went his careless way with a primitive hoofing and a grin."[20])

It is implied that such laughter is not to be won except by a disregard for traditional moral codes and for social obligations. To them nothing is good or bad, right or wrong in itself. A course of action must be chosen or not chosen in relation to the pleasure it brings or does not bring: "Ray's thoughts were far and away beyond the right and wrong of the matter. He had been dreaming of what joy it would be to go vagabonding with Banjo. Stopping here and there, staying as long as the feeling held in the ports where black men assembled for the great transport lines,

---

20) McKay, Claude: *Banjo*. p. 314.

loafing after their labors long enough to laugh and love and jazz and fight." The whole method of procedure followed by these Negroes of vagabond spirit is aptly summed up by Banjo: "'All we can do is grab our chance every time it comes our way.'"[21])

The note of recklessness and abandon is inseparable from the festive mood of a moon-light night, with societal inhibitions fully released through the magic effect of wine and song and dance. The instinctive life of these proletarians is quite another thing from that of the plantation-slave type. Theirs was the naturalness of ignorance and early morning, while our vagabonds are well-schooled in the ways of the world, along with all their simplicity of nature. They would have been extremely bored by the religious and social pastimes of the plantation community, and demand instead the strong stimulants of jazz and city night-life: "Black lovers of life caught up in their own free native rhythm, threaded to a remote scarce-remembered past celebrating the midnight hours in themselves, for themselves, of themselves, in a house in Fifteenth Street, Philadelphia."[22]) We can almost hear them "humming in harmony, barbaric harmony, joy-drunk, chasing out the shadow of the moment before."[23]) When a band of such Negroes is playing banjo, ukelele, mandolin, guitar, and horn together in the crowded cafés of Marseilles, the very atmosphere becomes charged with the intensity of the strong and ecstatic emotional response: "Shake to the loud music of life playing to the primeval round of life. Rough rhythm of darkly-carnal life. Strong surging flux of profound currents forced into shallow channels. Play that thing! One movement of the thousand movements of the eternal life-flow. Shake that thing! In the face of the shadow of Death. Treacherous hand of murderous Death, lurking in sinister alleys, where the shadows of life dance, nevertheless, to their music of life. Death over there! Life over here! Shake down Death and forget his commerce, his purpose, his haunting presence in a great

---

21) McKay, Claude: *Banjo*. p. 319.

22) McKay, Claude: *Home to Harlem*. p. 197.

23) Ibid. p. 54.

shaking orgy. Dance down the Death of these days, the Death of these ways in shaking that thing. Jungle jazzing, Orient wriggling, civilized stepping. Shake that thing! Sweet dancing thing of primitive joy, perverse pleasure, prostitute ways, many-colored variations of the rhythm, savage, barbaric, refined — eternal rhythm of the mysterious, magical, magnificent — the dance divine of life ..."[24])

There seems to be an identification here with some universal force too powerful, some well-spring of ecstasy too deep to be touched by the activity of race prejudice. The vitality of these characters is so positive that it cannot be easily poisoned. The arrows of would-be attackers seem to glance off without harming. This is in contrast to the mulatto heroines whose habit of introspection helped to make them more sensitive to the antagonism and injustices of a white world even while their habits of control and moderation enabled them to disguise the serious nature of the wounds and to refuse morbid and exclusive preoccupation with them. The very fact that they avoided direct and drastic treatment out in the open daylight meant often secret if slow infection. Prevention of the wounds in the first place was not likely in their case where the tendency to analyze their emotional responses caused them to be dominated by feelings, which are complex and derived and attached to concepts, rather than by emotions which are primary and possessing the strength of narrow concentration. A sensitively organized person subject to all the fine shades of feelings appears to be more receptive and exposed to unhappiness in all its degrees and varieties than the person whose extraverted nature calls for action rather than thought and sweeps him along on the full tide of his emotions in an uncomplicated stimulus-response fashion.

This means that novels dealing with such characters do not try to be psychological. Jake and Banjo and Shine are too obviously what they are to lend themselves to psychological treatment. They have not too many selves to know the one. There

---

24) McKay, Claude: *Banjo*. pp. 57—58.

is no need to use the method of dissection and probing beneath the surface. They stand squarely, and look us frankly in the face before going about their affairs. At the same time they do not lend themselves to all the dramatic action and set forms of a conventional plot. They escape stereotyped treatment of any kind and are quite unsuited to be the figures in a serious, sustained, and logical train of events. Banjo belongs perfectly to a story with such a subtitle as "A Novel Without a Plot". This corresponds to the evident non-propaganda purposes of these writers who are bent on evoking a mood of pleasure, adequately done by the relating of casual episode without stress on continuity and climax. We have already noted the dependence of the plantation tales on episode and the external events of daily life but there we found a certain finish of technique quite lacking, for example, in the formless drifting organization and the slangy vagabond style of Claude McKay's novels. In every way, then, the carefree mood of lively and spontaneous play is created, through the type of characters, through their reaction to their milieu, and through the particular manner of treatment chosen by the authors.

And this manner of treatment retains its casualness and its light-heartedness even when race issues are touched upon. Instead of the strained effect which the propaganda novel writers produced by earnest exhortation and fiery paragraphs, or the depressing effect which the next group of writers brings about by pictures of thwarted lives, whenever such issues are introduced, we find ourselves put into a state of relaxation by these writers and their predilection for humorous touch, ironical twist, and satirical thrust. Here is no one-sided, defensive point of view, or a call to reform of social abuses, but a capacity to make fun of both racial groups indiscriminately that indicates a remarkable freedom from subjectivity and emotionalism.

This is clearly evidenced by Rudolph Fisher's approach in "The Walls of Jericho". Neither black nor white characters are spared from a mischievous interpretation. We can visualize the two secretly devoted but ostensibly antagonistic companions, Jinx and Bubber, in the heat of daily argument: "Jinx was thin and elongated, habitually stooped in bearing, lean and sinewy, with freckled skin of a slick deep yellow and a chronically querulous voice" while "Bubber was as different from Jinx as any man could be, short, round, and bulging, with a complexion bordering on the invisible", so pitch black was it.[25]) Typical is the scene in the poolroom when even the weather proves a bone of contention:

"'Sho is hot,' Bubber had commented, missing a shot and wiping a glistening brow on his arm.

'Don' blame d' weather jes' 'cause you can't shoot pool', returned Jinx. 'I likes warm weather like this.'

'Can't see what fo'.'

'Well — we got to work outdoors, ain't we?'

'Yea — in d' heat.'

'Aw right. In warm weather you kin find some place out-doors to cool off, but when it's cold, damn if you kin find any place outdoors to git warm.'

'Cold weather fo' mine.' disagreed Bubber.

'Shuh!'

'Yas suh. We got to wear clo'es, ain't we?'

Uh-huh.'

'Well, when it's cold you kin put on enough to git warm, but when it's hot, damn if you kin take off enough to git cool!'"[26])

As is to be expected, the humour is more gentle in dealing with these proletarian characters whom we love the more for their innocent and refreshing foibles than with the altruistic and intellectual pretensions of the mulatto Mr. Potter or the white Miss Cramp. There is something ludicrous about "the ex-tremely proper J. Pennington Potter, a 'social worker' with a windy, pompous voice and a deep devotion to convention" especially when he is pictured to us as "a plump little sausage of a man, whose skin seemed stuffed to the limit with the importance of what it contained".[27]) But the satire of the social

25) Fisher, Rudolph: *The Walls of Jericho*. p. 6.
26) Ibid. pp. 143—144.
27) Ibid. pp. 39, 36.

reform attitude is best seen in the person of Miss Cramp who for fifteen years "had been devoting her life to the service of mankind": "Miss Agatha Cramp had, among other things, a sufficiently large store of wealth and a sufficiently small store of imagination to want to devote her entire life to Service; in fact, to Social Service on a large scale."[28]) The direction which it takes usually depends upon the racial groups to which her various maids belong, whether French, Polish, or Russian, and now that she has a Negro maid the possibilities of helping in their "uplift" occur to her for the first time. Hitherto it has only been the "remoter disasters" and distant fields which have stirred her imagination: "Over the slaughter of Armenians by Turks she had once sobbed bitterly and even over the devastation of the Japanese by earth-quake she had mourned a little — — But Negroes she had always accepted with horses, mules, and motors, and though they had brushed her shoulder, they had never actually entered her head."[29])

But the full measure of her ridiculous inadequacy is displayed when, once interested in these "savages" within her own country, she attends a large Negro dance in Harlem and unsuspectingly engages in earnest conversation on the subject the seemingly white but in reality mulatto Mr. Merritt. Typical of her naiveté is her remark to him on skin-color: "'But I was just thinking. These people have been out of their native element only three or four hundred years, and just see what it has done to their complexions! It's hard to believe that just three hundred years in our country has brought about such a great variety in the color of the black race — — Chiefly the climate, I should judge. Don't you think?'"[30]) We can hardly censor the sophisticated Merritt for not failing to take advantage of such gullibility.

But it is the author of "Black No More" who carries to its extreme point not only the humorous exposé of self-righteous and pretentious respectability as such, but the satire on its manifestations in both racial groups alike. As we have seen, this

28) Ibid.p. 59.
29) Ibid. p. 62.
30) Ibid. p. 113.

novel is not, strictly speaking, proletarian, and has much more of a plot, but it belongs to this group in spirit partly because of its reaction to middle class standards and conventions and partly because of its flippant and bantering attitude towards racial issues formerly regarded as a painful and serious business. There is no mercy shown to either white, mulatto, or black leaders who are often caricatured by a single phrase. We have Dr. Napoleon Wellington Jackson, "tall, lanky — — sooty black, very broad shouldered, with long, ape-like arms, a diminutive egg-shaped head" in contrasting color to Mr. Walter Williams, "a tall heavy-set white man with pale blue eyes, wavy auburn hair, and a militant lantern jaw" who can very safely feel "proud to be a Negro"![31]) Colonel Mortimer Roberts, "a great mountain of blackness" is an impressive figure beside Mr. Claude Spelling, "a scared-looking little brown man with big ears", or the statistician, Dr. Joseph Bonds, "a little rat-faced Negro with protruding teeth."[32]) The two profiteering white manufacturers are exposed, the "corpulent under-sized" Blickdoff, and Hortzenboff, "a beer barrel on stilts", as well as the exclusive Mr. Arthur Snobbcraft, president of the Anglo-Saxon Association, yet "suspiciously swarthy for an Anglo-Saxon!"[33])

Behind the physical appearances are the motives of individuals and groups, equally to be satirized. On the Negro side is the "National Social Equality League" battling for social equalities but actually rejoicing in that discrimination against Negroes on which their work and large salaries depend. According to the writer, characteristic of the seemingly idealistic but really opportunistic aims of these "race lovers" is their haughty and dignified leader, Dr. Shakespeare Agamemnon Beard: "For a mere six thousand dollars a year, the learned doctor wrote scholarly and biting editorials in "The Dilemma" denouncing the Caucasians whom he secretly admired and lauding the great-

---

31) Schuyler, George S.: *Black No More.* pp. 91—94.

32) Ibid. p. 96.

33) Ibid. p. 166.

ness of the Negroes whom he alternately pitied and despised. In limpid prose he told of the sufferings and privations of the downtrodden black workers with whose lives he was totally and thankfully unfamiliar."[34]) It is significant that many Negroes who are avowedly patriotic to their race take quick advantage of Dr. Crookman's medical treatment for changing them to white men in appearance. They are justified by the doctor: "They are all good Race men, you know, even if they have, like the rest of our staff, taken the treatment.'"[35])

On the white side is the "Knights of Nordica", modern version of the "Ku Klux Klan", capitalizing the ignorances and fears of "poor whites" through scheming leadership: "Rev. Henry Givens, Imperial Grand Wizard of the Knights of Nordica, was a short, wizened, almost-bald, bull-voiced ignorant ex-evangelist" who had not only "toiled diligently to increase the prestige, power and membership of the defunct Ku Klux Klan", but had also "been a very hard worker in withdrawing as much money from its treasury as possible."[36]) Publicity for this organization demands making speeches over the radio to large American audiences: "In his long address he discussed the foundations of the Republic, anthropology, psychology, miscegenation, coöperation with Christ, getting right with God, curbing Bolshevism, the bane of birth control, the menace of the modernists, science versus religion, and many other subjects of which he was totally ignorant."[37])

Employed to do research work for the Anglo-Saxon Association is the pedantic white scholar and statistican, Dr. Samuel Buggerie: "His well-known work, 'The Fluctuation of the Sizes of Left Feet among the Assyrians during the Ninth Century before Christ', had been favorably commented upon by several reviewers, one of whom had actually read it. — — — In several brilliant monographs he had proved that rich people have smaller families than the poor; that imprisonment does not stop

34) Schuyler, George S.: *Black No More*. p. 89.
35) Ibid. p. 83.
36) Ibid. p. 62.
37) Ibid. p. 161.

crime; that laborers usually migrate in the wake of high wages. In his most recent article in a very intellectual magazine read largely by those who loafed for a living, he had proved statistically that unemployment and poverty are principally a state of mind. This contribution was enthusiastically hailed by scholars and especially by business men as an outstanding contribution to contemporary thought."[38]) The particular task of Dr. Buggerie, himself a "professional Anglo-Saxon", is to separate "the poor whites from the imitation whites" by a study of their family trees and thus, by consequent laws against intermarriage, to protect that racial purity and Nordic supremacy which had produced such a fine specimen of humanity as himself![39])

While the farcical situations and the ironic observations of this novel are directed against various practices in the American scene as a whole from politics and government to religion, the main butt of ridicule is the practice in the field of race relations. When, through the fantastic and revolutionizing scheme of "Black No More" it grows more and more impossible to distinguish between the races except that the whitened Negroes are if anything whiter than those born white, the absurdity of the whole question becomes patent in the reversed situation: the beginnings of prejudice against white instead of dark skins, and of subsequent efforts to stain and darken the complexion artificially. The popular philanthropic organization now is the "Down - with - white - Prejudice - League"![40]) When the Negro novelist has reached the stage where he not only endeavors to show theoretically through the medium of his characters the strength and attractiveness of the instinctive gift of laughter, but also as in the case of Fisher and Schuyler, seeks to apply it on a more intellectual plane in his attitude towards both himself and others, Negroes and whites equally, then we are projected into an entirely new mood marking a distinctive stage in the development of race consciousness.

38) Schuyler, George S.: *Black No More*. p. 169.
39) Ibid. p. 170.
40) Ibid. p. 247.

But the fact that underneath the laughter and intense joy is sorrow and intense pain is a truth that even this group of novelists does not lose sight of. Characters like Ray and Sandy have already indicated to us that joy is the child of pain and attains to life only by struggle and courage and the will-to-live so inherent in their race, while books like "Cane" and "Tropic Death" would remind us that strong emotions have their black as well as their bright aspects. They concentrate not on the moonlight and revelry of the night known to the Banjos and Jakes, but on the silence and suffering in its deep shadows. This peasant-proletarian type is not immune from the tragic aspects of life, any more than the worldly, professional, middle class type, although the source is not particularized on race problems as in the characters of the propaganda novels, nor connected with the intellectual doubts and personality problems of the mulatto heroines in the psychological novels. Instead, theirs is the same instinctive and whole-hearted response to the elemental tragedy in life itself, not to be analyzed or understood, but only experienced directly, which is made at other times and places to joy.

The West Indian peasants in „Tropic Death" suffer at the hands of natural and supernatural forces as of something inevitable and incomprehensible. The drought brings death to Coggins' little daughter and "inertia swept over him".[41]) Miss Ella screams when she sees that her would-be lover is burned in the fire and afterwards, "it was then she realized how for nothing was her bucket of water".[42]) Philip, swimmimg in the sea, is powerless to escape the man-eating shark. The accident occurs before the eyes of his brother, and is over, simply and irrevocably: "And again the fish turned. It scraped the waters with its deadly fins."[43]) The death of Zink Diggs through the potency of the black magic she had designed for another is given sharp

41) Walrond, Eric: *Tropic Death*. p. 31.
42) Ibid. p. 58.
43) Ibid. p. 114.

actuality by the mere presence near her of the cat, "likewise dead".[44])

Lack of analysis opens the way for the intuitive and mystic approach to life. Clear understandings are replaced by dim and poignant realizations. We find characters in "Cane" seeking truth and knowing pain not through cold concepts but through an emotional awareness of throbbing universal forces. There is a difference about Fern and Avey whom many men have loved physically but never realized spiritually because they are in contact with something deep and mysterious and absorbing: "But though I held her tightly in my arms, she was way away — — it was an impersonal smile, never for me — — Avey was as silent as those great trees whose tops we looked down upon. She has always been like that."[45])

Fern is even more the embodiment of mystery and its accompanying pain: "Face flowed into her eyes — — — Her eyes, unusually weird and open, held me. Held God. He flowed in as I've seen the countryside flow in. Seen men. — — — They were strange eyes. In this, that they sought nothing — that is, nothing that was obvious and tangible, and that one could see, and they gave the impression that nothing was to be denied — — — — Fern's eyes desired nothing that you could give her; there was no reason why they should withhold."[46]) She has some deep source of reality inaccessible to her practical and plodding neighbors in southern Georgia. The intensity of her response to it finally breaks her silence and transports her into frenzy: "I must have done something — what, I don't know, in the confusion of my emotions. She sprang up. Rushed some distance from me. Fell to her knees, and began swaying, swaying. Her body was tortured with something it could not let out. Like boiling sap it flooded arms and fingers till she shook them as if they burned her. It found her throat, and spattered inarticulately in plaintive, convulsive sounds, mingled with calls to Christ Je-

44) Ibid. p. 182.

45) Toomer, Jean: *Cane.* pp. 79, 81—82.

46) Ibid. pp. 24—25.

sus. And then she sang, brokenly. A Jewish cantor singing with a broken voice. A child's voice, uncertain, or an old man's. Dusk hid her; I could hear only her song. It seemed to me as though she were pounding her head in anguish upon the ground. I rushed to her. She fainted in my arms."[47]) We have here an ecstatic abandon to spiritual suffering comparable to the ecstatic abandon of Claude Mc Kay's beach boys to joy and jazz, both of them evidently meant to be the expressions, at opposite ends, of an identification with universal forces far removed from problems of race, yet intimately connected with the emotional gifts of the race.

A brooding sense of strangeness and pain is instilled into the mood of these two books of Eric Walrond's and Jean Toomer's not alone through the kind of characters but through the use of poetic style and suggestive sketch in place of clear and prosaic style or orderly plot. A single phrase suffices to convey the unanswerable experience of physical atrophy or death, as we have seen in "Tropic Death", or of spiritual astrophy or death in "Cane". It is enough to tell us about Karintha that "the soul of her was a growing thing ripened too soon"[48]) or about another that "her soul is like a little thrust-tailed dog that follows her, whimpering".[49]) All the impotent sensitivity of Kabnis is revealed in his cry, "'God, do not torture me with beauty'" with its reaction, "'God, he doesn't exist, but nevertheless he is ugly'".[50]) When we learn that "emptiness is a thing that grows by being moved" and that "the space-dark air grows softly luminous" it is suggestive. The mood of night time is increased by a chance sentence in "Cane": "night winds in Georgia are vagrant poets, whispering",[51]) or in "Tropic Death": "All the thwarted sounds of creation rose to a mighty murmur in the obscuring night."[52]) When it is the intention

---

47) Ibid. p. 32.
48) Ibid. p. 4.
49) Ibid. p. 102.
50) Ibid. p. 162.
51) Ibid. p. 157.
52) Walrond, Eric: *Tropic Death*. p. 201.

to evoke a mood of suffering which has its roots in cosmic pain rather than in the local pain attendant on race prejudice, then lyrical and poetic prose may often be more effective than naturalistic and detailed prose. Also an atmosphere pervades each short story or sketch quite aside from any action on the part of the characters, dependent instead on situations and relationship. More than any other outstanding works of fiction by Negroes, "Cane" and "Tropic Death" reveal almost an entire absence of plot quite consistent with their greatest distance from those propaganda motives which tend to rely upon it. And as a result of such factors, these two books more than the others tend to arouse us by subtle means to a sense of the tragedy at the heart of existence itself, which colors the mood with the deepest poignancy.

Pain is all pervading here, and has a reality even separate from, no matter how much intensified by persons and situations. It is as if there were a throbbing presence in the air itself, and as if nature conspired to sustain it. In "Tropic Death" nature is not friendly to man. There is something brilliant and intense about it, something ominous and terrifying, and its beauty is the kind that hurts. The vividness of coloring has portent. It may be in the snakes crawling on the earth: "Gorgeously bedecked ones — two inches of blue, two of mauve, two of yellow, two of black. Some of the coral ones, a yard or more in length, lovely crown jewels. Green snakes, black snakes, reaching up to the shady bush and swamp — drowsy on the sandy road",[53]) so that we sense disaster ahead for the ignorant Seenie. Or it may be in the sunset clouds of the sky so that we anticipate the misfortune of Miss Ella: "The western sky of Barbadoes was ablaze. A mixture of fire and gold, it burned, and burned, — into one vast sulphurous mass. It burned the houses, the trees, the window panes. The burnt glass did amazing color somer- saults—turned brown and gold and lavender and red. It poured a burning liquid over the gap. It colored the water in the ponds a fierce dull yellowish gold. It flung on the corn and the peas

---

53) Walrond, Eric: *Tropic Death.* p. 194.

and the star apples a lavender glow. It pitched its golden, flaming, iridescent shadow upon the lush of paw-paw and sunflower. It withered the petals of rose or sweet pea or violet or morning glory. Its flame upon the earth was mighty. Sunset over the gap paralyzed."[54])

There is cruel intensity of heat as well as of color in these tropic lands. It is a furious "broiling hot" sun, a "roaring sun" which keeps up "its irrepressible sizzling", "bright as a scimitar", "immortal, barbaric".[55]) One gasps at "the consequences of the sun's wretched fury" bringing dizziness and the unrelieved dryness of draught. The soil becomes "hard, brittle", the crops withered, the roads covered with white marl dust, and even the village dogs, "hunting for eggs to suck, fowls to kill, paused amidst the yellow stalks of cork-dry canes to pant, or drop, exhausted, sun-smitten". "It was a dizzy spectacle" when the sun "wrung toll of the earth" this way.[56]) Under it, the sea "was angry", "shone like a sheet of blazing zinc", and "lay torpid, sizzling — — Another time it would turn with the cannon roar of the sun, red. Nor was it the red of fire or of youth, of roses or of red tulips. But a sullen, grizzled red — — the red of a red-hot oven".[57]) "O tireless, sleepless sun!" baking and frying, burning and blistering all living things and creatures to the point of exhaustion.[58]) After sunset comes night, and "falling night buried the sun's wreckage"[59]) but this only deepens the tragedy of night by adding to its natural burden of sorrow.

The aspect of nature is softer in "Cane". We are in the milder Southland, and between brilliant sunset and black night there is dusk, conveying its mood of mystery, haunting sights and sounds and silences. But the throbbing pain is still there, not sharp, but poignant and longing for the ease of fulfilment:

54) Walrond, Eric: *Tropic Death*. p. 54.
55) Ibid. pp. 257, 239, 143, 250, 261.
56) Ibid. pp. 17, 18, 19.
57) Ibid. pp. 239, 65.
58) Ibid. p. 241.
59) Ibid. p. 242.

"Dusk, suggesting the almost imperceptible procession of giant trees, settled with a purple haze about the cane. I felt strange, as I always do in Georgia, particularly at dusk. I felt that things unseen to men were tangibly immediate. It would not have surprised me had I had a vision — — — When one is on the soil of one's ancestors, almost anything can come to one."[60]) Associated with the dusk is an appeal to our various senses. "Up from the deep dusk" we see the full moon rise and smell the pine trees or the cane: "And all around the air was heavy with the scent of boiling cane — — — the scent of cane came from the copper pan and drenched the forest and the hill that sloped to factory town beneath its fragrance."[61] We either feel a palpitating silence or hear strange songs at this time: "The slow rhythm of her song grew agitant and restless. Rusty black and tan spotted hounds, lying in the dark corners of porches or prowling around back-yards, put their noses in the air and caught its tremor. They began plaintively to yelp and howl. Chickens woke up and cackled. Intermittently, all over the countryside dogs barked and roosters crowed as if heralding a weird dawn or some ungodly awakening. The women sang lustily. Their songs were cottonwads to stop their ears."[62])

These songs are called forth by the sadness of dusk and coming night, and by the evil of the moon: "Glowing like a fired pine-knot, it illumined the great door and soft showered the Negro shanties aligned along the single street of factory town. The full moon in the great door was an omen. Negro women improvised songs against its spell."[63]) Mysterious forces are at work as night draws near, and the shadow of Africa, the birth place of the race and its superstitions, seems to fall across this Southern community: "Echoes, like rain, sweep the valley. Dusk takes the polish from the rails. Lights twinkle in scattered houses. From far away, a sad strong song. Pungent and composite, the smell of farmyards is the fragrance of the wo-

---

60) Toomer, Jean: *Cane*. p. 31.
61) Ibid. p. 54.
62) Ibid. p. 53.
63) Ibid. p. 51.

man. She does not sing; her body is a song. She is in the forest, dancing. Torches flare — — — ju ju men, gree gree, witch doctors — — — torches go out — — — The Dixie pike has grown from a goat path in Africa."[64])

This night in "Cane„ has creative possibilities and would remind us again that hope arises out of the greatest darkness: "Night throbs a womb-song to the South. Cane-and-cotton-fields, pine forests, cypress swamps, saw-mills, and factories are fecund at her touch. Night's womb-song sets them singing."[65]) It is true that sunrise and a new day come after the night: "Outside, the sun arises from its cradle in the tree-tops of the forest. Shadows of pines are dreams the sun shakes from its eyes. The sun arises. Gold-glowing child, it steps into the sky and sends a birth-song slanting down gray dust streets and sleepy windows of the southern town."[66]) Yet we are never supposed to forget here that night, with all the forces in life it symbolizes, is fundamental, that it is the underlying condition out of which a new morning must emerge.

Our first impression of the mood which these different groups in Negro fiction have occasioned is one of variety. From the sunny pleasantness of the plantation stories we passed to the despair and hopelessness or the bitterness and revolt in the Southern small town of the propaganda novels, and then to the surface satisfaction and poise and underlying restlessness and discontent of the psychological novels, ending with the wholehearted joy or suffering associated with the instinctive lower classes of Negroes in city or countryside. There seems to be as wide a range of mood as can be brought by transition from idyllic early morning to noonday heat to afternoon troubled calm to night with its festivity and death, and as can be expected by a changing type of race consciousness. There is

64) Ibid. pp. 17—18.
65) Ibid. pp. 208—209.
66) Ibid. p. 239.

evidently a correspondence between the mild morning mood and the psychology of submission, between the strife in the middle of the day and the offensive-defensive psychology directly expressed, between the passive unrest of the cloudy afternoon and the offensive-defensive psychology indirectly expressed, and between the intense and all-absorbing pain of night time and the psychology of non-resistance to race issues.

Yet the more fully we open ourselves to these moods, the more we come to recognize a common element in most of them. From the moment we leave the slave-plantation milieu behind us, we leave also the note of unreflecting and unqualified optimism. Never again does unbroken and tranquil peace return to lull the spirit, for never again is there the same ignorance of real conditions, the same lack of self-respect and pride, of aspirations and the will-to-live. In some form or another, whether simple or derived, expressed, repressed, or sublimated, main stream or tributary, pain is the conditioning factor of all the other moods, and the pain of being a Negro in a hostile worlds is undoubtedly an integral part. We have seen that the last group of writers considered has the least visible connection with the race problem, and yet even here we sense a tragedy complex which may have its roots in the experience of race prejudice and may survive as a hang-over in their art even when the cause of the complex is not recognized. Experience of suffering on a personal score may lead to various results and attitudes and it may even identify itself with a larger world pain, but it can never be eradicated and will always tend to color the mood.

CONCLUSION

There seems to be much evidence to the effect that race consciousness is a dominant force in the experience of the American Negroes and in their literary expression. Approaching the question as far as possible from material offered by Negroes themselves, in both instances we perceived an apparently wide variation in the nature of the race consciousness. The group life has displayed certain reactions to race prejudice ranging from what we have characterized as submission through defence and offence to non-resistance. We see the seventeenth and eighteenth century slave psychology where the race consciousness is at best latent replaced by the aggressive positive attitudes accompanying the Civil War and Emancipation of the nineteenth century and the expanding opportunities of the twentieth century where the race consciousness is most virile, and in recent years supplemented by the strong self-feeling of an artistic and intellectual minority where the race consciousness is often so controlled or sublimated that we can sometimes become unconscious of it as such.

In the case of the literature, we analyzed the various kinds of milieu, character, and mood presented to us by the writers, in order to find whatever traces of race consciousness were there. We discovered certain natural groupings in all three instances within each category and in relation to each other. There were four major treatments of milieu classified as plantation-slave, small Southern town and ignorant masses, urban cosmopolitan and cultured middle class, and urban-proletarian — rural - peasant. In general, together with the first milieu were individuals characterized as acquiescent, virtuous and naive and a mood of pastoral calm, together with the second milieu individuals characterized as rebellious, active, professional and social minded and a mood of storm and stress, together with the third milieu individuals characterized as restless, passive, sophisticated, and individualistic and a mood tempered by undercurrents, and together with the fourth milieu individuals characterized as vital, uneducated, and instinctive or instinctive and intellectual and a mood of abandon to joy and sorrow.

These four main groups in turn correspond to the psychologies of submission, defence and offence directly expressed, defence and offence indirectly expressed, and non-resistance, observed in the group development. The parallel is striking and suggests a strong interdependence of life and literature in the case of the American Negroes. These people have found themselves in circumstances where they have been regarded and have had to regard themselves in terms of a problem. Writers have shown a marked tendency towards some kind of problem literature. Readers have undoubtedly had their sense of race consciousness increased which again has had its natural effect on the type of literature produced. But aside from any speculation as to a cause and effect relationship, we hope that at least the existence of a correlation in race consciousness is well established through the evidence presented.

When we view the nature of the Negro race consciousness in perspective, we tend to see an identity beneath its apparent variations. There are many indications that what we have designated as different kinds are only different forms of the same substance occasioned by changing time, place, and circumstances. We have seen, for instance, that the latest development of a non-resistant attitude with its belief in self-respect, self-reliance, and freedom in spirit and its parallel in literature through a mood of abandon to natural feelings, in reality is only one more reaction to the difficulties of being a Negro in a disharmonious environment. Here if anywhere we would expect the presence of race consciousness least, and yet the consciousness of identity in America with an unpopular race seems to be basic, no matter how disguised or sublimated. And what sublimation and refinement of attitude does exist comes only as a step in a long development. Even while we may judge the attitude of non-resisters towards race prejudice as superior, we have to remember that prevailing circumstances now are more fortunate than those their forefathers had, and that in a way they are standing on the past victories of the fighters. The probability is that American Negro fiction is destined to have direct or indirect connection with race consciousness as long as the race problem is kept alive by white America.

But perhaps the Negro's pain can be regarded as his salvation. It has certainly been a stimulus to an ever increasing mental activity and social endeavor. It has been the cause of great coöperation within the Negro group, unifying otherwise dissimilar elements. It has inspired lyrical outburst and dramatic scene, thoughtful essay, tragic story and poignant sketch. If he were fully accepted and free to adjust at will in the American scene, the situation would alter. In cases where in-group and out-group reconcile their animosities, the advent of certainty, comfort, and social solution can lead to staleness in the group experience and decadence in its literature. Apart from the question as to whether the values thus obtained would exceed any such danger, up to the present time we see that the Negro has used the fact of his changing status to constructive ends. His race consciousness has not stagnated and then silenced him but has grown apace. In proportion we find him articulate.

— 225 —

BIBLIOGRAPHY.

There have been numerous recent publications of bibliography in connection with the literature produced by the American Negroes. The University of North Carolina issued in 1928 an extension bulletin by Elizabeth Lay Green on "The Negro in Contemporary American Literature" consisting mostly of suggested readings and bibliography by and about the Negro since 1900. Vernon Loggins in his book "The Negro as Author" (Columbia University Press, 1931) has extensive bibliographies covering all types of Negro literature up to 1900. Benjamin Brawley gives selected lists, including magazine articles, in "The Negro in Literature and Art" (Duffield and Company, New York, 1930) while "The New Negro" edited by Alain Locke (Albert and Charles Boni, New York, 1925) contains bibliography of the artistic productions of Negroes in the fields of drama, music (folk songs and spirituals) and biography, as well as fiction. The reader who wishes more detailed information is referred to these sources.

The present bibliography is only partial, consisting exclusively of those books quoted or directly used in this particular study. Although additional material was read, including works of fiction about Negro life by white authors, reference to this material is omitted since it can be found in the above mentioned bibliographies and played no part in this investigation.

In the first section are given those books of a sociological, anthropological, or historical nature utilized as source material in the first part of this study. In the second section are listed those representative works of modern American Negro fiction selected for analysis in the second part.

1. General References.

ANNALS of the AMERICAN ACADEMY of POLITICAL and SOCIAL SCIENCE: *The American Negro.* Vol. 140, No. 229, November, 1928.

BOAS, FRANZ: *The Mind of Primitive Man.* The Mac Millan Co., New York, 1929.

DAVIS, JEROME; BARNES, HARRY ELMER (Editors): *An Introduction to Sociology.* D. C. Heath & Co., 1927.

DORSEY, GEORGE A.: *Why We Behave Like Human Beings.* Harper & Bros. New York and London, 1926. (popular).

*DU BOIS, W. E. B.: *The Souls of Black Folk.* A. C. Mc Clurg & Co., Chicago, 1911.

HERSKOVITZ, MELVILLE J.: *The American Negro. A Study in Raciai Crossing.* Alfred A. Knopf, New York, 1928.

*JOHNSON, CHARLES S. (Editor): *Ebony and Topaz.* Opportunity, New York, 1927.

*LOCKE, ALAIN (Editor): *The New Negro.* A. & C. Boni, New York, 1925.

*MOTON, ROBERT RUSSA: *What the Negro Thinks.* Doubleday Doran and Co., New York, 1930.

REUTER, EDWARD BYRON: *The American Race Problem.* Thomas Y. Crowell Co., New York, 1927.

SURVEY GRAPHIC, VOL. VI, No. 6, March, 1925. (Harlem number).

*WASHINGTON, BOOKER T.: *Up From Slavery.* Doubleday Page and Co., New York, 1901.

*WOODSON, CARTER G.: *The Negro in Our History.* The Associated Publishers, Inc., Washington, D. C., 1928.

*Negro writers.

2. American Negro Fiction.

CHESNUTT, CHARLES W.: *The Conjure Woman.* Houghton, Mifflin & Co., The Riverside Press, Cambridge, 1899.
The Marrow of Tradition. Houghton, Mifflin & Co., The Riverside Press, Cambridge 1901.
The Colonel's Dream. Doubleday, Page & Co., New York, 1905.

DUNBAR, PAUL LAURENCE: *The Sport of the Gods.* Dodd, Mead & Co., New York, 1902.
Folks From Dixie. Dodd, Mead & Co., New York, 1926. (Reprint).

DU BOIS, W. E. BURGHARDT: *Dark Princess.* Harcourt, Brace & Co., New York, 1928.

FAUSET, JESSIE REDMON: *There is Confusion.* Horace Liveright, New York, 1924.
Plum Bun. Frederick A. Stokes Co., New York, 1929.

FISHER, RUDOLPH: *The Walls of Jericho*. Alfred A. Knopf, New York and London, 1928.

HUGHES, LANGSTON: *Not Without Laughter*. Alfred A. Knopf, New York and London, 1930.

JOHNSON, JAMES WELDON: *The Autobiography of an Ex-Coloured Man*. Alfred A. Knopf & Co., New York, 1927. (Garden City Pub. Co.).

LARSEN, NELLA: *Quicksand*. Alfred A. Knopf, New York and London, 1928.

Passing. Alfred A. Knopf, New York and London, 1929.

McKAY, CLAUDE: *Home to Harlem*, Harper & Brothers, Publishers, New York and London, 1928.

Banjo. Harper & Brothers, Publishers, New York and London, 1929.

SCHUYLER, GEORGE S.: *Black No More*. The Macaulay Co., New York, 1931.

THURMAN, WALLACE: *The Blacker the Berry*. The Macaulay Co., New York, 1929.

TOOMER, JEAN: *Cane*. Boni & Liveright, New York, 1923.

WALROND, ERIC: *Tropic Death*. Boni & Liveright, New York, 1926.

WHITE, WALTER F.: *The Fire in the Flint*. Alfred A. Knopf, New York, 1925.

Flight. Alfred A. Knopf, London, 1926.

INDEX